Aidan Ellis is a barrister at Temple Garden Chambers practising in credit hire and personal injury. He has written and lectured on credit hire and is also the co-editor of the Personal Injury Brief Update Law Journal (www.pibriefupdate.com).

Ellis On Credit Hire

Eighth Edition

Ellis On Credit Hire

Eighth Edition

Aidan Ellis Barrister,
Middle Temple, MA (Hons)(Cantab) LLM

Law Brief Publishing

Published 2026 by Law Brief Publishing, an imprint of Law Brief Publishing Ltd
30 The Parks
Minehead
Somerset
TA24 8BT

www.lawbriefpublishing.com

Paperback: 978-1-918241-38-9

PREFACE

This Eighth Edition aims to bring this text back up to date, by including the latest authorities relating to credit hire.

The most significant recent development is the Court of Appeal decision in Tescher v Direct Accident Management Ltd, which finally gives clear guidance on the exercise of the discretion to order costs against a non-party, in this case the hire company. In Chapter 16, the impact of this decision is discussed, in the context of prior cases concerning credit hire organisations.

Chapter 16 also contains an expanded section on illegality, to address the Court of Appeal decision in Ali v HSF Logistics Polska. In that case, the Insurer was unsuccessful in arguing that a claim for hire charges failed by reason of illegality where the claimant did not have a valid MOT for their own vehicle. The application of the relevant principles to other forms of illegality, including driving without a valid driving licence, remains controversial.

For the first time, this edition is fully indexed. It is hoped that this will make it easier for readers to locate the topics, cases and legislation that they need.

The structure of this book has not been altered. Rates and mitigation remain at the heart of credit hire litigation. They will need to be considered in every credit hire case. These chapters have been updated lightly to add new cases and material, where applicable, but they have not been fundamentally altered. In particular, the chapter on impecuniosity has been updated to reflect the latest authorities on the practical effect of debarring orders in the credit hire context.

In relation to enforceability, much of the material on the consumer credit legislation and the cancellation regulations is now mainly of historical interest. Instead, new developments have focussed more on clarifying the position in relation to misrepresentation and other contractual issues.

This book has always been aimed not only at seasoned litigators, but also at garages, credit hire companies, insurers and indeed anyone who wishes to gain more understanding of the issues which arise in these cases. It hopes to provide a clear summary of the issues for both those tackling the subject for the first time and those experienced in its intricate details. It does not pretend to be fully comprehensive, noting that there are weighty specialist tomes already dealing with consumer credit, costs and civil procedure.

This edition continues the approach of previous editions to focus on appellate decisions, particularly from the higher courts. There is so much credit hire litigation that producing a mass of inconsistent first instance decisions is unlikely to help anyone. This edition therefore tries to extract the principles from higher court decisions on which the first instance decisions should be founded.

To my surprise, more than fifteen years have passed since I first agreed to help Tim Kevan update his textbook 'Kevan on Credit Hire'. I take this opportunity to mark my gratitude to Tim for his industry in creating a book about credit hire in the first place, his generosity in allowing me to take over his creation and his personal support and friendship over many years.

I am also grateful for the support of my colleagues and former colleagues at Temple Garden Chambers. In particular to Dean Norton (senior clerk), Dominic Adamson KC, Paul McGrath, Jonathan Hough KC, Marcus Grant, Tim Sharpe and James Yapp among others. Any mistakes are my own, for which I apologise.

The law is stated as I understand it on 1 April 2026. In such a contentious field, it is likely that there will be new decisions which need to be reflected in a further edition in due course.

For the benefit of those who are not overly familiar with these cases, I should say that the discussion of principles and cases which follows often assumes the same basic facts. A Claimant's vehicle is damaged in a road traffic accident by a Defendant. Whilst the Claimant's vehicle is off the road (being repaired or replaced), the Claimant hires a replacement vehicle from a Credit Hire Organisation. The vehicle is provided on credit so that the Claimant does not have to lay out any money. The Claimant and the Credit Hire Organisation then look to recover the credit hire charges from the Defendant's motor Insurer. The Defendant's Insurer will look to reduce or eliminate its liability by challenging the daily rate of hire, the reasonableness of the Claimant's conduct and / or the enforceability of the agreement. These issues are addressed in turn in the following chapters.

In keeping with previous editions, this book is not a substitute for legal advice. Readers researching a particular problem or case may find inspiration in these pages, but should not rely upon them in isolation or without reading the underlying cases and materials. A textbook can never be a substitute for legal advice from appropriately qualified practitioners.

Aidan Ellis
April 2026

CONTENTS

TABLE OF CASES

TABLE OF LEGISLATION

Secondary Legislation (Regulations and Orders)

PART ONE

RATES

CHAPTER ONE

INTRODUCTION TO RATES

> *"the major protection for the defendant and his insurers is that the claimant can only recover the 'spot' or market rate of hire"*

In *Copley v Lawn,*[1] in considering the proper scope of arguments relating to mitigation of loss in credit hire cases, the Court of Appeal identified the market rate of hire as the 'major protection' for the defendant in credit hire cases. As set out below, subsequent cases suggest a greater role for mitigation in credit hire cases than the Court of Appeal suggested in *Copley*. But the identification of the market rate of hire as the major protection for the defendant is far less contentious. County Courts still regularly grapple with credit hire cases in which the daily rate is the main issue. The determination of the market rate of hire remains highly contentious and retains its place in the first Part of this revised edition.

Disputes over the rate of hire reflect a fundamental dispute between the insurance and credit hire industries. Insurers have long complained that credit hire rates cost substantially more than the equivalent market rates. But the method of determining the 'equivalent' market rate has always been controversial. Moreover, credit hire companies argue that they provide a different service – for example, providing hire vehicles on favourable insurance terms for a period which cannot be defined in advance – which is not matched by ordinary hire companies or which, if ordinary hire companies could match it, may cost more the basic hire rate.

---

1 Copley v Lawn, [2009] EWCA Civ 580 at para. 6.

The present position, frequently restated in the leading cases, is that an ordinary claimant is not entitled to recover the full credit hire rate because it is said to incorporate irrecoverable benefits additional to the provision of a vehicle. As a result, only the equivalent market hire rate is recoverable. We will consider the exception which arises in relation to impecunious claimants in Part Two of the book. In this Part, we will consider the authorities for this general principle and the reasoning behind it in Chapter Two. We will then go on to consider the leading Court of Appeal cases on the determination of the equivalent market hire rate in Chapter Three. Evidential issues which commonly arise in practice are then addressed in Chapter Four.

As explained in Chapter Two, the additional benefits issue is separate from arguments about reasonableness and mitigation. The principles applicable to mitigation are set out in Part 3.

CHAPTER TWO

CREDIT HIRE RATE OR BASIC HIRE RATE?

It is perhaps helpful to start by stating the general rule again. In *Dimond v Lovell*,[2] after emerging from the thicket of consumer credit issues to address the issue of rates, Lord Hoffmann (with whom Lord Browne-Wilkinson agreed) stated that:-

> *"in the case of a hiring from an accident hire company, the equivalent spot rate will ordinarily be the net loss after allowance has been made for the additional benefits which the accident hire company has provided."*

It should be acknowledged at the outset that this part of the speech was *obiter dicta*. The *ratio* of *Dimond v Lovell* related to the enforceability of the hire agreement under the Consumer Credit Act 1974. This led Lord Saville to abstain from deciding the rates issue on the basis that it:-

> *"does not arise for decision in the present case. This is a question of great importance and difficulty, the answer to which may well have widespread ramifications. It is accordingly a question that I would prefer to consider in a case where it does arise for decision."*

Although the other four Judges did address the issue, Lord Nicholls dissented on the basis that the full credit hire rate should be recoverable and Lord Hobhouse agreed that the credit hire rate should not be recoverable, but proposed a different way of ascertaining the recoverable

2 Dimond v Lovell, [2002] 1 AC 384.

damages. Only Lord Browne-Wilkinson agreed entirely with Lord Hoffmann.

Nevertheless it would, in practice, be very difficult to argue that lower courts should not follow Lord Hoffmann's approach. As the Court of Appeal explained in *Sayce v TNT*:

> *"There are circumstances in which, although not technically bound by a decision of a higher court, a lower court should follow and apply that decision, even though it may disagree with it. There may be room for legitimate disagreement between judges of co-ordinate jurisdiction and in those circumstances reasoned difference of opinion may provide a useful springboard for an appeal. That is not the case, however, where a higher court has decided a question of principle, albeit obiter, for the purpose of clarifying the law for the profession at large. It would not be right, for example, for this court to disregard those parts of their Lordships' speeches in Dimond v Lovell that deal with the recovery of that part of the credit hire costs that relate to additional benefits on the grounds that they are obiter".*[3]

Moreover, many subsequent cases confirm that Lord Hoffmann's *dicta* have become firmly entrenched in the jurisprudence. They have been repeatedly confirmed in subsequent cases. Thus in *Burdis v Livsey*, the Court of Appeal endeavoured to follow the House of Lords' *"guidance as to the principles to be applied in arriving at the correct measure of damages for loss of use"*.[4]

In a similar vein in *Bee v Jenson*, the Court of Appeal noted that *"the House held, secondly, that even if the claimant could have recovered he could have recovered no more than the spot charge and not the charges made for an*

3 Sayce v TNT, [2011] EWCA Civ 1583 paragraph 24.

4 Burdis v Livsey, [2003] QB 36 paragraph 136.

agreement that entitled the claimant to more benefit than the cost of hire itself".[5]

In *Copley v Lawn*, the Court of Appeal *"regarded it as well settled that, although a claimant can recover the cost of hiring a replacement car, he can only recover the reasonable rate of such hire; that has been held in Dimond v Lovell to be the market or spot rate"*.[6]

In *Bent v (1) Highways and Utilities Construction Ltd (2) Allianz Insurance* ("Bent no1"),[7] the Court of Appeal summarised the authorities thus "*The authorities establish that in the case of "pecunious" (as the Judge described Mr Bent) claimants, the damages to be awarded are normally to be assessed at "spot hire" rates – the rate at which a broadly similar car could be had on the market.*"

In *Bent v (1) Highways and Utilities Construction Ltd (2) Allianz Insurance no2* ("Bent no2"), the Court of Appeal repeated *"If the claimant could afford to hire a replacement car in the normal way, ie. without credit terms and by paying in advance,[8] then the damages recoverable for loss of use of the damaged car will be that sum which is attributable to the basic hire rate of the replacement car"*.[9]

Similarly, in *Stevens v Equity Syndicate Management Ltd*, the Court of Appeal summarised the general principle in these terms: *"If he [the claimant] could have afforded to hire a replacement vehicle in the normal way, that is to say without credit hire terms and by paying in advance, then*

---

5 Bee v Jenson, (2007) 4 All ER 791 para. 6.

6 Copley v Lawn, para. 3.

7 Bent no1, [2010] EWCA Civ 292, see para. 6 in particular.

8 Note that this does not exactly encapsulate the definition of impecuniosity offered by the House of Lords in Lagden v O'Connor, which will be explored in more detail in the next chapter.

9 Bent no2, [2011] EWCA Civ 1384.

the damages recoverable will be that sum which is attributable to the basic hire rate (or BHR) of the replacement vehicle".[10]

The result is that, although it was strictly *obiter*, the general rule established by Lord Hoffmann in *Dimond* is now deeply entrenched in the jurisprudence. Unless the issue returns to the Supreme Court (and unless the claimant is impecunious) the general rule is therefore that the claimant is restricted to recovering "the equivalent spot hire rate".

The Reason for the General Rule

Before going on to consider how the Court should determine the basic hire rate, it is necessary to explain the reason for this general rule. Understanding the reason for the rule, should guide the application of the rule to the evidence.

In *Dimond*, Lord Hoffmann, with whom Lord Browne Wilkinson agreed, stated:

> *"My Lords, I would accept the judge's finding that Mrs. Dimond acted reasonably in going to 1st Automotive and availing herself of its services . . . She cannot therefore be said not to have taken reasonable steps to mitigate her damage.*
>
> *But that does not necessarily mean that she can recover the full amount charged by 1st Automotive. By virtue of her contract, she obtained not only the use of the car but additional benefits as well."*

This finding is significant because by accepting that Mrs Dimond acted reasonably in going to the credit hire company, as the Court of Appeal and the trial Judge had already held below, Lord Hoffmann made it clear that the reason for not allowing the claimant to recover the credit hire

10 Stevens v Equity Syndicate Management Ltd, [2015] EWCA Civ 93 para. 11.

rate is nothing to do with mitigation or reasonableness. Rather it is a matter of betterment.

The point is that a credit hire company typically provides a range of accident management services to a claimant, which go beyond the simple provision of a replacement vehicle. Lord Hoffmann identified the additional benefits inherent in the credit hire contract at page 401 as:

i. <u>the credit charge itself</u>

   "She was relieved of the necessity of laying out the money to pay for the car."

ii. <u>the costs of the action</u>

   "She was relieved of the risk of having to bear the irrecoverable costs of successful litigation and the risk, small though it might be, of having to bear the expense of unsuccessful litigation". Lord Hoffmann also referred to other associated costs: "Paying commission to brokers"; "checking that the accident was not the hirer's fault."

iii. <u>possibly avoiding a residual liability</u>

   "Depending upon the view one takes of the terms of agreement, she may have been relieved of the possibility of having to pay for the car at all."

iv. <u>relieving the anxiety of the claim</u>

   "She was relieved of the trouble and anxiety of pursuing a claim against Mr. Lovell or the C.I.S."

Lord Hoffmann continued:-

"My Lords, English law does not regard the need for any of these additional services as compensatable loss. As Sir Richard Scott V.-C.

> *said (at [1999] 3 W.L.R. 561, 580) "damages for worry and for the nuisance caused by having to deal with the consequences of an accident are not recoverable." If Mrs. Dimond had borrowed the hire money, paid someone else to conduct the claim on her behalf and insured herself against the risk of losing and any irrecoverable costs, her expenses would not have been recoverable. But the effect of the award of damages is that Mrs. Dimond has obtained compensation for them indirectly because they were offered as part of a package by 1st Automotive. There is in my opinion something wrong with this conclusion."*

He then referred to the cases of *British Westinghouse Electric and Manufacturing Co. Ltd. v. Underground Electric Railways Co. of London Ltd* [1912] A.C. 673 and *Bellingham v. Dhillon* [1973] Q.B. 304 which emphasised that only compensatory damages were recoverable. In other words, additional benefits received whilst mitigating loss should not be taken into account in quantifying the claim. But how does this impact on the assessment of damages? Lord Hoffmann explained:-

> *"How does one calculate the additional benefits that Mrs. Dimond received by choosing the 1st Automotive package to mitigate the loss caused by the accident to her car? . . . I do not think that a court can ignore the fact that, one way or another, the other benefits have to be paid for . . . How does one estimate the value of these additional benefits that Mrs. Dimond obtains? It seems to me that prima facie their value is represented by the difference between what she was willing to pay 1st Automotive and what she would have been willing to pay an ordinary car hire company for the use of a car . . . I quite accept that a determination of the value of the benefits which must be brought into account will depend upon the facts of each case. But the principle to be applied is that in the British Westinghouse case [1912] A.C. 673 and this seems to me to lead to the conclusion that in the case of hiring from an accident hire company the equivalent spot rate will ordinarily be the net loss..."*

Thus, the only way to strip out the additional and irrecoverable benefits from the credit hire charges is by reference to the "equivalent spot rate".

On the face of it, Lord Hobhouse adopted a similar analysis. He expressly said that he agreed with Lord Hoffmann that the judge and the majority of the Court of Appeal had approached the issue in the wrong way. He also decided that Mrs Dimond had acted reasonably and went on to emphasise the additional benefits contained in the credit hire contract. He described these at pages 406 – 407 as:

i) <u>the credit charge itself</u>

"It is financing the transaction until the expected recovery is made from the other party".

ii) <u>the costs of the action</u>

"it is bearing the cost of handling the claim and effecting that recovery"; "something in respect of costs".

iii) <u>possibly avoiding a residual liability</u>

"it is bearing a commercial (though not normally the legal) risk that there may be a failure to make that recovery".

Thus aside from one (removing the anxiety of litigation), Lord Hobhouse identified the same additional benefits as Lord Hoffmann.

However, his analysis of how the recoverable damages should be calculated differed from that of Lord Hoffmann. Lord Hobhouse favoured *"the approach of making a commercial apportionment between the cost of hiring a car and the cost of the other benefits included in the scheme."*

He explained that Mrs Dimond would not have been able to recover <u>the whole cost</u> of the credit hire charges *"as the cost of mitigating the loss of use of her car"*. He said later, *"The elements to which the uplift in the charges of the accident hire company was attributable were (and inevitably must be) elements which were not properly included in the claim for damages for loss of use."*

In other words, the claim for the uplift was not recoverable in the claim for loss of use. This may have left open the possibility that it may be recoverable in other ways. Indeed, this is supported by his further statement that *"As appears from what I have said, some might be recovered from the wrongdoer in another form"*. In practice, however, it is difficult to see how the Claimant could recover for these additional benefits via any other route. First, the Claimant would not be able to recover for the same thing twice:

> *"The necessity to make some apportionment or other reduction in the claim is demonstrated by the need to avoid double counting. Prima facie, the court should award statutory interest on the claim; but here the claim already included some element of interest. Similarly the claim included something in respect of costs; to award costs as well would involve some duplication."*

Second, Lord Hobhouse stated that, *"it is unlikely that any scheme could be devised which would enable the insurance element to be recovered"*. This appears to refer to the additional benefit which comprised the possibility of avoiding a residual liability.

The heart of the difference between Lord Hoffmann and Lord Hobhouse is this: Lord Hoffmann thought that the measure of the Claimant's recoverable loss could safely be approximated by looking to the equivalent spot hire rate while Lord Hobhouse seemed to prefer an approach based on stripping out the unrecoverable additional benefits from the credit hire charges.

As the caselaw set out above and below illustrates, it is Lord Hoffmann's approach – searching for the equivalent basic hire rate – which is most often adopted in practice. However, that does not mean that the Courts have not expressed certain reservations. From time to time, the Court of Appeal has flirted with the idea that the credit hire company could disclose details of its charging structure in order to allow the charge for credit to be stripped out in a manner reminiscent of Lord Hobhouse's approach. Most recently, in *Stevens v Equity Syndicate Management Ltd* the Court of Appeal canvassed "whether credit hire companies could, as a matter of course, disclose their estimate of the BHR alongside every quoted credit hire rate".[11] It later suggested that the selection of the lowest reasonable rate was justified by the absence of evidence from the credit hire company to "elaborate upon and give disclosure relating to its charging structures".[12]

On the whole, however, the Courts have retreated from the disclosure and costs implications of any attempt to strip out the elements of the credit rate.[13] Nevertheless, in theory it remains open to credit hire companies to seek to avoid the analysis of basic hire rates altogether by providing appropriate disclosure of their charging structures and an analysis breaking down the credit hire charges into their constituent elements.

For completeness, in dissent in *Dimond* Lord Nicholls accepted that the credit hire contract incorporated additional benefits but argued that the uplift should be recoverable. He identified the same "additional services" as Lord Hobhouse:

<u>the credit charge itself</u>

> "The hirer does not have to produce any money . . . at the time of the hiring".

<u>the costs of the action</u>

> "The hire company pursues the allegedly negligent driver's insurers"; "The hire company is not deterred by having to bring court proceedings should this become necessary".

---

11 Stevens, para. 30.

12 Stevens, para. 36.

13 Stevens, para. 30.

possibly avoiding a residual liability

> "The hirer does not have to produce any money, either at the time of the hiring or at all"; "If the claim is unsuccessful, in practice the hire company does not pursue the hirer".

Lord Nicholls then went on to explain why these additional benefits ought, in his view, to be recoverable:-

> *"The additional services . . . redress the imbalance between the individual car owner and the insurance companies. They enable car owners to shift from themselves to the insurance companies a loss which properly belongs to the insurers but which, in practice, owners of cars often have to bear themselves. So long as the charge for the additional services is reasonable, this charge should be part of the recoverable damages.*
>
> *A measure of damages which does not achieve this result would be sadly deficient. The law on the measure of damages should reflect the practicalities of the situation in which a wronged person finds himself. Otherwise it would mean that the law's response to a wrong is a right to damages which will often be illusory in practice. I do not believe this can be the present state of the law in a situation which affects thousands of people every year."*

However, Lord Nicholls' was a lone voice in dissent. As set out above, the majority approach in *Dimond* is now firmly entrenched in the jurisprudence. His dissent is now mainly interesting from a historical perspective.

CHAPTER THREE

DETERMINING THE BASIC HIRE RATE

Identifying that the equivalent spot hire rate will ordinarily be the amount of recoverable damages, as the House of Lords did in *Dimond*, is helpful as a general principle. But it does not guide the County Courts in determining what the equivalent spot hire rate is in specific cases. This issue has been addressed by the Court of Appeal on no fewer than five occasions. It remains highly contentious. We will set out each decision in detail before attempting to draw some conclusions.

A. Burdis v Livsey

In the first case, *Burdis v Livsey*, the Court of Appeal began by identifying the difficulty of the task. They pointed out that hire rates are "in constant flux". This is no doubt correct: they vary depending on the season and depending on the availability of particular vehicles. Furthermore the rates charged by different companies may vary considerably. Thus there is no single market rate as such.

At first instance in *Burdis*, the Judge had considered a number of ways of arriving at the right measure of damages:-

- Analysing the charges made by the credit hire company to uncover which charges related to irrecoverable additional benefits and which simply related to hiring the car. Note that this appears to be the approach that Lord Hobhouse in *Dimond* had preferred. But both the Judge and the Court of Appeal considered that this approach was too *"cumbersome"* to apply. It would lead to disproportionate costs and lengthy disclosure exercises.

- Applying an arbitrary *"reasonable discount"* to the credit hire charges. The Court of Appeal also dismissed this approach, *"we do not believe it appropriate in the absence of agreement between the parties or without cogent evidence as to what the discount should be. Further, as the judge pointed out, once the courts start applying a particular discount the total charge may be increased."*

- Considering the actual hire rates locally. This creates its own difficulties such as what companies to survey and whether to take the highest or the lowest rate. With some modifications as to the detail, this was the route which was eventually approved.

- The approach that the Judge in fact adopted was based on expert evidence given by Mr Mainz on behalf of the Insurers. Mr Mainz had carried out a survey of car hire rates including those charged by the best-known national hire companies and a random selection of smaller companies. His figures thus provided a band of rates, which were a snapshot of the hire market as at January 2001.[14] The Judge decided to award an average based on the Mainz report. He then applied a 10% uplift to the average of these rates, to take account of the fact that the survey was carried out in January whereas the actual hire was in peak season.

The Court of Appeal rejected this approach. They held:

> *"146 ... That cannot be right. A person who needs to hire a car because of the negligence of another must, subject to mitigating his loss, be entitled to recover the actual cost of hire not an average derived from the Mainz report. If the principle adopted by the judge is correct then it would seem appropriate also to apply that principle to the cost of car*

---

14 In Burdis v Livsey, the Court of Appeal heard five appeals together. The Court used one set of illustrative facts as the basis for its decision, which were drawn from Sen v Steelform Engineering Co Ltd. Dr Sen the claimant in that case had hired a car for three days from 3 – 5 June 1999.

> *repair, namely a claimant may only recover the average of the charges of garages. But a person whose car is damaged should in appropriate circumstances recover the cost to him of repair and loss of use. His recovery should not be restricted to an average of car repair or hire rates nor should he be able to recover that average cost if the actual cost is less. We believe that the solution is to apply normal legal principles.*

The Court of Appeal also expressly accepted the criticisms advanced by the claimant that (1) the claimant should be entitled to recover the true cost of hire not simply an average (2) the uplift of 10% was arbitrary and (3) the adoption of the Mainz report was not a "cheap and workable" solution since the Mainz report would not be admissible or applicable in the mass of other cases which were pending.

The Court of Appeal then set out the correct approach to take. This section of the judgment is crucial and so is set out in full below.

> *147. The fundamental principle is that a person whose car has been damaged is entitled to compensation for the loss caused. In a case where such loss includes loss of use and he establishes a need for a replacement, he is entitled to the cost of hiring a replacement car. He can go round to the nearest car hire company and is prima facie entitled to recover the amount charged whether or not the charge is at the top of the range of car hire rates. However the basic principle is qualified by the duty to take reasonable steps to mitigate the loss. What is reasonable will depend on the particular circumstances.*
>
> *148. We do not anticipate that the application of the correct legal principles will lead to disproportionate costs in small cases. The claim will be based on evidence as to the rate charged by a car hire company in the relevant area. Perhaps the rate will be at the top end of the range of company rates. Thereafter the evidential burden passes to the insurers to show that it would not have been reasonable to use that particular car hire company and that the reasonable course would be to use another company which charged a lower rate. What is reasonable and whether a loss is avoidable are questions of fact, not law, which District*

and County Court judges regularly decide. It can arise in many different types of cases, ranging from damage to chattels to a failure to take action. We do not believe that a decision on such issues in respect of car hire charges will be any more difficult than in respect of car repair charges."

We will return to try to reconcile this passage with the later Court of Appeal decisions. But it is worth making one observation on terminology at this stage. In its decision, the Court of Appeal consistently refers to credit hire companies as "accident hire companies". The reference in paragraph 148 to a "car hire company" must therefore be to a spot hire company. But if this is correct, then the Defendant might argue that the Court of Appeal was placing the burden of proof on the Claimant, at least initially, to provide evidence of spot hire rates. This is supported by the Court of Appeal continuing that "thereafter the evidential burden passes to the insurers". In order for the burden to pass to the insurers "thereafter", it must have been on the Claimant initially. As set out below, however, subsequent cases make it clear that the burden of proof rests on the Defendant to show that the equivalent spot hire rate was lower than the credit hire rate.

B. Bent No1

In the first appeal in the Bent case, the trial Judge had rejected the evidence of spot hire rates tendered by the Defendant primarily on the basis that it was evidence of comparable rates in 2009 when the hire actually occurred in 2007. The trial Judge was also concerned that the rates related to different vehicles and that given that the Claimant was only 23 it was not clear that ordinary hire companies would hire any vehicle, let alone a powerful vehicle, to him. As a result, at first instance the credit hire rates were awarded in full.

The Court of Appeal disagreed. In relation to the timing point, Jacob LJ giving the leading judgment held that:

> *"Working with comparables and making adjustments is the daily diet of judges concerned with valuation in all sorts of fields. Clearly evidence of the spot rate a year or so later than the relevant date is likely to throw considerable light on what the spot rate would have been at the time."*[15]

In relation to whether the Defendant needed to provide rates evidence for an identical vehicle, Jacob LJ continued that:

> *"one must not be hypnotised by any supposed need to find an exact spot rate for an almost exactly comparable car. Normally, the replacement need be no more than in the same broad range of quality and nature as the damaged car. There may be a bracket of spot rates for cars rather "better" and rather "worse". A Judge who considered that bracket and aimed for some sort of reasonable average would not be going wrong."*[16]

Perhaps the unusual features of this decision will be immediately apparent. It certainly has the merit of brevity. The Court of Appeal judgment is barely more than two pages long. It makes very little reference to earlier jurisprudence and no reference at all to *Burdis v Livsey*. This might be thought surprising given that the suggestion that Judges could adopt "some sort of reasonable average" apparently contradicts the express rejection of averages in *Burdis*.

The result was that the issue of spot hire rates was then referred back to the County Court for determination at a fresh hearing at which the Claimant was allowed the opportunity to enter his own rates evidence. This sets the scene for the second Bent case in which the resulting assessment of the equivalent spot hire rate was appealed again, this time by the Claimant.

---

15 Bent no1, para. 8.

16 Bent no1, para. 9.

C. Bent No2

In order to explain this decision, it is necessary to start by setting out the facts in more detail. The Claimant, Darren Bent, was a well-known Premier League footballer. He was not impecunious. He was 23 at the time of the accident. He hired an Aston Martin DB9 as a replacement for his Mercedes-Benz CLS 63 AMG Coupe. It is perhaps unfortunate that a leading case on the calculation of spot hire rates should concern two such specialised and prestigious vehicles, when the vast majority of cases before the courts concern rather more standard vehicles.

The Claimant relied on written and oral evidence from the Chief Executive of the credit hire company, which attached tables of spot rates for vehicles in category SP9 in Spring 2009 and also further evidence about 2007 figures from smaller specialist hirers. The Defendant relied on a rates survey carried out on the internet and by telephone to gain the hire rates from five ordinary car hire companies.

The Court of Appeal began by setting out the legal background. As set out above, it confirmed that *"the damages recoverable for loss of use of the damaged car will be that sum which is attributable to the basic hire rate of the replacement car."*[17]

Thus far in this chapter, we have adopted the phrase 'spot hire rate' to reflect the market cost of hiring a replacement vehicle. This was the phrase used by Lord Hoffmann. However *Bent no2* states that "Spot hire rates" is a misnomer and that "it would be better if, in the context of credit hire cases, the term "spot rate" were not used in future and the term "basic hire rate" or BHR were used instead".[18] We will follow the Court of Appeal's guidance and refer to basic hire rates from this point forwards.

---

17 Bent No2, para. 33.

18 Ibid. para. 34.

The Court of Appeal continued that *"it is for a defendant to demonstrate, by evidence, that there is a difference between the credit hire charge agreed between the claimant and the credit hire company and the BHR"*.[19] The Court of Appeal supported this proposition in a footnote by saying that it is well established that it is for the Defendant to prove that the Claimant has benefitted from betterment so that the damages recovered must be reduced.

The Court then considered how the basic hire rate might be established. It held that a court could consider two types of evidence: direct evidence and indirect evidence. Direct evidence would consist of *"published rates, from the actual credit hire company that hired the replacement car which demonstrates either that the credit hire rate and the BHR for that type of car is the same or it is different and what the difference is"*. According to the Court, *"if there is such direct evidence it might be the best evidence of any difference between the credit hire rate charged and the BHR for that type of car in that area at the time the replacement car was hired"*.[20] The second type of evidence, termed "indirect evidence", is *"evidence of the BHR charged by other car hire companies in the area for the type of car actually hired"*.[21]

The reference to direct evidence might encourage credit hire companies to consider whether it would be in their interests to publish a basic hire rate tariff. They might argue that a credible tariff is all that is required to demonstrate the BHR, after all the Court of Appeal recognised that this might represent the "best evidence" on the point. Insurers might respond that this would be misleading because many credit hire organisations

---

19 Ibid. para. 35 and note that the Court of Appeal repeated this at paragraph 73: "has the defendant proved a difference between the credit hire rate actually paid for the car hired and what, in the same broad geographical area, would have been the BHR for the model of car actually hired".

20 Ibid. para. 38.

21 Ibid. para. 41.

purely specialise in credit hire. Their rates are not available to ordinary customers, or not attractive to them. Practical issues would likely arise in relation to the extent of disclosure which is proportionate and necessary to support any such tariff.

In returning to the case at hand, in a section headed discussion and conclusion, the Court restated the test: *"the aim of the judge's fact finding exercise is to ascertain the BHR for the model of car that the claimant actually hired and to do so on an objective basis".*[22] This was later confirmed by saying that on the facts the question was *"what was the BHR for the Aston Martin DB9 that was actually hired".*[23]

In considering the discussion of rates in *Burdis v Livsey*, the Court interpreted the earlier decision as meaning that:

> *"the court has to calculate the BHR on the basis that the claimant notionally went round to an equivalent non-credit hire company. If there is a difference between the two rates [ie between credit hire and BHR], the claimant will recover the BHR that the non-credit car hire company would have charged, even if the BHR that the car hire company charged was at the top end of the range, provided that the claimant acted reasonably."*[24]

The logic of this passage may well be sound. But it rather avoids tackling the interesting question, which is whether the Court of Appeal in *Burdis* was correct to place an initial evidential burden on the claimant.

In relation to the discussion of averages in *Bent no1*, the Court said that:

> *"it may be difficult to produce evidence of an exact BHR for the car that was actually hired on credit terms. The judge has to deal with the*

---

22 Ibid. para. 74.

23 Ibid. para. 80.

24 Ibid. para. 76.

> *evidence available. It is in that sense that Jacob LJ said that a judge would not be going wrong if he considered a bracket of BHRs for cars rather better or rather worse than the one actually hired. But, whether the judge has evidence of BHRs for the type of car actually hired on credit, or has evidence of BHRs for other types of car which are within a bracket that is comparable, the aim of the exercise remains the same. It is to make a calculation of what the BHR was for the car actually hired and so compare it with the credit hire rate actually paid.*
>
> *"I do not believe that Jacob LJ intended to suggest that "some sort of reasonable average" of a bracket of "spot rates" for cars rather better or worse than that actually hired on credit terms would produce the BHR to which a claimant was entitled. Such an approach would be inconsistent with this Court's statement in Burdis v Livsey at [146], where it expressly rejected the suggestion that a claimant should recover the average cost of car hire, whether the actual cost to him was more or less than the average. I think that all Jacob LJ was doing was to give an indication of one way by which a judge might identify the BHR of the actual car hire on credit hire terms by mean of what, in [38] above, I have called indirect evidence."*[25]

One possible confusion is that when turning back to paragraph 38, the reference there to indirect evidence is only to say that *"it is unlikely that indirect evidence from the car hire company (such as its assertion of what its BHR would have been had they had one) will be useful"*. This is plainly not the same indirect evidence referred to in the paragraph above. Perhaps the reference is misplaced and it should refer to paragraph 41 (evidence of hire rates charged by other companies) and not 38.

The reader might also be forgiven for emerging from these paragraphs wondering whether the use of averages is sanctioned or not. After all the judgment starts by noting that the Court of Appeal had expressly rejected the use of averages in *Burdis*, but appears to end by saying that what

25 Ibid. paras 78 and 79.

Jacobs LJ had suggested in *Bent No1* (which was the use of averages) was *"one way by which a judge might identify the BHR"*. Though *Bent No1* was plainly not followed, nor was it expressly said to be wrongly decided. Perhaps the point is simply that the Court of Appeal wished to make it clear that, where no rate is available for an exactly comparable vehicle, the Courts can still consider a bracket of rates for better and worse vehicles in arriving at a basic hire rate.

On the facts, the Court of Appeal concluded that the trial Judge had *"erred in concentrating on the 2009 figure when 2007 figures were available"*. Moreover *"the judge erred in concentrating on the range of figures for a Mercedes SL 55 AMG when BHR figures for an Aston Martin DB9 were available"*. The Court held that *"the best evidence on which to make a finding relates to the contemporaneous 2007 rates for an Aston Martin DB9."* These figures were available within the Claimant's rates evidence.

In relation to the Defendant's survey, whilst the Court described it as *"useful evidence"*, there was a flaw: *"all the quotations stipulated a minimum age for a driver, the lowest of which was 25…Mr Bent was, of course, 23 at the time"*. As a result, the claimant would have had to arrange cover through his own insurance, yet *"there is no firm evidence that Mr Bent's insurers would have been prepared to insure him to hire an Aston Martin DB9 so that it cannot be demonstrated that the lower rates discovered by Miss Goeting would have been applicable"*.[26]

The result on the facts was that the Defence had failed to prove that that the BHR was lower than the credit hire rate and the Claimant therefore recovered the credit hire rate in full. This result cannot logically be limited to cases where there is a difficulty in hiring a vehicle based on the Claimant's age; Claimants may rely on this principle in all circumstances

26 Ibid. paras 87 and 89.

where the ordinary car hire companies will not hire to the Claimant, for instance where they have speeding convictions.

D. Stevens v Equity Syndicate Management

The fourth case to reach the Court of Appeal was *Stevens*. The Claimant had hired a replacement Audi A4 for a period of 28 days whilst his own vehicle was unroadworthy. An issue arose as to the recoverable rate of hire. At first instance, guided presumably by *Bent No1*, the Recorder allowed an average of four equivalent basic hire rates. It was agreed on appeal that adopting averages was not the correct approach.[27]

The Court of Appeal began by citing paragraph 73 of *Bent No2* with approval, because it explains a structured approach which may usefully be adopted in these cases. Paragraph 73 of *Bent No2* reads:-

> *"to summarise, the questions are: (i) did the claimant need to hire a replacement car at all; if so, (ii) was it reasonable, in all the circumstances, to hire the particular type of car actually hired at the rate agreed; if it was (iii) was the claimant 'impecunious'; if not, (iv) has the defendant proved a difference between the credit hire rate actually paid for the car hired and what, in the same broad geographic area, would have been the BHR for the model of car actually hired and if so what is it; if so, (v) what is the difference between the credit hire rate and the BHR"*

In the High Court, Burnett J had held that the search for the BHR should be for the figure that the claimant would have been willing to pay had he gone into the ordinary car hire market. That clearly indicated a subjective test based on what that specific Claimant would have done. Burnett J acknowledged this by indicating that "questioning of the claimant on this issue, should be directed to exploring what he would have been willing

27 Stevens, para. 25.

to pay on the hypothesis that he would have gone into the market to hire a vehicle".

The Court of Appeal rejected the subjective approach. It held that the reason for looking at basic hire rates is in order to strip out additional benefits from the credit hire contract. This is an objective exercise. Evidence about what the specific claimant would have done is "likely to be of very little assistance".[28]

The Court acknowledged that Courts "are still experiencing practical difficulties in calculating the BHR". It identified the problem as being that the claims are often for small sums and lawyers and judges have to approach them "at proportionate cost".[29]

The Court also expressly acknowledged that some uncertainty is inherent in the nature of the exercise of assessing the BHR: *"any attempt to value the benefits at a later stage in a proportionate way must necessarily involve a degree of imprecision. The best that can be hoped for, absent a very expensive exercise of disclosure and analysis, is a reasonable approximation"*.[30]

That goes some way to answering many of the criticisms that Claimants typically make of rates evidence. It suggests that exactly comparable rates are not required and a degree of imprecision is acceptable. The aim is to arrive at a practical and proportionate solution.

With proportionality in mind, the Court of Appeal concluded that: "the lowest reasonable rate quoted by a mainstream supplier for the hire of a vehicle to a person such as the claimant is a reasonable approximation to the BHR."[31] In so doing, it expressly rejected the Claimant's contention that he should recover the highest figure in the range of rates as

28 Stevens, para. 39.

29 Ibid. para. 30.

30 Ibid. para. 34.

31 Ibid. para. 35.

"manifestly unjust" because it was the credit hire company that was in the best position to disclose its actual charging structure.[32]

A key passage sets out the principle:-

> *"it follows that a judge faced with a range of hire rates should try to identify the rate or rates for the hire, in the claimant's geographical area, of the type of car actually hired by the claimant on credit hire terms. If that exercise yields a single rate then that rate is likely to be a reasonable approximation for the BHR. If, on the other hand, it yields a range of rates then a reasonable estimate of the BHR may be obtained by identifying the lowest reasonable rate quoted by a mainstream supplier or, if there is no mainstream supplier, by a local reputable supplier."*

Thus, it was for the defendant to prove that there was a difference between the BHR and the credit hire rate. If the defendant identifies a single basic hire rate, that is likely to be the measure of loss. If the defendant identifies a range of rates, the Court should adopt the lowest reasonable rate from a mainstream supplier. If there is no mainstream supplier, the Court should adopt the lowest reasonable rate from a local reputable supplier.

One final curiosity of the case is that the subjective rate adopted by Burnett J and the lowest reasonable rate adopted by the Court of Appeal both led to a figure only slightly less than the average which the Recorder had awarded (wrongly) at first instance.

32 Ibid. para. 36.

E. McBride v UK Insurance Ltd[33]

Within two years of the decision in *Stevens*, the credit hire organisations sought to overturn it. Two appeals were brought together to the Court of Appeal. The first, *McBride v UK Insurance Ltd*, concerned the hire of a Jaguar XK for a period of 77 days at a daily credit hire rate of £409 which had been reduced to £270 at first instance. The appellant argued directly that *Stevens* was wrongly decided and inconsistent with earlier decisions, that the basic hire rate suppliers were not 'mainstream' and that the assessment of the basic hire rate was flawed because it did not provide a nil excess. In the conjoined appeal, *Clayton v EUI Ltd*, the Claimant hired a BMW M3 and later a Mercedes E350 which were held to be reasonable replacements for his 1973 Ford Mustang. The daily rate was again substantially reduced at first instance, as a result of the Court deciding that it could rely on the basic hire rates set out in the Defendant's evidence but increase them by 10% to allow for an appropriate excess waiver and 15% to allow for a rate for a seven day period rather than the 28 day period on which the Defendant's evidence was premised.

The attempt to overturn the 'lowest reasonable rate' rule from *Stevens* was roundly rejected. The Court of Appeal expressly addressed the consistency of the decision in *Stevens* with previous authority. It noted that the rates mentioned by Lord Hobhouse in *Dimond* suggested that even in that case he *"had in mind that the lowest locally available hire rate represented a reasonable approximation of the BHR"*.[34] It held that the approach outlined in *Stevens* was consistent with *Dimond* and with Burdis. In relation to *Bent No. 2*, the Court of Appeal held that there was no *"real conflict"* between the decisions because where the top end of the range of basic hire rates exceeds the lowest reasonable rate

---

33 McBride v UK Insurance Ltd, [2017] EWCA Civ 144.

34 Ibid. para. 37.

> *"the claimant will not recover more than that lowest reasonable rate, unless he or she can demonstrate that it was appropriate on the facts of the particular case to take some higher rate, which is extremely unlikely ever to be the case. In a modern context, where it is no longer necessary to pore through the yellow pages and telephone a whole series of car hire companies, but comparable prices can be obtained very quickly and painlessly through an internet search, the reasonable person in the position of the claimant will not wish to pay more than the lowest reasonable rate charged by a mainstream supplier or a local reputable supplier".*[35]

The result is that the rule established in *Stevens* that the lowest reasonable rate charged by a mainstream supplier or a local reputable supplier is likely to represent a reasonable estimate of the basic hire rate has been authoritatively re-affirmed. Moreover, the discussion in *McBride* is generally consistent with the approach to rates evidence in *Stevens*. The language used by the Court of Appeal is similar to the *"reasonable approximation"* referred to in *Stevens*. Thus in *Clayton*, the Court confirmed that the exercise in relation to basic hire rates is *"necessarily approximate and artificial"* and that a *"rigorous and exacting"* approach to rates evidence may be unjust.[36]

As to the second argument in *McBride*, the Court of Appeal refused permission to appeal against the finding that the basic hire companies in that case – Coretec, Dream Car Hire and Premiere Velocity – were mainstream suppliers. This was, the Court held, a finding of fact which was open to the Judge on the evidence and could not be disturbed on appeal.[37]

The Court of Appeal then considered the nil excess point. This had not been previously addressed in detail by a higher court. In essence, the issue

---

35 Ibid. para. 53.

36 Ibid., paras 95-96.

37 Ibid. para. 57.

arises because credit hire companies often charge a daily collision damage waiver in order to reduce the insurance excess payable in relation to any damage to the hire car to zero. Ordinary car hire companies also offer collision damage waivers but, particularly in relation to prestige vehicles, these waivers often limit the applicable excess rather than removing it altogether. How should the Court assess the equivalent basic hire rate, where the credit hire rate was offered with a nil excess but the proposed basic hire rates all carry an excess?

In *McBride* the Court held that where the evidence demonstrates that the basic hire rate is cheaper than the credit hire rate (without considering excess waivers) then the credit hire rate contains additional benefits which should be stripped out. That ordinary car hire companies are not prepared to offer a nil excess should not *"be used as a smokescreen to enable credit hire companies to recover their charges in full"*.[38]

The critical passage then continues:-

> *"where a nil excess is not available from car hire companies, the correct approach is to treat the nil excess separately from the comparison exercise between the default credit hire rate and the basic hire rate with an excess. It will almost invariably be the case that it was reasonable for the claimant to seek a nil excess for the reasons given in Bee v Jenson and, on that hypothesis, the only question for the Court will be how much should be recoverable as the cost of the purchasing a nil excess"*.[39]

That is a striking proposition because it makes it clear that, where basic hire rates do not offer a nil excess, the Court should not award the credit hire daily rate but should award the basic hire daily rate and then assess an additional amount for the cost of reducing the excess to zero.

---

38 Ibid. para. 68.

39 Ibid. para. 76.

The Court's approach to the assessment of the cost of a nil excess was also interesting. First, in *McBride* itself, the Court rejected the online products relied on by the defendant because the terms and conditions of that insurance did not apply to a vehicle as valuable as the one hired. It therefore awarded the basic hire daily rate plus the credit hire company's daily collision damage waiver.[40]

Second, in *Clayton*, though it did not arise on the facts of that case, the Court highlighted the potential importance of online stand-alone products:

> *"I consider that where there is evidence of the availability of an excess elimination insurance as a stand-alone product from Questor or other providers such as Insurance4carhire.com, the Courts should admit and accept such evidence as evidence of the reasonable cost of obtaining a nil excess, provided of course that the quote obtained from such a provider is for a car which is comparable with the one hired from the credit hire company and is for the same period as the period of actual hire from the credit hire company. Certainly, the Court should not reject such evidence because the judge or the claimant has not heard of the product, as the district judge did here. The exercise is an objective one and such evidence should be admissible irrespective of the subjective knowledge or lack of it of the Court or the claimant. Information about the available of such products can, in any event, be readily accessed on the internet [...] the admission and acceptance of evidence of these stand-alone products should be the norm".*[41]

Third, in *Clayton*, the Court declined to overturn the trial Judge's approach which had been to increase the basic hire daily rate by 10% to allow for the cost of a nil excess. On the analysis of the available evidence,

---

40 Ibid. para. 77-78.

41 Ibid. para. 105.

the 10% figure was *"closely parallel"* to the credit hire company's collision damage waiver.[42]

For the avoidance of doubt, if the basic hire rates relied on have quoted for a nil excess, then there is no further issue because *"only the lowest reasonable basic hire rate (including in such cases the cost of a nil excess) will be recoverable, on the assumption that the defendant has demonstrated that this is less than the charges of the credit hire company"*.[43]

Finally, in *Clayton*, the Court of Appeal rejected the challenge to the trial Judge's decision to increase the basic hire rate by 15% to reflect the reasonableness of obtaining rates for a seven-day period rather than a 28-day period. The Claimant's evidence in re-examination had been that although hire ultimately took 52 days, he had hoped it would be done very quickly in about a week. The Defendant's only rates evidence was based on a hire period of 28 days. The Court of Appeal held that taking a realistic approach to the manner in which these cases are handled and tried, the Judge was entitled to increase the 28 day rate by 15% to approximate the seven day rate, noting that this was consistent with the 12% discount to the 7 day rate which had been allowed in Bent No.2 to reach a 28 day rate.[44] On the other hand, the Court also noted that if the Judge had not made the 15% adjustment *"there would have been much to be said for the judge using the rates he did have in evidence, the 28 day rates, and taking those a reasonable approximation of the basic hire rate"*.[45]

---

42 Ibid. para. 103.

43 Ibid. para. 79.

44 Ibid. para. 100.

45 Ibid. para. 99.

F. Conclusion

In previous editions of this book, we noted the number of occasions on which the issue of rates has gone to the Court of Appeal and the number of rates dispute still litigating and expressed doubt that *Stevens* would remain the final word on this issue. *Stevens* has now been reconsidered and approved by *McBride*. The decisions in those cases are being accepted and applied in lower courts, including the High Court.[46] Although it is difficult to be confident that *McBride* will result in a permanent resolution of the correct approach to this difficult issue, for the time being this is the approach being applied – though, of course, its practical application to individual cases may still result in difficulties.

Standing back from the detail for a moment, the difficulty in these cases is usually that the Court is confronted by a range of different rates, sometimes provided by both parties and sometimes provided by the Defendant and rebutted by the Claimant, which can cover a range of different vehicles, terms and conditions and dates. But in order to award damages, the Court needs to arrive at a single figure. How should it turn the range of rates evidenced by the parties into a single basic hire rate?

It will not have escaped the reader's attention that the first four Court of Appeal decisions advocated a different solution to this problem. Indeed, the whole spectrum of possible solutions has been advocated: in *Burdis* it appeared that the Court was suggesting that a figure towards the top of the range of rates should be selected, in *Bent no1* an average of the rates was put forward and, finally, in *Stevens* the lowest reasonable rate was selected. That inconsistency invited the appeal in *McBride* that *Stevens* was inconsistent with earlier decisions. The failure of that appeal, however, has added authority to the "lowest reasonable rate" approach.

---

46 See, for example, Bunting v Zurich Insurance Plc, [2020] EWHC 1807, para. 10.

The starting point in arguing rates evidence in practice must now be the decisions in *Stevens* and *McBride.* Those decisions may also be the most straightforward to apply in practice – for Courts looking to find a single rate, it is easier to look for the lowest reasonable rate than to struggle with the more circuitous reasoning in *Bent No2.*

It is submitted that it is now clear that the burden of proof is on the Defendant to establish the BHR. Despite the ambiguous wording in *Burdis v Livsey, Bent no2* clearly places the burden of proof on the Defendant and *Stevens* agrees with *Bent no2* on that issue. Moreover, as explained in those cases, that result is also consistent with the law of betterment generally.

It is then clear that the task facing the court is to try to identify the BHR for the type of vehicle that the Claimant actually hired (or a reasonable equivalent). In assessing this rate, in the absence of direct evidence of a basic hire tariff from the credit hire company, the best evidence would be evidence of the right type of vehicle in the right location and at the right time. However, Defendants may argue that the references in *Stevens* to a "reasonable approximation" and "a degree of imprecision" when read together with the statement in *Bent No1* – never expressly overruled – that one should not be "hypnotised" by a need to find an exactly comparable vehicle, suggest that the Courts need not reject rates evidence altogether if it does not exactly replicate the original hire. Further support for that approach can be found in the reference in *McBride* to the exercise being *"approximate and artificial"* and the refusal to criticise the trial Judge for estimating percentage adjustments to the daily hire rates that he was presented with.

Finally, although the guidance in *Stevens* (endorsed in *McBride*) that the Courts should adopt the "lowest reasonable rate" appears clear, a number of aspects of the decision leave arguments open to both parties. First, what exactly is meant by the lowest ***reasonable*** rate? Claimants may argue that the word "reasonable" qualifies the rates that the Court should adopt so that the Court can discard any rates that impose onerous conditions such as a high deposit or excess. Defendants may argue that it only excludes rates which are obviously not comparable. Second, which hire companies qualify as "mainstream suppliers" or "local reputable suppliers"? Presumably, mainstream suppliers include household names such as Enterprise, Europcar or Avis. But what are the "mainstream" suppliers for more prestigious vehicles or private hire vehicles? And it is more difficult to identify what qualifies as a local reputable supplier. Where the hire companies involved are less well known, the Defendant may be well advised to ensure that the rates evidence addresses whether they are reputable suppliers though what exactly is required to meet this test remains open to argument. It is suggested that the number of years that a company has been established may well be relevant. But at one extreme, the parties could adduce evidence about online reviews of the company in an attempt to demonstrate that it is or is not reputable. The refusal of leave to appeal a similar point in *McBride* does not weaken the force of these observations, rather it emphasises that whether particular companies are mainstream or reputable is a factual issue which can be challenged at first instance.

CHAPTER FOUR

EVIDENTIAL MATTERS ON RATES

Where the court is evaluating one or more pieces of rates evidence it will still have to weigh the credibility and reliability of the evidence in reaching its conclusions as to the BHR.

Advocates and lawyers working in this area will quickly develop their own approach to tackling the merits of different pieces of evidence. A 'menu' of the more common issues is set out below. But this is an area in which the devil always lies in the detail. Often this requires an analysis of the raw data, which is buried in annexes to a statement, to ensure that it really supports the summary table which is usually offered. Many of the best points need to be discovered on a case-by-case basis in the detail of individual items of evidence.

However, it is necessary to underscore that recent cases tend to emphasise the importance of County Court Judges doing the best that they can with imperfect evidence, rather than rejecting basic hire rates evidence altogether on the basis of minor challenges. In *Bunting v Zurich Insurance Plc*, the High Court began by highlighting "the tradition of the Court of Appeal that County Court judges should be encouraged to do their best with imperfect evidence."[47] The High Court continued that, in the light of the Claimant's criticisms of the rates evidence, "the judge was fully entitled to use his experience to make a rough and ready adjustment to the hire cost".[48] Making a rough and ready allowance for the issues identified by the Claimant was considered "precisely the sort of matter

47 Bunting v Zurich Insurance, [2020] EWHC 1807, para, 13.

48 Ibid, para. 17.

which is open to a first instance judge" and the challenge to it on appeal was dismissed as "nit-picking".[49]

A similar approach was taken in *Axa Insurance Plc v Lakhani*, in which the High Court emphasised that since the issue was not strictly one of mitigation, it was wrong for the trial judge to have considered that the defendant had "a high hurdle to cross" to establish the basic hire rate.[50] These cases suggest that, at least in cases where only the Defendant has produced rates evidence, it may be difficult a claimant to argue that the rates evidence should be dismissed altogether (though still possible if a fatal flaw can be identified). However, there is clearly scope in appropriate cases for claimants to seek adjustments to increase the figures put forwards in rates evidence, for instance to reflect a 7-day rate rather than a 28-day rate as set out below.

Excess Waivers

In the previous edition of this book, we included a lengthy section on the issue of excess waivers, referring to the statements of principle in relation to the reasonableness of obtaining a nil excess in *Marcic v Davies*[51] and *Bee v Jenson*[52] and the inconsistent decisions in County Court cases such

49 Ibid, para. 19.

50 Axa Insurance Plc v Lakhani, [2021] EWCA Civ 873, paras. 12-13.

51 Marcic v Davies, Court of Appeal, 20 February 1985.

52 Bee v Jenson, [2006] EWHC 3359.

as *Dhami v Amlin Corporate Member Ltd*,[53] *Cheung v UK Insurance Ltd*[54] and *Lawson v Mullen*.[55]

Those cases have now been overtaken by the detailed and binding discussion of this issue in *McBride* (set out in the previous chapter). In short, the lack of availability of a nil excess from basic hire rates providers should not be used as a "smokescreen" to allow recovery of the full credit hire rate. Instead, the Court should separate the daily rate of hire from the excess waivers and consider them separately. The Court expressly encouraged reliance on stand-alone excess reduction products available online, provided that their terms and conditions are appropriate to the specific facts of the case (care is needed on this point – we note that in *McBride* the product was rejected as unsuited to the value of the hire vehicle).

The result is that the Court may allow a mix and match of rates; it may allow the basic hire daily rate plus the credit hire excess waiver; or it may allow the basic hire daily rate plus an excess waiver product available online. Whilst there may be some criticism of the reality of this approach (since the Claimant could never actually hire from a basic hire company but add on a credit hire company's excess waiver), the resulting guidance is clear, binding on the County Courts and relatively straightforward to apply in practice.

A related issue is whether the basic hire rates contain reasonable insurance arrangements. It may be open to the Claimant to argue that it would have been unreasonable for him to utilise basic hire rates which only provide

[53] Dhami v Amlin Corporate Member Ltd, Unreported, HHJ Oliver Jones QC, 23 July 2013.

[54] Cheung v UK Insurance Ltd, Unreported, HHJ Worster, 27 March 2015.

[55] Lawson v Mullen, Unreported, HHJ Freedman, 12 June 2015.

for third party insurance. As explained in *Bee v Jenson*,[56] upon receiving the hire vehicle, the Claimant is obliged to return it in the same condition that he received it. That means that if the Claimant is involved in another accident, he is in a worse position than if he was using his own vehicle because he would not have the option to delay repairs, choose not to repair the vehicle or effect amateur or temporary repairs. The Claimant's insurance needs are therefore different than they were prior to the accident. This may allow the Claimant to argue that basic hire rates which only provide for third party insurance are not a reasonable option (assuming that the credit hire insurance arrangements were comprehensive). This point cannot be met by waivers which have the effect of reducing the applicable excess but do not convert the insurance from third party to fully comprehensive.

Methodology

It is sometimes worth attacking the methodology of the rates survey. The aim is to demonstrate either that it is not truly representative of the basic hire market or that the resulting rates would not really have been available to the claimant. It is worth noting, however, that in *Lakhani*, the High Court recognised that "[c]herry picking is [...] a legitimate part of the exercise".[57] If the aim of the exercise is to identify the lowest reasonable rate, then the evidence cannot fairly be criticised for choosing the lowest available rates.

The following points can arise:-

a) The rates may not be comparable with the rate offered by the credit hire company. In addition to the excess waivers addressed above, the basic hire rates might impose a mileage restriction or limit the number of additional drivers. The significance of these

56 Bee v Jenson, [2006] EWHC 3359, para. 15, cited at McBride, para. 58.

57 Axa Insurance Plc v Lakhani, para. 14.

points depends on the facts. If, on the evidence, the mileage restriction would pose no problem to the claimant, it is not relevant.[58] Similarly, while claimants have sometimes attacked basic hire rates for requiring the claimant to pay a deposit, where impecuniosity is not in issue this is unlikely to be relevant;[59]

b) Where the hire lasts for more than 28 days or even more than 7 days, the BHR may be based on hiring for 7 days or 28 days whereas the credit hire may be on a daily rate. Depending on the evidence, the Claimant might argue that he did not know at the start of the hire period how long he needed the hire vehicle for. This might have the result that the claimant would have been unable to take advantage of the discounted rate for longer periods of hire.

In *Bent no2*, the Court of Appeal rejected the submission that the trial Judge was wrong to take the 28-day rate. At paragraph 90, the reason given was that it was clear from the outset that *"it was going to take a considerable time to effect the repairs on this specialist car which needed specialist parts that had to come from Germany."*

It is worth noting two features of this decision. First, claimants may argue that it follows from that decision that it might be appropriate to take a daily or a 7-day rate in any case where it would not have been clear to the claimant that repairs were going to take a long time.

Second, the result reached in *Bent no2* is puzzling. At paragraph 91, the Court of Appeal accepted the trial Judge's finding that there was a discount to the daily rate in respect of longer hires and therefore discounted the BHR by 12%. It is not clear where this figure of 12% came from (the suggestion is that it was a

58 Bunting v Zurich Insurance Plc, para. 18.

59 Ibid.

concession by counsel at first instance, though what the concession was based on remains unclear). But in the absence of any statistics to support it, this might be considered an arbitrary discount of the type criticized by the Court of Appeal in *Burdis v Livsey*.

Nevertheless, in *McBride*, the Court of Appeal approved the approach of a trial Judge using his general experience to assess that a 28-day rate needed to be increased by 15% to reach a 7 day rate. The arbitrary nature of that increase was highlighted by the trial Judge himself describing it as *"guesswork"*, though the Court of Appeal held that *"he must in reality have been drawing on his considerable experience of such cases and the judicial knowledge … that you pay more for a 7 day hire than for a long term hire"*.[60]

In *Bunting*, the High Court also endorsed the ability of the trial judge to make rough and ready adjustments to the figures.[61] The Court accepted the rates evidence that, despite an apparent 30-day limit on the basic hire rates, the evidence was likely reflective of the rate over a longer period.[62]

The result is that where rates evidence is based on a period of hire which the Court finds inappropriate on the facts, this is not likely to lead to the evidence being rejected out of hand but can lead to the Court adjusting the evidence by a rough and ready percentage to reflect the likely greater daily cost of a shorter-term hire.

c) The person obtaining the rates evidence is likely to be a specialist in carrying out similar surveys. They may therefore be in a better position than the Claimant would have found himself in. In this regard, it is particularly important to consider how the witness

---

60 McBride, para. 101.

61 Bunting, para. 17.

62 Ibid., para. 16.

selected which companies to ask for a quote. Have they selected companies that they know belong at either the top or bottom end of the market? Have they only been able to source a vehicle after a series of referrals?

d) It is worth checking whether the basic hire rates come from a genuinely local company, or local branch of a national company, rather than from a London company which offers a delivery service. In this context, however, we note the observation of Recorder Smith in *Grice v Atos Origin IT Services UK Ltd*[63] that *"in an era when the internet is the first resort for anyone researching anything, the concept of locality is immediately enlarged; this is further exemplified by the preparedness of organisations to win commerce by offering delivery and collection services"*.

e) If the Claimant uses their vehicle for business use, it is necessary to check whether the basic hire rates allow for business use. Some hire companies, for instance, will not allow the vehicle to be used for the purposes of a courier or delivery driver. Any other peculiarities of the Claimant, such as age or driving convictions arguably also need to be taken into account.

f) Beware, in particular, of rates from hire companies located at airports. These companies are likely to be targeting the specific tourist market, they may well be in direct competition with a number of other companies in close proximity. They may not be truly representative of the local market as a result.

g) Where the rates evidence covers a selection of vehicles, it is worth considering whether these vehicles are truly comparable to the vehicle actually hired. A common flaw in rates evidence is that it assumes a certain level of knowledge about models of car, and

63 Grice v Atos Origin IT Services UK Ltd, Unreported, Bradford County Court, 26 August 2016.

neglects to explain properly why they are considered to be comparable.

h) In line with the decision in *Stevens*, it is now permissible to investigate whether the hire companies involved are "mainstream" and whether they are "reputable local suppliers".

A particular issue which often arises in these cases is whether the basic hire rates evidence actually proves that an appropriate vehicle was available to the Claimant at the material time. This is, of course, potentially more difficult for the Defendant to establish since it would require a detailed telephone enquiry or a contemporaneous database search, rather than a simple online search after the event. Defendants may argue, in line with the approach taken in *McBride* and *Stevens*, that availability is a red herring and the hypothetical exercise being undertaken does not require actual proof of availability. Claimants have historically responded that the burden of proving that the basic hire rate was cheaper than the credit hire rate is on the Defendant and that necessarily requires proof of availability.

This issue was addressed squarely in *Bunting*. The High Court held not only that the judge was entitled to accept the rates evidence that a comparable car would have been available at the time, but also that "the court does not necessarily require evidence as to the availability of a particular car at a particular date".[64] This decision makes it difficult for claimants to rely upon availability in most cases, though the argument may retain some attraction in cases concerning unusual vehicles or remote locations.

In many lower-value claims it is common for rates evidence to be assessed on paper only. It is usually to the advantage of the person seeking to challenge the rates evidence to try to get the witness to attend court for

64 Bunting, para. 16.

cross-examination. Unexpected flaws may become apparent under questioning.

Credibility

Another way to attack rates evidence, in appropriate cases, is to undermine the credibility of the witness who puts the rates forward. Often their objectivity might be challenged, particularly if the witness is linked to the credit hire company or to the insurer. Alternatively, it might be worth exploring what proportion of their instructions come from claimants and defendants (as a litigant would assess a medical expert in a personal injury case) and how much they get paid for each statement.

A related point is that some cases suggest that witness statements (therefore including evidence of hire rates) should not be given by a solicitor with conduct of the case. This point was taken in a credit hire context in *TNT UK Ltd v Gregory*, in which the Court described the rule that a solicitor should not give evidence as "well-established" and explained that it was necessary to prevent conflicts of interest.[65]

It is not our intention to comment in detail on the contempt of court cases brought against the employees of a certain rates surveying company.[66] Suffice it to say that, returning to first principles, rates evidence is ordinary factual evidence and, like any other witness, the person who completed the survey must sign a statement of truth. The consequences if the statement of truth is compromised – including contempt of court (which as these cases illustrate carries a prison

65 TNT UK Ltd v Gregory and Choudry, Unreported, HHJ Hampton, 25 June 2010 para. 9.

66 For a summary of the facts, see Dickinson and others v Tesco Plc and others, [2013] EWCA Civ 36. For the sentences ultimately imposed, see R (on the application of Accident Exchange Ltd) v Broom and others, [2017] EWHC (Admin) 1530.

sentence) – should in principle be no different for a witness as to basic hire rates than for any other witness.

The Form of Rates Evidence

A dispute sometimes arises about whether rates evidence is expert evidence. Procedurally, permission is required to rely on an expert report. Evidentially, the crucial difference is that an expert witness may give opinion evidence. Defendants may seek permission to rely on expert evidence on rates, in order to lend extra authority to their evidence or to allow their witness to answer questions with their opinion. By contrast, particularly on the small claims track where the courts are reluctant to give permission for expert evidence, the Claimant may argue that the rates evidence is expert and should be excluded. Defendants may respond by arguing that a person who carries out a survey is not exercising any particular expertise. Simply contacting hire companies is a task that anyone could perform. The point is arguable either way, however, many Courts now adopt a standard direction in relation to rates evidence, which specifies that it is factual evidence to be given in the form of a witness statement.

Where a witness is giving lay evidence about basic hire rates, unless the directions specify otherwise, the usual rules of evidence apply. This means that if the party does not intend to call the witness to give oral evidence, they must give the other party notice of this intention (different rules and considerations apply on the small claims track). Failure to do so could have serious consequences, including the exclusion of the evidence.

In small claims, where the strict rules of evidence do not apply, Defendants might choose to rely simply on quotations printed from the internet, perhaps even without a witness statement in support. In support of this approach, Defendants may rely on *Smith v Burney*.[67] In that case

67 Smith v Burney, Unreported, HHJ Behrens QC, 27 April 2007.

HHJ Behrens QC upheld the decision at first instance to admit evidence of basic hire rates which was simply printed off the internet and was sent to the Claimant's Solicitors only three working days before trial. The Court held that there was no prejudice to the Claimant since the evidence was easily verifiable and the limitations of the evidence were apparent on its face without the need for cross-examination. Insurers may rely on this case to support the admission of evidence printed off the internet, and indeed late evidence of basic hire rates mores generally. Claimants may argue that the decision was influenced by the fact that this was an extremely small claim, worth less than £1,000. The same approach might not apply even to cases still within the small claims track but worth say £9,500.

Standard Directions

It is becoming increasingly common for Courts to issue standard directions in relation to credit hire cases, which can include mandatory provisions about the contents of rates evidence. The precise terms of the directions vary, however it is not uncommon for them to prescribe the minimum number of quotes required or even to require evidence of availability.

Where the Court makes an order in those terms, the parties should comply with it and, in default, they run a risk that the Court will refuse to admit the evidence. It is noteworthy that in Bunting, the High Court proceeded on the basis that the rates evidence had been admitted at first instance (without objection) notwithstanding concerns that it did not fully comply with the directions order.[68]

As a result, where the Defendant objects to the terms of such orders, it should make an application to vary them within the seven-day time limit

68 Bunting, para. 4.

allowed under the CPR. Alternatively, it may be necessary to consider applying for relief from sanctions in writing prior to trial.

Simultaneous Exchange or Rebuttal Evidence

The usual rule in civil cases is that the parties exchange their evidence at the same time, so that neither party has the benefit of seeing the other's evidence first. However, in a number of recent cases, the Claimant has argued that rather than filing their own rates evidence simultaneously, the Claimant should be permitted to file evidence rebutting the Defendant's rates. County Court practice is currently inconsistent. The Claimant's argument was accepted by District Judge Bloom in *Gonzalez v Dignity Funerals Ltd*[69] but rejected by District Judge Bell in *Miller v AIG Europe Ltd.*[70]

ABI Rates

It is not appropriate for Defendants to rely upon ABI Rates. As the Court of Appeal said in *Burdis* at paragraph 150:

> *"No doubt the scheme is, and will be, of benefit to insurers, the accident hire companies and the public; but the ABI figures cannot be taken in hostile litigation as being the appropriate figures of loss. They reflect a compromise agreed between the parties rather than an assessment of loss."*

The simple truth is that the ABI Rates are not relevant to the court's task in these cases. They will be left out of account.

---

69 Gonzalez v Dignity Funerals Ltd, Unreported, Willesden County Court, 14 March 2016.

70 Miller v AIG Europe Ltd, Unreported, Guildford County Court, 15 January 2016.

PART TWO

IMPECUNIOSITY

CHAPTER FIVE

IMPECUNIOSITY

A. Introduction

There is only one clearly recognised exception to the rule in Di*mond v Lovell.* It arises where the Claimant was impecunious at the time of the hire. As we will see, the precise definition of impecuniosity remains contentious, but the essence of impecuniosity is that, at the relevant time, the Claimant could not afford to pay the basic hire rate.

In this chapter, we will consider the analysis of impecuniosity in the leading case of *Lagden v O'Connor,*[71] recent cases applying the test of impecuniosity including *Irving v Morgan Sindall Plc* and *Putta v Royal Sun Alliance Insurance Plc* and the practical implications of this issue including on applications for pre-action disclosure.

B. Lagden v O'Connor

The Facts of Lagden

At first instance, HHJ Harris found as facts that Mr Lagden was:-

> *"an unusual man, an ex press photographer, now an unemployed Jehovah's witness in poor physical and mental health, with memory difficulties and a house on Canvey Island. He had very little money, he was indeed at all material times subject to an administration order."*[72]

---

71 Lagden v O'Connor, [2004] 1 AC 1067.

72 Lagden, para. 34.

From these facts HHJ Harris drew the conclusion that Mr Lagden had no other choice but to enter a credit hire contract.[73]

These findings are intriguing. The factual findings about Mr Lagden's means are remarkably brief. The Judgment gives no detail at all about whether Mr Lagden had any available savings, nor does it stop to analyse his income and outgoings. There is nothing in the Judgment to suggest that detailed disclosure was obtained or considered.

As a result, there is room to doubt the factual basis for the legal conclusion that he was impecunious. Lord Scott, in the minority of the House of Lords, drew attention to this: *"I do not regard the factual basis on which Dimond v Lovell has been distinguished as very persuasive...the proposition that Mr Lagden had no choice does not seem to me satisfactorily based given the rather sparse facts."*[74]

Moreover, these findings were made against a background of doubts about the claimant's credibility. HHJ Harris held that *"Mr Lagden was not a wholly convincing witness...he seemed for no very obvious reason to be anxious to assist Helphire if he could"*.[75] It is interesting that the courts were content to make a finding of impecuniosity against this limited factual background. Perhaps the explanation is that, given the administration order, Mr Lagden's case was so clear-cut that no further detail was required. As set out below, in most cases a more comprehensive analysis of the claimant's means is likely to be required.

The Principle Established in Lagden

In *Lagden*, the Claimant argued that it is one thing to say that credit hire rates incorporate irrecoverable additional benefits and so an ordinary claimant can only recover the equivalent basic hire rate. But it is quite

73 Ibid, para. 82.

74 Ibid, paras 74-75.

75 Ibid, para. 35.

another to apply this principle without modification to an impecunious claimant. Such a claimant could not afford to pay hire charges and so does not have a choice between the credit hire rate and the basic hire rate: for him / her it is credit hire or nothing. The argument runs that for such a person the additional benefits inherent in a credit hire contract are incidental to the cost of obtaining a replacement vehicle. Therefore, the Claimant argued, an impecunious claimant should recover the credit hire charges in full.

The Insurers responded that this line of argument was foreclosed by the House of Lords decision in *Dimond* itself, which established a clear principle which did not allow for any exceptions. Moreover they relied on *the Liesbosch*[76] to assert that where damages are augmented by the Claimant's lack of financial resources, those additional damages are too remote to be recoverable from the Defendant.

By a narrow majority, the House of Lords found in favour of the Claimant.

Lord Hope delivered the most detailed of the three speeches in the majority. He began by setting out the House of Lords decision in *Dimond*. Then he described the problem in the following terms:

> *"But what if the injured party has no choice? What if the only way that is open to him to minimise his loss is by expending money which results in an incidental and additional benefit which he did not seek but the value of which can nevertheless be identified? Does the law require gain to be balanced against loss in these circumstances? If it does, he will be unable to recover all the money that he had to spend in mitigation. So he will be at risk of being worse off than he was before the accident. That would be contrary to the elementary rule that the purpose of an*

[76] Owners of Liesbosch Dredger v Owners of SS Edison ("the Liesbosch"), [1933] AC 449.

> *award of damages is to place the injured party in the same position as he was before the accident as nearly as possible."*[77]

He reviewed the authorities and concluded:

> *"the facts in these two cases were quite different from those in this case. But I think that the principles on which they were decided are of general application, and it is possible to extract this guidance from them. It is for the defendant who seeks a deduction from expenditure in mitigation on the ground of betterment to make out his case for doing so. It is not enough that an element of betterment can be identified. It has to be shown that the claimant had a choice, and that he would have been able to mitigate his loss at less cost…So if the evidence shows that the claimant had a choice, and that the route to mitigation which he chose was more costly than an alternative which was open to him, then a case will have been made out for a deduction. But if it shows that the claimant had no other choice available to him, the betterment must be seen as incidental to the step which he was entitled to take in the mitigation of his loss and there will be no ground for it to be deducted".*[78]

And he later repeated:

> *"But it is reasonably foreseeable that there will be some car owners who will be unable to produce an acceptable credit or debit card and will not have the money in hand to pay for the hire in cash before collection. In their case the cost of paying for the provision of additional services by a credit hire company must be attributed in law not to the choice of the motorist but to the act or omission of the wrongdoer. That is Mr*

77 Lagden, para. 30.

78 Ibid, para. 34.

> *Lagden's case. In law the money which he spent to obtain the services of the credit hire company is recoverable."*[79]

One criticism of these passages in Lord Hope's speech is that they seem to elide issues arising from mitigation and issues arising from betterment. It is striking that Lord Hope often refers to both issues in one sentence, which creates the impression that the same conclusions necessarily apply to both. Of course this is not necessarily the case, as the House of Lords decision in *Dimond* itself demonstrated.

Lord Hope also rejected the Defendant's arguments based on *The Liesbosch*. In that case the House of Lords had held that the damages payable by a Defendant could not be increased by virtue of a Claimant's impecuniosity. Lord Hope stopped short of saying that *the Liesbosch* was wrongly decided. However, he said that: *"it is clear that the law has moved on"*.[80] In the same paragraph he continued that, the present position is that a wrongdoer must take his victim as he finds him: *"this rule applies to the economic state of the victim in the same way as it applies to his physical and mental vulnerability"*.

The other two majority speeches were shorter. Lord Nicholls (with whom Lord Slynn agreed) attacked the case from a common sense point of view:

> *"the law would be seriously defective if in this type of case the innocent motorist were, in practice, unable to obtain the use of a replacement car. The law does not assess damages payable to an innocent plaintiff on the basis that he is expected to perform the impossible. The common law prides itself on being sensible and reasonable. It has regard to practical realities"*.[81]

79 Ibid, para. 37.

80 Ibid, para. 61.

81 Ibid, para. 6.

In the same paragraph he continued

> *"Here, as elsewhere, a negligent driver must take his victim as he finds him. Common fairness requires that if an innocent plaintiff cannot afford to pay car hire charges, so that left to himself he would be unable to obtain a replacement car to meet the need created by the negligent driver, then the damages payable under this head of loss should include the reasonable costs of a credit hire company".*

The result of *Lagden* is thus that a claimant who was impecunious at the time of hire can, subject to any arguments about mitigation, recover the credit hire daily rate.

The Definition of Impecuniosity

It is plain from the dissenting speeches that Lord Scott and Lord Walker were concerned that it would prove difficult to give a workable definition of impecuniosity. Thus Lord Scott said

> *"the impecuniosity, no other choice, exception that your Lordships are introducing...is conceptually imprecise. It will, I believe, prove an obstacle to the swift and economical settlement of a very large number of simple cases. I think it will be a disservice to the development of the law".*[82]

Lord Walker expressed himself in similar terms:

> *"The concept of a claimant being unable to hire a replacement car (otherwise than through an accident hire company) because of impecuniosity is, as was acknowledged in the course of argument, a vague one... To allow the exception would be liable to lead to an increase in contested small claims, contrary to the public interest."*[83]

[82] Ibid, para. 88.

[83] Ibid, para. 106.

It is easy to understand the minority's concern. The Courts (and, of course, the parties) need to resolve many low-value credit hire cases in a proportionate and fair way. But questions related to a claimant's means are inevitably fact specific, may require significant volumes of disclosure and may be open to different interpretations. As a result, whether or not the claimant falls within the definition of impecuniosity is often a contentious issue.

Lord Nicholls and Lord Hope both discussed the definition of impecuniosity. We will consider the relevant passages in both speeches and whether there is any substantial difference in their approaches.

The first definition of impecuniosity was suggested by Lord Nicholls:

> *"There remains the difficult point of what is meant by 'impecunious' in the context of the present type of case. Lack of financial means is, almost always, a question of priorities. In the present context what it signifies is inability to pay car hire charges without making sacrifices the plaintiff could not reasonably be expected to make."*[84]

Thus Lord Nicholls propounded one single test: was the claimant unable to pay car hire charges without making sacrifices that he / she could not reasonably be expected to make.

Lord Nicholls himself described this test as "open-ended", thereby showing that he appreciated that this might give rise to difficulties in applying it to the facts of real cases. Of course, there will be a number of claimants who are obviously impecunious (like Mr Lagden) and obviously pecunious (perhaps having significant savings). But a significant number of claimants will fall somewhere in the middle; they would be able to raise the money to pay for hire charges, but using the money for hire charges would have a knock-on effect on the rest of their finances. Should the law treat these individuals as impecunious? The answer according to Lord Nicholls is that the court should look at the

84 Ibid, para. 9 (underlining added).

sacrifices that the claimant would have to make in order to pay the hire charges, and determine if they are reasonable or unreasonable. But the problem is that this incorporates ideas of reasonableness which can lead to uncertainty; the reasonableness of particular decisions is inherently open to argument on the facts of individual cases.

Applying Lord Nicholls' test, the courts must consider a wide range of circumstances. One claimant might have had the right sum of money saved in a bank account, but have intended the money to pay for a family holiday. Another claimant might have £20,000 in savings, but say that this was a redundancy payment which they needed to keep in case they weren't able to find a new job. To take a more extreme example, another claimant might have £200,000 in a savings account but give evidence that they intended to use the money immediately to buy a yacht which they needed to maintain their status as the yacht club president. It is open to argument whether the sacrifices required of any or all of these hypothetical claimants in order to pay for hire charges would be reasonable or unreasonable and hence whether they would be regarded as impecunious.

A different definition of impecuniosity was set out in the speech of Lord Hope. He began by saying:

> *"The wrongdoer is not entitled to demand of the injured party that he incur a loss, bear a burden or make unreasonable sacrifices in the mitigation of his damages."*[85]

This, of course, sounds similar to the test suggested by Lord Nicholls: where one judge in the majority speaks of *"unreasonable sacrifices"* and another judge in the majority speaks of *"sacrifices the plaintiff could not reasonably be expected to make"*, it seems artificial to try to draw a distinction between them. There is, however, something odd about the wording chosen by Lord Hope because incurring hire charges will always

---

[85] Ibid, para. 34.

mean incurring a loss and bearing a burden. In fact, it transpires from the following paragraphs that Lord Hope had a rather different test in mind. He continued in the very next sentence:-

> *"He [the defendant] is entitled to demand that, where there are choices to be made, the least expensive route which will achieve mitigation must be selected".*

In expanding on the meaning of impecuniosity, Lord Hope returned to the notion of choice:-

> *"the criterion that must be applied is whether he had a choice – whether it would have been open to him to go into the market and hire a car at the ordinary rates from an ordinary car hire company.*[86]
>
> *In practice, for reasons that are obvious, companies which offer cars for hire in the open market insist on payment of the rental up front before the car is collected, together with a sum to cover the risk of damage to the car while it is on hire. Payment is usually made by means of a credit card or a debit card. Some companies may accept cash, but if they do the sum that will have to be paid up front will not be small. Many car owners are, of course, well able to provide what is needed to satisfy the hirer that the money which is needed to pay for the hire is available. If they choose to use the services of a credit hire company they must accept as a deduction from their expenditure the extra cost of doing so. The full cost of obtaining the services of a credit hire company cannot be claimed by the motorist who is able to pay the cost of the hire up front without exposing himself or his family to a loss or burden which is unreasonable.*
>
> *But it is reasonably foreseeable that there will be some car owners who will be unable to produce an acceptable credit or debit card and will not have the money in hand to pay for the hire in cash before collection. In their case the cost of paying for the provision of additional services*

86 Ibid, para. 34.

> *by a credit hire company must be attributed in law not to the choice of the motorist but to the act or omission of the wrongdoer."*[87]

It is submitted that these passages indicate that the test which Lord Hope propounds is a test of choice: whether or not it would be 'open to' the Claimant to pay basic hire charges.

Clearly this test would produce different results compared with the test suggested by Lord Nicholls. In the examples previously given, the yacht club president, the redundant worker and the person saving for a family holiday all have a choice – it would be 'open to' all of them to hire a vehicle. As a result, applying Lord Hope's test all would be pecunious. The advantage of the test described by Lord Hope is that it is clearcut and easy to apply. The disadvantage is that it does not allow the Court to take account of an individual claimant's needs and circumstances and, as a result, it is capable of leading to unattractive results in practice.

The minority did not agree that "choice" was a workable test. Lord Scott commented that *"there are nearly always choices"* and continued that *"to say that he [Mr Lagden] had no other choice seems to me somewhat implausible"*.[88] Lord Walker agreed, suggesting that the test is rather artificial: *"the choice is likely to depend on temperament and resourcefulness, rather than on some minute calculation of their margin of solvency."*[89]

In an attempt to answer the criticism that the test for impecuniosity would lead to an increase in contested cases, Lord Hope laid down a rule of thumb:

> *"In practice the dividing line is likely to lie between those who have, and those who do not have, the benefit of a recognised credit or debit card. It ought to be possible to identify those cases where the selection*

---

87 Ibid, paras 35 – 37.

88 Ibid, para. 75.

89 Ibid, para. 106.

> *has been made on grounds of convenience only without much difficulty."*[90]

Again, the advantage of this rule of thumb is that it would bring clarity and certainty. It is straightforward to establish whether any individual claimant had a debit / credit card.

But, claimants may argue that such a test is too blunt an instrument. Lord Scott pointed out two problems with it. First, he said that *"there are still many people in this country who keep cash in their houses, would be accounted quite well-off by most standards, but who do not have credit or debit cards."*[91] Whether or not this remains factually accurate, the basic point remains that possession of a credit or debit card is not a true guide to wealth. It is easy to imagine a claimant with many credit cards, all with varying amounts of debt on them, being in a far worse financial position than a person with no credit cards.

Second, Lord Scott pointed out that there will be many people who lack spare cash to pay for hire charges, but could make use of a facility to borrow – perhaps through a credit card. The result of Lord Hope's test is that Mr Lagden who had no spare cash and so made use of credit hire could recover the cost of credit inherent in the hire charges. But another claimant who had no spare cash but could have paid for hire charges on a credit card, would logically only recover the basic hire rate and so could not recover the cost of credit. Lord Scott suggested that no sensible distinction can be drawn between these cases – they simply involve claimants using different sources of credit.

This in turn raises the spectre of whether a claimant who could only afford to pay for basic hire charges on a credit card can increase his damages by claiming the cost of the basic hire charges plus the cost to him of putting those basic hire charges on his credit card (i.e. the interest

---

90 Ibid, para. 42.

91 Ibid, para. 87.

on those charges). Although inevitably difficult to calculate (it would depend on the terms applicable to his credit card), since *the Liesbosch* is no longer good law, claimants may argue that there is no barrier to such a claim.

As set out above, there are differences between the approach adopted by Lord Nicholls and Lord Hope. No subsequent higher court cases have expressed a preference for one test over the other. As a result, defendants may wish to emphasise Lord Hope's more clear-cut test of 'choice', whilst claimants may prefer to emphasise Lord Nicholls' test of 'unreasonable sacrifices'. There remains ample scope for argument on the facts of specific cases.

Further issues of principle remain to be resolved. For example, how far is the court entitled to take account of the earnings of the Claimant's partner in determining impecuniosity? In this context, the case of *Fettes v Williams*[92] is interesting because HHJ Hull QC was quite prepared to take account of the Claimant's husband's earnings in deciding that she was not impecunious.

C. Cases Applying Impecuniosity

Although there are few reported appeals and it would not be practical to set out every first instance decision on impecuniosity, it may be helpful to set out a number of decisions below as an illustration of the way in which the courts apply the definitions of impecuniosity in real cases.

In the High Court, Turner J had to consider an appeal against the first instance finding that the Claimant was not impecunious in *Irving v*

92 Fettes v Williams, HHJ Hull QC, unreported 22 January 2003.

Morgan Sindall Plc.[93] The relevant section of the Judgment is relatively short and it is worth setting it out in full:-

> *The material before the judge on the issue of impecuniosity was relatively straightforward. The claimant was employed at a modest basic wage of £472 per month. She was able to improve on this figure by working overtime the extent of which fluctuated but which could raise her total income to about £700 per month. Her current account statements reveal a cyclic pattern reflecting monthly peaks upon the crediting of wage payments which are gradually eroded by expenditure over the course of the month which follows. The troughs are marked by a balance in the region of £250. She had an ISA savings account containing about £250. However, the claimant also had a Graduate Bank Account which, although not accumulating interest charges, was overdrawn to the extent of a little over £700 at the material time. She had a credit card with a limit of £500.*
>
> *The pre–accident value of the claimant's car was £775.*
>
> *The judge concluded that the claimant could have raised about £900 by depleting those of her accounts which were in credit and spending up to her credit card limit. Thus she would be able to buy a replacement car of the value of that written off.*
>
> *What the judge failed to appreciate, however, was that his calculations were based on the assumption that the claimant could be expected to have bought a replacement car immediately after the accident. Such an assumption was untenable. A fortnight had elapsed before her car had been written off. At the very least, the claimant would have needed a further fortnight thereafter within which to buy a replacement. Over this period of four weeks, the claimant would have been entitled, even if pecunious, to have hired a car at the basic hire rate. Such evidence as was before the court revealed that the cost of hiring a replacement*

93 Irving v Morgan Sindall Plc, [2018] EWHC 1147 QB.

> *vehicle on this basis would have been about £700 over this period. Accordingly, when the hire charges and the capital cost of a replacement vehicle are added together, the sum which the claimant would have needed to raise was far in excess of that upon which the judge based his calculations.*
>
> *I take into account the fact that the judge had suggested that further sums could have been raised if the claimant had applied to extend the limit on her credit card or had made importunate approaches to her family for loans. Neither option in the circumstances of this case was sufficient to bring the claimant outside the parameters of impecuniosity. Furthermore, I cannot ignore the fact that by reducing her capital to the bare minimum and increasing her debt, the claimant would have been exposing herself to the risk of a serious financial challenge in the event that even a modest but unexpected financial reverse might have afflicted her before her claim was satisfied. Impecuniosity need not amount to penury.*
>
> *It will only be in rare cases in which an appellate court will interfere with a judgment on the issue of impecuniosity reached at first instance. Nevertheless, in the very particular circumstances of this case, I am satisfied that the judge below, experienced as he is, was wrong.*[94]

A number of observations can be made about that decision. First, it re-affirms that the question of impecuniosity is a question of fact for the trial judge and, despite the result in that case, is unlikely to be overturned on appeal.

Second, the factual findings summarised at paragraph 32 are hardly promising from the defendant's point of view. The Claimant had a monthly income of £700 (at best), minimal savings, a credit card limit of £500 and an overdraft on one bank account of £700. It is hardly

[94] Ibid. paras 32 – 37.

surprising that the High Court ultimately concluded that she was impecunious.

Third, the Court concluded that in assessing whether the Claimant could have afforded to replace her vehicle, it was relevant to consider the cost of hiring during the initial period before a replacement could have been bought. It was the addition the cost of four weeks' hire to the cost of a replacement vehicle which put impecuniosity beyond doubt. Defendants may, however, question whether this really establishes that where the issue is when and whether the Claimant ought reasonably to have incurred the cost of replacing their vehicle, the Court must also always bring into account the cost of hire in addition to the cost of replacement. It must surely be open to Defendants to contend, for instance, that the Claimant could have hired on credit for a short period before replacing the vehicle. Further, the well-known Court of Appeal decisions in *Umerji v Zurich* and *Opoku v Tintas Ltd* (discussed in detail in chapter 7) make no mention of bringing the cost of hiring into account in the manner suggested in *Irving*.

Fourth, the Court concluded – without much discussion – that an application to extend the credit limit on the Claimant's credit card or an approach to the Claimant's family for a loan was not "sufficient to bring the Claimant outside the parameters of impecuniosity". It is not clear what evidence there actually was about the possibility of a family loan or the option of extending the credit card limit. Claimants may argue that *Irving* supports the submission that claimants are not obliged to take on additional debt to family members or on credit cards, building on Lord Hope's words that the defendant is not entitled to demand that the claimant "incur a loss" or "bear a burden". Defendants may argue that the issue is inevitably fact specific and if the evidence shows that a particular claimant had ready access to family money or credit, that may be a relevant (and potentially decisive) factor in relation to impecuniosity.

Finally, the Court emphasised that the approach to impecuniosity should not be too restrictive. It observed that *"impecuniosity need not amount to penury"*. It was sensitive to the fact that *"by reducing her capital to the bare minimum and increasing her debt, the claimant would have been exposing herself to the risk of a serious financial challenge in the event that even a modest but unexpected financial reverse might have afflicted her before her claim was satisfied".* That is an important point to bear in mind. Claimants are not necessarily expected entirely to deplete their financial reserves in order to hire a replacement vehicle. Exposing a claimant to a risk of a serious future financial challenge is likely to be considered an unreasonable sacrifice.

In the High Court in *Stevens v Equity Syndicate Management Ltd,*[95] the Claimant appealed a finding that he was not impecunious. Burnett J described the factual evidence as "sketchy": the Claimant's witness statement asserted briefly that he could not have afforded to pay for hire charges and statements had been adduced from one current bank account which showed a balance between £2,500 and £3,500 whilst his car was with the repairer.[96] He also had an overdraft facility of £1,000. Hire charges at the basic hire rate were assessed at less than £1,500.

However, the Claimant asserted that once he had paid his mortgage and a loan, he only had around £500 per month for all other expenses (in fact, the analysis of his accounts suggested that the surplus was £750 not £500 but nothing turns on this). In oral evidence he added that he needed to keep a cushion of money to protect him against future events and gave the example that he later had to find money to pay for a child to have a tonsillectomy.

---

95 Stevens v Equity Syndicate Management Ltd, [2014] EWHC 689. As set out in Chapter Three, the Claimant appealed to the Court of Appeal on the rates issue but not on the impecuniosity issue.

96 Ibid, para. 18.

Burnett J concluded that the trial Judge was entitled to find that the Claimant was not impecunious and to base that finding on the "continuous healthy balance" in his current account.[97]

There are two interesting features of the decision. First, Burnett J noted that the single bank account disclosed "could not conceivably reflect the totality of economic activity of a man, still less a family man". Few withdrawals were evident from the current account, including no cash withdrawals and only one related to a supermarket and one relating to petrol. The plain inference must either be that the claimant or his family had access to another account or he dealt largely in cash. This shows that it can be important for defendants to look beyond the basic figures in bank accounts and to question whether they really reflect the claimant's full financial position.

Second, Burnett J remarked that the trial Judge was entitled to find that the claimant was not impecunious *"particularly in the context of a case where there was no dispute on liability and thus no question about the recoverability of reasonable hire charges".*[98] This reasoning has not been explored in other cases. But it raises an interesting question. Should the Courts assess whether it was open to the claimant to pay hire charges / whether the claimant could pay hire charges without making unreasonable sacrifices in absolute terms or on the basis that the claimant would have to part with money upfront but then be reimbursed? Defendants may argue that *Stevens* suggests that it is more difficult for a claimant to establish that he/she could not afford to pay hire charges, where liability is not in dispute and hence the claimant could expect to be repaid the money within a relatively short period. Claimants may respond that the issue is really about what they could afford at a particular moment in time and how likely they are to be able to recover the money – which may not be obvious at the time – is unlikely to be determinative.

97 Ibid, para. 21.

98 Ibid, para. 21.

In *Thompson v Vincent Haulage Ltd,*[99] a claimant with savings of £2,000 and a credit limit on his credit card of £1,000 was found not to impecunious in circumstances where the evidence suggested a basic hire rate in the region of £2,400. The argument that the claimant intended to use the £2,000 for the purchase of a property in Bulgaria was rejected partly for lack of evidence and partly because there was no indication that the money was required "within a short time".[100]

In *Boardman v Byrne,*[101] the claimant's assertion that he was impecunious was rejected based partly on his own admission that he would probably have been able to borrow the money and partly due to the *"enormous resources"* of the claimant's business which was the part owner of the damaged vehicle.[102]

In *W v Veolia Environmental Services UK (PLC),*[103] the evidence suggested that the claimant actuary was only earning enough to cover the costs of his business. He had not taken a salary for five years. He was under financial pressure due to an earlier divorce, and he was likely to retire in not many more years. He was overdrawn at the time, but had an overdraft facility of up to £30,000. He had savings of £50,000 – £100,000. He also had income from pensions, bringing in around £20,000 per annum.[104] The basic hire rate was in the region of £485 per

---

99 Thompson v Vincent Haulage Ltd, HHJ Benson QC, Preston County Court, 15 April 2008, unreported.

100 Ibid, para. 21.

101 Boardman v Byrne, Walsall County Court, 18 April 2008, unreported.

102 Ibid, para. 15.2.

103 [2011] EWHC 2010.

104 All findings of fact in this regard are set out in paragraph 7 of the judgment.

day.[105] HHJ Mackie QC held that the Claimant was impecunious.[106] His credit cards would not have withstood the basic hire rate for more than a brief period. He reasonably needed his limited capital for his old age.

In *Putta v Royal Sun Alliance Insurance Plc*,[107] on appeal the claimant contended that using his resources to pay basic hire rates would have left him with expensive credit card debts and more consideration should have been given to his expenses and need to provide for unexpected events. In dismissing the appeal, the High Court analysed the funds available to the claimant at the start of each week of the seven week period of hire.[108] The Court concluded that at the beginning of each week, the Claimant had substantial funds available to him and he would not have been left in penury.[109] The case is an interesting example of the precise analysis which may be required – rather than simply asking whether the Claimant could afford the total basic hire charges, it may be more revealing to break them down and look at whether the Claimant could reasonably have paid them on a week by week basis.

D. Practical Issues

Burden of Proof

One issue which has been controversial is which party bears the burden of proving whether or not the claimant was impecunious.

---

105 The Claimant hired a new Bentley in replacement for his 21-year old Bentley, explaining the scale of the basic hire rate. Perhaps a different result might have been reached had the Defendant challenged the reasonableness of hiring a new Bentley as a replacement.

106 Ibid, para. 61.

107 Putta v Royal Sun Alliance Plc, [2020] EWHC 117.

108 Ibid, paras. 34-40.

109 Ibid. paras 41-42.

An issue arose as to the burden of proof in relation to whether the Claimant could have afforded to repair / replace his vehicle in the Court of Appeal decision in *Zurich Insurance Plc v Umerji.*[110] In that case as a result of the directions order, having failed to disclose all his financial documents, the claimant was debarred from relying on impecuniosity. The Court of Appeal held that that debarring order applied to all issues to which the Claimant's finances were relevant. It considered that it made no practical sense to treat the burden of proof regarding impecuniosity differently as regards mitigation or as regards rates – the concept is the same and depends on the same evidence.[111] It added that since a claim for hire charges is a claim for expenditure incurred in mitigation of the primary loss (the loss of use of a vehicle), the burden is on the claimant to "prove (and therefore plead) that such expenditure was reasonably incurred".[112] Whilst this discussion was primarily in relation to the burden of proof on mitigation and the meaning of a specific unless order, it is plain from the discussion that the Court of Appeal considered that the burden of proof in relation to impecuniosity (as it applies to rates) was on the Claimant.

Claimants may argue that this is not consistent with earlier authorities which suggested that it was for the Defendant to prove that the Claimant was not impecunious. Thus Lord Hope in *Lagden* had said that *"it is for the defendant who seeks a deduction from expenditure in mitigation on grounds of betterment to make out his case for doing so…it has to been shown that the claimant had a choice."*[113] That approach was supported by the cases on betterment cited in that case.

Defendants, however, may argue that the burden of proof properly rests on the Claimant for three reasons. First, it is the Claimant who asserts

110 Zurich Insurance Plc v Umerji, [2014] EWCA Civ 357.

111 Ibid, paras 35 and 37.

112 Ibid, para. 37.

113 Lagden, para. 34.

that he is impecunious. In civil law it is generally for the party who relies on an assertion to prove it. Second, impecuniosity arises by way of an exception to the general rule in *Dimond*. It is generally for the party who seeks to take advantage of an exception to prove that they fall within it. Third, all of the evidence related to impecuniosity is exclusively in the Claimant's possession or control. It would be ridiculous, so Defendants might argue, if the Claimant could fail to disclose this material and then benefit from this failure to disclose, because the Defendant would be unable to prove that he was not impecunious.

In *W v Veolia Environmental Services UK (PLC)* HHJ Mackie QC elegantly summarised the problem which may arise: *"the burden of showing a lack of impecuniosity may rest upon the defendant but this is a matter peculiarly within the knowledge of the claimant."*[114] The Court of Appeal decision in *Umerji* resolved that problem by placing the burden of proof on the claimant in relation to impecuniosity.

Pleading and Standard Directions

The approach of the Courts to the pleading of impecuniosity has changed since previous editions. The current approach is to require the Claimant to plead facts relevant to impecuniosity. In many cases, the standard directions will impose a debarring order if the Claimant fails to comply with the obligation to plead impecuniosity and the relevant directions as to disclosure. This approach reflects the importance of the parties being able to assess the merits of the case at an early stage, with a view to settlement.

Movement in this direction began in *Umerji*, where the Court of Appeal drew attention to the Practice Direction to Part 16 (as it then stood) and observed that, consistent with their conclusion that credit hire charges were expenses incurred in mitigation of the primary loss, *"the claimant*

[114] W v Veolia, para. 60.

should plead his case as to reasonableness, including any assertion of impecuniosity".[115]

Since then, the Practice Direction to Part 16 of the Civil Procedure Rules has been amended. It now sets out that the claimant must state in the Particulars of Claim "if the claim relates to credit hire, whether the claimant could afford to pay in advance to hire a replacement car, and, if not, why not ("impecuniosity")".[116] Moreover, paragraph 6.4(2) states that the obligation to plead such matters "includes an obligation to state relevant facts."

Many standard directions in credit hire cases now impose a debarring order which prevents the claimant from relying on impecuniosity, unless they plead their position on impecuniosity in a Reply and provide the appropriate disclosure (usually bank statements and earnings information for the period from three months prior to the hire period to the end of the hire period).

The effect of such an order was considered by the Court of Appeal in *Diriye v Bojaj.*[117] In that case, despite an unless order requiring the claimant to plead "all facts" in support of impecuniosity, his Reply simply stated 'As he earned cash as a minicab driver, he expended the same on bills and daily living allowances for his family'.[118] The Court of Appeal, however, considered that the Reply needed to address the claimant's income, his expenditure and explain how those figures showed that he could not afford to pay hire charges.[119] It was instrumental to that decision that the Court considered that, first, the claimant was not

115 Umerji, para. 13 fn. 2.

116 Civil Procedure Rules 16PD para. 6.3(5).

117 Diriye v Bojaj, [2020] EWCA Civ 1400.

118 Ibid., para. 48.

119 Ibid.

entitled to "advance a rubbishy case in stages"[120] and, second, that the defendant is entitled to know the case which it has to meet.[121] The Court therefore concluded that the Reply did not comply with the debarring order.

Other cases illustrate the correct application of the approach in *Diriye*. In *Probyn v Noordin*,[122] at first instance the claimant had succeeded in an oral application for relief from sanctions in relation to impecuniosity, despite being in breach of a debarring order. The High Court held that faced with such a breach, the Court had to either refuse to grant relief or to grant relief and proceed in a fashion which would allow the trial to run fairly. It was not, however, open to the Court to grant relief and then allow the Claimant to rely on new evidence on impecuniosity which was not contained in his pleadings or disclosure.[123]

It follows from the decision, that if relief is to be granted in such a situation, then Claimant would have to amend the Reply to comply with the debarring order and provide full disclosure, presumably entailing an adjournment of the trial to allow the Defendant to consider the position.

The issue of compliance with an unless order also arose in *Braciforte v Williams*,[124] in circumstances where despite disclosing considerable financial disclosure, the Claimant was in default because she did not disclose statements from a Brazilian account which she could no longer access without travelling to Brazil. On appeal, the Court held that the trial Judge can make an "evaluative assessment" of whether the missing material affects the court's ability to determine impecuniosity. The Court

120 Ibid., para. 52.

121 Ibid., para. 53.

122 Probyn v Noordin, [2023] EWHC 3314.

123 Ibid., para. 47-50.

124 Braciforte v Williams, Liverpool County Court, 8 January 2025 (HHJ Wood KC).

distinguished between cases of wholesale non-compliance and cases where a substantial amount of material was disclosed. On the facts of that case, the trial Judge was not wrong to refuse to debar the Claimant from arguing impecuniosity.[125]

The Court in *Braciforte* also gave general guidance regarding impecuniosity to the effect that, first, the disclosure of accounts should not be cursory or half-hearted and should not be limited to the claimant's main account. Second, the Court retains a discretion to permit the claimant to rely on impecuniosity even if some non-disclosure is identified during the hearing, depending on the extent of the disclosure failure and its impact on the defendant's ability to challenge impecuniosity. Third, the parties should consider the disclosure on impecuniosity in advance of trial and identify any issues. The defendant should consider applying to debar the claimant at the outset of trial, if failings are identified. Claimants, by contrast, should consider whether an application for relief from sanctions is required.[126]

Finally, in *Motor Insurers' Bureau v Houston*, the High Court considered the effect of an unless order which provided that unless the Claimant provided financial disclosure he would be debarred from relying on impecuniosity "for the purposes of determining the appropriate rate of hire".[127] The Claimant failed to provide complete financial disclosure. The Court concluded that, giving the words in the order their ordinary and natural meaning, the effect of the wording of this debarring order was that the Claimant was only debarred from asserting impecuniosity for the purpose of rates but could assert impecuniosity as regards

---

125 Braciforte, paras. 54-57.

126 Braciforte, para. 65.

127 Motor Insurers' Bureau v Houston, [2025] EWHC 3178, paras. 17, 36.

mitigation and the period of hire.[128] The precise wording of the debarring order therefore remains highly significant.

<u>*Disclosure / Part 18 Questions*</u>

Given the uncertainties inherent in the definition of impecuniosity and the risk of a claimant being able to give new information about his finances in oral evidence, it is usually beneficial for the Defendant to try to obtain clear information and disclosure about impecuniosity at an early stage. After all, in *Lagden*, Lord Nicholls suggested that *"Motor insurers and credit hire companies should be able to agree on standard enquiries, or some other means, which in practice can most readily give effect to this test of impecuniosity"*.[129]

For claims that are in the fast track and multi-track, the Claimant must comply with standard disclosure. This means that he / she is obliged to disclose those documents *"on which he relies"* and which *"adversely affect his own case"*.[130] Where impecuniosity is in issue, it is likely that all bank statements, wage slips, credit card statements and other financial statements will either be documents on which the claimant relies or documents which adversely affect his own case. They should therefore be disclosed. The Defendant may also request further information from the Claimant pursuant to CPR Part 18 should clarification be required.

On the small claims track, the disclosure provisions are more limited. However, the parties are still required to disclose the documents on which they rely, and Civil Procedure Rule 27.2(3) additionally provides that the Court may *"order a party to provide further information if it considers it appropriate to do so"*.

---

128 Motor Insurers' Bureau v Houston, paras. 37-41.

129 Lagden, para. 9.

130 Civil Procedure Rules 31.6.

As a result, it is likely to be difficult for the Claimant to avoid the disclosure of relevant information and documents.

As mentioned above, many Courts now issue standard form orders in credit hire cases, which require the Claimant to disclose all relevant financial statements for a fixed period (usually three months before and three months after the period of hire). Close attention should be paid to the wording of those Orders. The Court should address the issue of compliance with the directions as a preliminary matter and, in the absence of full compliance, there is a real risk that the Claimant could be debarred from relying on impecuniosity.

Claimants should be aware that cases have been struck out for failure to disclose the relevant documents: *Saeed v Ellis*.[131] In more extreme cases, failure to disclose obviously relevant document may be held to amount to fundamental dishonesty: *Haider v DSM Demolition Ltd*.[132] In many other cases, concerns about partial disclosure feature as a reason for finding against the Claimant: see for example *Singh v Aqua Descaling Ltd*.[133]

It is, however, worth highlighting that standard disclosure only applies to documents which are or have been in the claimant's control (see CPR Part 31.8(1)). In *Morgan-Rowe v Woodgate*, the High Court confirmed that married couples are not in control of their spouse's bank or credit card statements.[134] As a result, the claimant will not be debarred by reason of a failure to disclosure their spouse's bank statements. If the

131 Saeed v Ellis, Nicol J, High Court of Justice, Queen's Bench Division, Manchester District Registry, 4 June 2009, Unreported.

132 Haider v DSM Demolition Ltd, [2019] EWHC 2712

133 Singh v Aqua Descaling Ltd, HHJ Oliver-Jones QC, Walsall County Court, 6 June 2008, unreported. Many more examples could be given.

134 Morgan-Rowe v Woodgate, [2023] EWHC 2375, para. 44.

defendant seeks disclosure of such documents, they retain the option of applying for non-party disclosure pursuant to CPR 31.17.

The modern approach to litigation is to front-load the costs so far as possible. Consistent with that approach, it is suggested that Claimants should ideally consider the position in relation to impecuniosity before issuing proceedings – including obtaining the relevant documents. If this groundwork is done, the Claimant will be well placed to plead the issue properly in the Particulars of Claim (with the aim of discouraging the Defendant from investigating rates evidence at all) and overcome any procedural hurdles.

Pre-Action Disclosure

In recent years, attention has switched to the extent to which defendants can oblige claimants to provide documents relevant to impecuniosity at the pre-action stage. From the insurer's point of view that is desirable, because it allows the insurer to consider the likely position in relation to impecuniosity at an early stage. From the claimant's point of view, however, it is an early stage of litigation to be asked to provide personal disclosure such as personal bank statements.

The test in relation to pre-action disclosure is set out in CPR 31.16(3) which provides that the Court may order pre-action disclosure where four conditions are satisfied:-

1. The respondent is likely to be a party to subsequent proceedings;
2. The applicant is also likely to be a party to subsequent proceedings;
3. If proceedings had started, the respondent's duty of standard disclosure would extend to the documents or categories of documents sought;

4. Disclosure before proceedings have started is desirable in order to:-

    a. Dispose fairly of the anticipated proceedings;

    b. Assist the dispute to be resolved without proceedings; or

    c. Save costs.

Provided these four jurisdictional preconditions are met, the Court then has a discretion whether to order pre-action disclosure.

In Holt v Allianz Insurance Plc,[135] the issue of pre-action disclosure in the context of impecuniosity reached the High Court on appeal, disclosure having been ordered at first instance. Somewhat unfortunately, the appeal was allowed on the technical basis that the applicant insurance company had failed to establish that it was likely to be a party to subsequent proceedings, with the respondent claimant arguing that they intended to issue only against the negligent driver.[136] The second condition was therefore not satisfied and the application for pre-action disclosure failed.

Although the High Court noted that its conclusions on the other issues were obiter and hence not binding, it went on to consider the remaining elements of the test.[137] The approach of the High Court was that it will generally be sensible for the claimant to grapple with impecuniosity, whenever a claim for credit hire charges is met with a response that the basic hire rates are lower.[138]

135 Holt v Allianz Insurance Plc, [2023] EWHC 790.

136 Ibid., paras. 73-75.

137 Ibid. para. 75.

138 Ibid., para. 39.

On the third condition (standard disclosure), the High Court considered that impecuniosity was very probably going to be asserted and disputed and hence the documents sought fell within standard disclosure.[139] The reasoning suggests that unless the Claimant has disavowed impecuniosity, the third condition is likely to be satisfied in credit hire cases.

On the fourth condition (desirability for a specified purpose), the High Court agreed with the first instance decision that, where impecuniosity is likely to be an issue, it would be contrary to the letter and spirit of the Practice Direction not to give serious consideration to it at the pre-trial stage.[140]

Finally, in relation to the exercise of discretion, notwithstanding the disclosure relating to personal information, the High Court (like the Court at first instance) would have exercised its discretion in favour of granting the application.[141]

These finding were largely consistent with the earlier decision on seven applications heard together in the County Court in Cardiff by HHJ Harrison, under the name of the first case *EUI Ltd v Charles*.[142]

Although the decision in *Holt* turned on the identification of the likely defendant, if it possible for insurers to overcome that technical hurdle, the remaining reasoning – which lower courts are likely to find persuasive – was, in general terms, in favour of granting pre-action disclosure. However, there would remain ample scope for disputing requests for pre-action disclosure on the facts of specific cases (for instance if the

139 Ibid., paras 80-82.

140 Ibid., para. 88.

141 Ibid. paras 91-93.

142 EUI Ltd v Charles, Unreported, 21 September 2018.

defendant failed to set up the point correctly in pre-action correspondence).

Finally, it is worth noting that CPR 46.1 provides that the usual costs order in relation to pre-action disclosure is that the applicant seeking pre-action disclosure should pay the costs of the application and the cost of complying with the order. CPR 46.1(3), however, provides the Court with the discretion to make a different order having regard to all the circumstances including (a) the extent to which it was reasonable to oppose the application and (b) compliance with relevant pre-action protocols.

Other Potential Exceptions to Dimond

One of the criticisms that Lord Walker advanced of the "choice" test is that it is not expressly limited to a claimant's financial resources. As Lord Walker put it:

> *"This claimant's choice was restricted by his extreme impecuniosity. The freedom of choice open to other claimants might be restricted by all sorts of other circumstances, such as the remote geographical location in which an accident occurred, the specialised character of the claimant's vehicle or a dislocation of the normal market caused by exceptional demand. The proposed modification of the principle in Dimond v Lovell seems dangerously open-ended"* [143]

Defendants may well argue that *Lagden* is a narrow decision focussing on the question of impecuniosity alone. Indeed, throughout their speeches (at least the speeches in the majority) their Lordships were focussing only on the question of financial means. It is therefore misleading, so the argument runs, to submit that the judgement has any wider implications: instead, it might be said, that it creates one narrow exception only.

---

143 Lagden, para. 104.

Claimants may respond, however, that the ratio of *Lagden* is not tied to financial means but is that if the Claimant has no choice but to hire on credit, the additional benefits that he thereby receives are purely incidental to obtaining a replacement vehicle. Thus, where freedom of choice is limited by any other factor including those described by Lord Walker, the Claimant may argue for recovery of the full credit hire rate.

In this regard, the Claimant's age is likely to be an important consideration. Many car hire companies will not hire to individuals younger than a certain age (or indeed older than a certain age), particularly where the vehicle in question is powerful or high value. Such a Claimant can argue convincingly that they had no alternative but to hire on credit and so that they should recover the credit hire charges in full. As we have already seen in Chapter Three, a related argument was accepted in *Bent No2*, on the basis that the defendant's basic hire rates evidence was not truly comparable to the credit hire rate, and hence the defendant had failed to discharge the burden of proof in that regard, because none of the surveyed hire companies would actually have hired to someone of the claimant's age.

PART THREE

MITIGATION

CHAPTER SIX

INTRODUCTION TO MITIGATION OF LOSS

A. Introduction

A further way for Defendant Insurers to attack credit hire charges is to argue that the Claimant has failed to mitigate his loss. In short, that the Claimant has acted unreasonably.

In assessing the strength of arguments based on mitigation of loss it is important to start with a firm grip on the general principles of mitigation. We will summarise them first. In this regard, we should add one word of caution. Mitigation is a difficult subject, about which whole books have been written. This chapter is not a substitute for such works as McGregor on Damages, which contains an excellent account of the law on mitigation.

But in addition to the general principles, the practitioner also needs to be aware of the increasing volume of cases applying these general principles to credit hire scenarios. These cases are the primary focus of this Part.

We should also note that in *Copley v Lawn*[144], the Court of Appeal expressed doubts about the application of mitigation of loss in this area:

> *"judges should, in my view, be reluctant to become too readily involved in complicated mitigation arguments since the major protection for the defendant and his insurers is that the claimant can only recover the "spot" or market rate of hire as explained in Dimond v Lovell. One rarely encounters mitigation arguments in ordinary sales of goods cases*

144 Copley v Lawn and Maden v Haller, [2009] EWCA Civ 580 at para. 6.

> *precisely because the relevant statute provides that damages are to be prima facie assessed by reference to the market value of the goods. The reason is that it is usually open to the innocent buyer or seller to go into the market to acquire other goods or dispose of the contractual goods and that is what he ought to be doing by way of mitigation of his loss. There is no reason why loss of use claims based on the hire of goods should be any different. I would, therefore, look with some scepticism on arguments that an innocent claimant should take further steps (over and above ensuring that he is not hiring a replacement car for more than the market rate) by way of mitigating his own loss or protecting the tortfeasor's position."*

For a period, this suggestion that mitigation arguments should be approached with some scepticism together with disappointing results for defendants in cases such as *Mattocks v Mann*, meant that the sting appeared to have been drawn out of mitigation arguments.

There has, however, been a resurgence of interest in mitigation in recent years. Significant Court of Appeal decisions such as *Zurich Insurance Plc v Umerji* and *Opoku v Tintas Ltd* have re-asserted the important restraint that mitigation of loss can place on excessive claims for hire charges. The net result is that mitigation arguments can no longer be lightly dismissed in this area.

The structure of this Part will be that the general principles of mitigation are set out below. The following five chapters will then look at some specific examples of common mitigation arguments in credit hire cases: need for a hire vehicle; courtesy cars; like for like; period of hire; and self-employed claimants / businesses.

B. General Principles

It is generally accepted that Claimants should take reasonable steps to limit their losses following an accident. Thus, the Claimant whose car is damaged is expected to investigate alternative means of getting to work, rather than presenting a vast claim for loss of earnings. This is usually labelled the 'duty to mitigate'.

Although this label is almost universal, even the phrase "duty to mitigate" is not without its difficulties. For a start the Claimant is not actually under an obligation to do anything at all. As Pearson LJ put it in *Darbishire v Warran*:- [145]

> *"The plaintiff is not under any actual obligation to adopt the cheaper method: if he wishes to adopt the more expensive method he is at liberty to do so and by doing so commits no wrong against the defendant or anyone else. The true meaning is that the plaintiff is not entitled to charge the defendant by way of damages with any greater sum than that which he reasonably needs to expend for the purpose of making good the loss. In short, he is fully entitled to be as extravagant as he pleases but not at the expense of the Defendant"*

The reasoning in *Darbishire v Warran* has since been strongly criticised on other grounds.[146] Nevertheless, it is submitted that the passage cited above represents the correct state of the law on mitigation; mitigation of loss is not about compelling the Claimant to take a particular course of action. It is simply about calculating what part of the Claimant's loss can be charged against the Defendant.

Burden of Proof

The Court of Appeal recently specifically addressed the burden of proof in a credit hire context in *Umerji*.[147] In that case, the Claimant had argued that whilst he bore the burden of proving impecuniosity (that he could not afford to pay basic hire rates without making unreasonable

[145] Darbishire v Warran, [1963] 1 WLR 1067 at 1075

[146] See Coles and others v Hetherton and others, [2013] EWCA Civ 1704, at paras 30 – 31.

[147] Zurich Insurance Plc v Umerji, [2014] EWCA Civ 357.

sacrifices), the Defendant bore the burden of proving that he could have afforded to purchase a replacement vehicle and so bring the period of hire to an earlier end. The issue before the Court turned on the wording of an unless order in relation to the disclosure of financial documents. But the Court went on to address the argument based on the different burdens of proof:-

> *"The correct analysis would appear to be as follows. A claim for the cost of hire of a replacement vehicle is, strictly, a claim for expenditure incurred in mitigation of the primary loss, namely the loss of use of the damaged vehicle: see the speech of Lord Hope in Lagden v O'Connor at para. 27 (p. 1077H). The burden is thus on the claimant to prove (and therefore plead) that such expenditure was reasonably incurred: see the authorities reviewed by Sir Mark Potter P in Beechwood Birmingham Ltd v Hoyer Group UK Ltd…There is no doubt a grey area about how much needs to be pleaded and proved to establish reasonableness before the evidential burden shifts to the defendant to show that the expenditure was unreasonable"*[148]

It is submitted that this analysis explains why it is often said that the Claimant bears the burden of proving that he needed to hire a replacement vehicle at all. There is an initial burden on the Claimant to show the expenditure on credit hire charges was reasonably incurred. If the Claimant does enough to discharge that burden, then the baton passes to the Defendant to show that the Claimant nevertheless acted unreasonably.

<u>*Standard of Mitigation*</u>

The standard of mitigation has been described in different terms in different cases. Some of these formulations are more favourable to the Claimant and others to the Defendant.

---

[148] Ibid., para. 37.

Thus Claimants often rely on the purple prose of Lord MacMillan in *Banco de Portugal v Waterlow and Sons Ltd:*[149]

> *"Where the sufferer from a breach of contract finds himself in consequence of that breach placed in a position of embarrassment the measures which he may be driven to adopt in order to extricate himself ought not to be weighed in nice scales at the instance of the party whose breach of contract has occasioned the difficulty. It is often easy after an emergency has passed to criticise the steps which have been taken to meet it, but such criticism does not come well from those who have themselves created the emergency. The law is satisfied if the party placed in the difficult by reason of the breach of a duty owed to him has acted reasonably in the adoption of remedial measures and he will not be held disentitled to recover the cost of such measures merely because the party in breach can suggest that other measures less burdensome to him have been taken."*

Of course, Lord MacMillan was speaking specifically about breach of contract. However his comments apply equally to tort. This was affirmed (for example) by Nourse LJ in *Mattocks v Mann*[150], Davies LJ in *Moore v DER.*[151]

In borderline cases, Claimants may wish to rely on the reasoning of Sedley LJ in *Wilding v British Telecommunications.*[152] Although an employment case, the doctrine of mitigation applies equally in both jurisdictions. In that case the Respondent argued that *"you act unreasonably if you do not act reasonably"*. Sedley LJ rejected this reasoning:-

---

149 Banco de Portugal v Waterlow and Sons Ltd, [1932] AC 452 at 506.

150 Mattocks v Mann, (1993) RTR 13 at 21E.

151 Moore v DER, [1971] 1 WLR 1476.

152 Wilding v British Telecommunications, (2002) ICR 1079.

> *"it is not enough for the wrongdoer to show that it would have been reasonable to take the steps he has proposed: he must show that it was unreasonable of the innocent party not to take them. This is a real distinction. It reflects the fact that if there is more than one reasonable response open to the wronged party, the wrongdoer has no right to determine his choice. It is where, and only where, the wrongdoer can show affirmatively that the other party has acted unreasonably in relation to his duty to mitigate that the defence will succeed."*[153]

On the other hand, there are other cases which suggest that the standard is wholly objective and that economic considerations may be overwhelming. Thus, Defendants may point to the following:-

> *"The person who has broken the contract is not to be exposed to additional cost by reason of the plaintiffs not doing what they ought to have done as reasonable men, and the plaintiffs not being under any obligation to do anything otherwise than in the ordinary course of business."*[154]

A similar point was made by Pearson LJ in *Darbishire v Warran*:

> *"It is vital, for the purpose of assessing damages fairly between the plaintiff and the defendant, to consider whether the plaintiff's course of action 'was economic or uneconomic, and if it was uneconomic it cannot (at any rate in the absence of special circumstances, of which there is no evidence in this case) form a proper basis for assessment of*

153 Ibid, para. 55.

154 James L.J. in Dunkirk Colliery Co. v Lever (1878) 9 Ch.D.20 at 25, cited with approval by Viscount Haldane in British Westinghouse Electric and Manufacturing Co. Ltd v Underground Electric Railways Company of London Ltd [1912] AC 673 (at 689).

> *damages. The question has to be considered from the point of view of a business man"*[155]

The phrases the "ordinary course of business" and "economic or uneconomic" are useful for Defendants, particularly in cases where the Claimant is a company or a self -employed individual. The reason is that it suggests that the court should look simply at the costs of the choice made by the Claimant. This is often helpful because the high costs of credit hire often enable Defendants to argue that they are out of the "ordinary course of business" or "uneconomic".

It may also be worthwhile for the Defendant to point out that the standard of reasonableness is objective. In the classic case of *Marcroft v Scruttons Ltd*,[156] concerning a claimant's refusal to undergo medical treatment, the Court of Appeal had to consider whether the standard is objective or subjective. It held that the Court should not take into account subjective factors:-

> "*The difficult question in this case is whether we are to admit this subjective condition of his as a reason for refusing medical treatment. I think not.*"

Question of Fact

It is commonly asserted that issues of mitigation are questions of fact for the trial Judge to determine. One source for this principle is *Payzu v Saunders*:-

155 Darbishire v Warran. We note that in Coles v Hetherton, the Court of Appeal described the discussion of mitigation in Darbishire v Warran as an "aberration" because the Court wrongly applied concepts of mitigation to the cost of repairing a vehicle. Although this does not mean that the description of the principles of mitigation in that case was wrong, it would be unwise to rely too heavily upon it in the light of that criticism.

156 Marcroft v Scruttons Ltd, 1954 Lloyds Reports Vol. 1 395.

> *"It is plain that the question what is reasonable for a person to do in mitigation of his damages cannot be a question of law but must be one of fact in the circumstances of each particular case."*[157]

However this statement requires qualification. It is clear that whilst questions of mitigation are still regarded as findings of fact, they are not treated in the same way as findings about, for example, the speed of a vehicle involved in a road traffic accident. Thus the Court of Appeal observed in overturning the trial Judge's findings on mitigation in *Copley v Lawn*:-

> *"There is no question of any interference with any finding of primary fact; questions of mitigation are however, questions of evaluation and judgment and there is no reason why this court should not interfere, if the judge's conclusions are, in its considered opinion, wrong".*[158]

It is submitted that this analysis is correct. Primary factual findings – for instance in a credit hire context, the date when repairs started or when the claimant became that his vehicle was a write-off – are in a different league from findings in relation to mitigation, which involve applying the test of unreasonableness to the facts. Accordingly, it is right that less deference is accorded to the findings at first instance in relation to mitigation and there is more scope for appellate intervention.

---

157 Payzu v Saunders, [1919] 2 KB 581 at 588.

158 Copley v Lawn para. 23.

CHAPTER SEVEN

NEED FOR A HIRE CAR

It is unreasonable for a Claimant to hire a replacement vehicle, if in truth he had no reason to use the replacement vehicle whilst his own was unavailable.

This flows from the general principle explained in *Umerji* and set out above, that the Claimant bears an initial burden of showing that the expense of hire charges was reasonably incurred in mitigation of the loss of use of his vehicle.

As Lord Hope explained in *Lagden*:-

> *"The motorist cannot claim for the cost of hiring another vehicle if he had no reason to use a car while his own car was being repaired – if, for example, he was in hospital during the relevant period or out of the country on a package holiday."*[159]

In fact, need for a hire car was identified as an issue in the very first credit hire case to reach the House of Lords. In *Giles v Thompson,*[160] which dealt primarily with issues arising from champerty, Lord Mustill went on to give useful guidance regarding need to hire a replacement vehicle. He stated that: *"the need for a replacement car is not self-proving."* He went on to say that it was for the Defendant to *"displace the inference"* which otherwise arose.

He explained that:

---

159 Lagden v O'Connor, para. 27.

160 Giles v Thompson, [1994] AC 142.

> *"I agree with the Court of Appeal that it is not hard to infer that a motorist who incurs the considerable expense of running a private car does so because he has a need for it, and consequently has a need to replace it if, as a result of a wrongful act, it is put out of commission."*

Lord Mustill went on to warn against permitting exaggerated claims for car hire:

> *"What matters is that the judges should look carefully at claims for hiring, both as to their duration and as to their rate. This will do much to avoid the inflated claims of which the defendants' insurers are understandably apprehensive, and will also discourage the promotion of over-optimistic claims by motorists, who if the present forms of agreement are enforced in accordance with their terms may be left with residual liabilities for hiring charges. The discipline imposed by judges who have the acumen and experience to detect greed and slapdash claims procedures will in my opinion do much more to forestall abuse than a dusting-down of the old law of champerty."*

He continued at pages 164 -165:

> *"And as to the possibility that the scheme will encourage motorists to hire cars which they do not need, at the ultimate expense of the insurers, I am confident that resourceful lawyers are well able to press by interlocutory measures for a candid exposure of the motorist's true requirements, and, if all else fails, to fight the issue at an oral hearing, as happened in the present case. If the motorists are found to have been tempted by the hire companies into the unnecessary hiring of substitute vehicles, the claims will fail pro tanto, with consequent orders for costs which will impose a healthy discipline upon the companies."*

Despite this warning, Lord Mustill only gave two examples of situations in which the Claimant might fail to establish need: "*The motorist may have been in hospital throughout . . . ; or he may have been planning to go abroad for a holiday leaving his car behind; and so on. . . .*"

Whilst this was plainly not intended as an exhaustive list, the examples chosen should be familiar. The very same examples were used by Lord Hope in the passage from *Lagden* set out above and in the Court of Appeal in *Giles v Thompson*[161] by Steyn LJ (as he then was).

In explaining his conclusions, Steyn LJ added that the Claimant *"clearly"* did not have to show that the car was *"essential"*. Rather *"[i]t is sufficient to show that he acted reasonably"*.[162]

These citations indicate that whilst it is correct to say that the Claimant bears an initial burden of showing that hire charges were reasonably incurred, in relation to his need to hire, this is not a heavy burden. The only examples given in the above cases of situations in which need would not be established are extreme cases – sickness or holidays. In most ordinary situations, an individual claimant is likely to be able to establish a need for a replacement vehicle.

Nevertheless, experience shows that the Defendant can successfully challenge need to hire on the facts in a variety of situations. These include situations where the Claimant had access to other vehicles through family members or business connections, or where the Claimant clearly managed without a vehicle either before or after the hire period (though here it may be on the facts that the Claimant's situation has changed).

In relation to practice and pleadings, it may be worth noting that paragraph 8.2 of the Practice Direction to Part 16 of the Civil Procedure Rules provides that *"[t]he claimant must specifically set out the following matters in his particulars of claim where he wishes to rely on them in support of his claim: [...] any facts relating to mitigation of loss or damage"*. In *Bricklebank v Quinn*,[163] the Defendant argued that the claim for credit

161 Times, 13 January 1993, at page 337H.

162 Ibid, at 337G.

163 Bricklebank v Quinn, Unreported, Central London County Court, 15 December 2017.

hire charges should be struck out because the Claimant had failed to plead her need to hire a replacement vehicle. The Court accepted that the Claimant should have pleaded facts relating to her need to hire a replacement vehicle because they were facts relating to mitigation of loss. However, the Court found that striking out the claim for credit hire charges was disproportionate and that the Claimant should have the opportunity to file and serve an amended Reply. This recognition that claimants should plead facts relating to their need to hire a replacement vehicle (and other issues of mitigation) is a relevant factor which defendants may raise during the trial process.

Need and Companies

A particular difficulty sometimes arises where the Claimant is a company and the damaged vehicle is one of a number of fleet vehicles. How can such a Claimant prove that they needed to hire a replacement vehicle? If they cannot establish need, does this extinguish the claim altogether?

Establishing Need in relation to a Corporate Claimant

If a corporation intends to argue that it needed to hire a replacement vehicle, it should provide evidence to justify that need. In two significant cases, the evidence provided was inadequate with disastrous consequences for the claims.

First, in *Park Lane BMW v Whipp*,[164] HHJ Harris found that there was no need to hire, in part because the Claimant had produced no evidence of the size and utilisation of its fleet, no evidence of what either vehicle was used for or was intended to be used for and no evidence about whether there were any other vehicles available to it.

[164] Park Lane BMW v Whipp, HHJ Harris, unreported 20 May 2009.

Second, in *Singh v Yaqubi*,[165] the Court of Appeal upheld a first instance finding that the Claimant had failed to prove a reasonable need for a replacement vehicle. In that case, the Claimant sought to recover hire charges of £99,439.06 for charges associated with two vehicles: a Bentley and a Rolls Royce. In upholding the first instance decision that he had failed to establish need, the Court of Appeal said this:-

> *"Very large hire claims such as this one should be scrutinised carefully by the court and particularly when the business partnership, which was required to establish the need, had a fleet of seven prestigious cars on the same insurance. For such a business claim to succeed, the judge was entitled to require specific evidence of need, such as evidence of the actual use of the vehicle for business purposes before the accident and the use to which the hired vehicle was put during the period of hire. Such evidence as was given, was vague and non-specific and the judge was entitled to hold that the need for a replacement Rolls Royce had not been established."*[166]

It is apparent from the passages cited from the first instance decision that there were real evidential gaps in that case. The Claimant himself had been abroad for part of the hire period and could say nothing specific about the use of the hire vehicle whilst he was away; he believed it was used for moving clients around. Moreover, no work diary or equivalent document was disclosed to show the use of either the hire vehicle or (before the accident) the damaged vehicle. As a result, a claim for almost £100,000 was dismissed in its entirety.

These cases might create the impression that it is very difficult for a company with a fleet to establish need. But that is not necessarily right; it is all a question of establishing the right evidence. For example, in *R S*

---

165 Singh v Yaqubi, [2013] EWCA Civ 23.

166 Ibid, para. 39.

Fleet Installations Ltd v Southern Rock Insurance Company Ltd,[167] the Claimant called evidence from its Fleet Manager who was able to explain that all of its vehicles were already allocated to specific employees. HHJ Gregory did not hesitate to find that need was established.

It is suggested that in preparing cases, Claimants could usefully read *Singh* and *Park Lane BMW* as providing a shopping list of the evidence that is likely to be required to establish need in similar cases. Careful thought should be given to disclosure; particularly if there are documents demonstrating the utilisation of the Claimant's fleet of vehicles. Moreover, care is needed in the selection of witnesses – the driver of the vehicle may not be best placed to answer questions about the potential availability of other vehicles and an additional witness may be required to plug this gap.

Conversely, of course, Defendants should analyse the Claimant's evidence against these decisions to highlight what evidence is missing. Tactically, Defendants may wish to think carefully before putting Part 18 Questions or seeking specific disclosure on these issues. Depending on the circumstances, the Defendant may do better by arguing the point at trial than by providing the Claimant with a second chance to provide the necessary evidence.

What is the measure of loss if need is not established?

Suppose that a company fails to establish need on the basis that it could have re-allocated another vehicle from its fleet. Does that mean that it can recovery no damages for loss of use or that there must be some other measure of loss?

---

167 RS Fleet Installations Ltd v Southern Rock Insurance Company Ltd, Unreported, Walsall County Court, 4 May 2014.

In *Beechwood Birmingham Ltd v Hoyer Group UK Ltd,*[168] this point reached the Court of Appeal on unusual facts. The Claimant was a substantial Audi dealer, with a fleet of 64 vehicles. When one of its fleet vehicles was damaged, it hired a replacement from a credit hire company. Apparently the Claimant admitted that it had no need to hire a vehicle. In other similar situations it had just re-allocated a vehicle from its fleet. Rather the evidence was that it wanted to test the efficacy of the credit hire process, in order to decide whether to refer its customers in the future. It is no surprise that at first instance there was a finding that the Claimant had no need to hire.

The Court of Appeal reviewed the authorities and concluded:-

> *"the net result of the shipping cases can be stated as follows. Where a substitute vessel is hired in to fulfil the role of the damaged vessel, the costs of hiring in are recoverable. Where the claimant's fleet is sufficient to provide a standby, then an award may be made based upon the expenses of keeping that standby, which means not only the expenses of daily upkeep but something representing the amount of capital employed in having another ship available. Where there is no substitute ship hired and no standby ship kept available the damages awarded are generally to be calculated on the basis of interest on the capital value of the damaged ship at the time of the collision."*[169]

The Court held that cases brought by corporations for loss of use of a chattel used for the business form a distinct class of cases from those brought by private individuals. In cases involving corporations, the loss *"should be the subject of an award of such sum as reasonably compensates for the nature and extent of the financial loss suffered as a result of the neutering*

168 Beechwood Birmingham Ltd v Hoyer Group UK Ltd, [2010] EWCA Civ 647.

169 Ibid., para. 45.

of the damaged vehicle as an asset employed in the claimant's business and the redeployment of any other such asset."[170]

The Court of Appeal then discussed how best to quantify this loss. It settled on this formulation: *"an award based on the interest and capital employed and any depreciation sustained over the period of repairs, allowed in respect of the vehicle of the type damaged in the accident."*[171]

The result appears to be that:-

- If a company can show that it needed to hire a replacement vehicle, it can recover those hire charges (subject to the usual arguments about mitigation and rate);

- If the company's fleet was large enough to provide a standby, and hence there was no need to hire, then a more limited award should be made based on the interest and capital employed on the damaged vehicle and the cost of having a substitute available

Finally, it is perhaps worth noting that in credit hire cases the Court is rarely provided with the information on which to quantify the damages in the manner suggested by the Court of Appeal. In *Beechwood Birmingham* itself, the Court of Appeal had no evidence about how to quantify the loss and hence invited the parties to agree the appropriate figure based on their guidance. The Court of Appeal noted that *"the figures produced by any further exercise on the lines I have indicated would scarcely justify the time and cost involved in further remission to the Judge"*. This was perhaps a little generous to the Claimant who had failed to provide the relevant evidence to prove this loss. Defendants might rely on *Park Lane BMW v Whipp*, in which confronted with the same problem HHJ Harris had simply dismissed the claim for hire charges. It appears that the Claimant also recovered nothing in *Singh v Yaqubi*.

170 Ibid., para 49.

171 Ibid., para 52.

Given that Claimants should now be familiar with the decision in *Beechwood Birmingham*, it is more likely that other Judge will take this course in the future should Claimants fail to provide the necessary evidence.

CHAPTER EIGHT

COURTESY CARS

The issue here can be stated shortly: is it reasonable for a Claimant to hire a replacement vehicle in circumstances where they have been offered a courtesy car either through their own insurance or by the Defendant?

The cases show that a different approach should be taken depending on whether the offer comes from the Claimant's own insurer or the Defendant's insurer.

A. From the Claimant's Own Insurer

If the Claimant's own insurer offers the Claimant a courtesy car, is it a failure to mitigate for the Claimant to take a credit hire vehicle instead?

This is one example of a broader issue which is whether the Claimant's failure to utilise their own insurance is capable of amounting to a failure to mitigate. In addition to the availability of a courtesy car, the issue may arise in cases where the hire period is prolonged because the Claimant elects not to progress the repairs through their own insurance.

In the late 1990s inconsistent results were reached in the County Courts on these issues.[172] However, the current state of the authorities presents

---

172 Thus the defendant succeeded in Callender v Ray Braidwood & Sons [1999] 1 CL, Bucknall v Jepson [1998] CLY 1456, Spence v United Taxis [1998] CLY 1465 and Ball v Howells Transport [1999] CL, DJ Ackroyd and Lyons v Metcalf [1999] CLY 2494 (save that in Lyons this was obiter since the claim failed in any event); whereas the claimant succeeded on the same issue in Perehenic v Deboa Structuring [1998] CLY 1467 and Cockburn v Davies and Provident Insurance Plc [1997]

a number of obstacles in the way of the Defendant succeeding on such an argument.

The first obstacle is that Claimants may argue that benefits received under an insurance policy should be left out of account. This builds on the principle of res inter alios acta, an early account of which was given in *Bradburn v the Great Western Railway Company.*[173] The defendant sought to deduct the proceeds of an accident insurance policy from the damages to which the claimant was entitled in compensation. The Court held that the insurance policy should be left out of account. Pigott B explained:

> *"He [the claimant] does not receive that sum of money because of the accident, but because he has made a contract providing for the contingency; an accident must occur to entitle him to it, but it is not the accident, but his contract, which is the cause of his receiving it"*

The same point was picked up in *Parry v Cleaver.*[174] This case is familiar to personal injury lawyers as it holds that payments that the Claimant has received from occupational disability pensions do not have to be deducted from his damages. In so holding, Lord Reid stated at page 14:

> *"As regards moneys coming to the plaintiff under a contract of insurance, I think that the real and substantial reason for disregarding them is that the plaintiff has bought them and that it would be unjust and unreasonable to hold that the money which he has prudently spent on premiums and the benefit from it should enure to the benefit of the tortfeasor. Here again I think that the explanation that this is too remote is artificial and unreal. Why should the plaintiff be left worse off than if he had never insured?"*

CLY 1805.

173 Bradburn v Great Western Railway Co, (1874) LR 10 Ex 1.

174 Parry v Cleaver, [1970] AC 1.

This result was applied in a credit hire context by HHJ Harris in *Seddon v Tekin*.[175] HHJ Harris stated that *"There is no reason why a Defendant should be able to take advantage of the fact that the plaintiff is insured to reduce his own loss."* This is entirely consistent with *Parry v Cleaver*. But HHJ Harris also gave a further reason: *"and if the plaintiff did so by taking the car from his own insurer then his own insurer could recover the cost from the Defendant anyway, so the defendant's position would not be improved"*.

This line of authority was also considered in *Rose v the Co-operative Group*,[176] in which the Circuit Judge concluded *"whether or not the Claimant knew or ought to have known he had a choice of car free of charge through his own insurance, the availability of such a choice by use of his own insurance should be disregarded."*

This suggests that Claimants may be able to argue that as a matter of principle any benefits coming to the Claimant under a contract of insurance (including a courtesy car) should be left out of account in assessing damages. This would be fatal to any contention that the Claimant failed to mitigate by failing to take a courtesy car.

The second obstacle is that there is a line of authority suggesting that where the Claimant has a choice between recovering from the Defendant and recovering from another source (for example, their own insurer), it is generally not unreasonable to look to recover the loss from the Defendant in the first instance.

In *Martindale v Duncan*,[177] the Court of Appeal held that on the facts of that case it was not a failure to mitigate for the Claimant to seek to recover damages from the Defendant in the first instance rather than his own insurer. Davies LJ said at page 577:

---

175 Seddon v Tekin, [2001] GCCR 2865.

176 Rose v The Co-Operative Group, Unreported 7 February 2005.

177 Martindale v Duncan, [1973] 1 WLR 547.

> *"The plaintiff was seeking in the first instance to recover his damage from the defendant's insurers and, if anything went wrong with that claim, although he obviously would not want to forfeit his "no claims" bonus, the second string to his bow would be to recover the money from his own insurers, and until he had had authorisation for doing the work he could not be at all certain that he would stand in a good position vis-a-vis the insurance company."*

The Court of Appeal went on to hold that it was not a failure to mitigate on the facts of that case for the Claimant to seek to recover damages in the first instance from the Defendant's insurers rather than claiming against his own insurers.

This line of argument is also be supported by *the Liverpool (No 2).*[178] In that case, the Court of Appeal held that where the victim of an accident has differing and alternative rights for the same loss against a tortfeasor and against another in contract he is not required to take steps to recover his loss from the other party from whom he could recover in contract.

The *Liverpool No2* was recently discussed and reaffirmed by the Court of Appeal in *Peters v East Midlands Strategic Health Authority.*[179] In that personal injury case, the Defendant argued that rather than claiming the cost of care from the Defendant, the Claimant should make use of NHS care, which the local authority was under a statutory duty to provide. This argument was rejected in these terms:

> *"we can see no reason in policy or principle which requires us to hold that a claimant who wishes to opt for self-funding and damages in*

[178] The Liverpool (no 2) [1963] P64.

[179] Peters v East Midlands Strategic Health Authority, (2009) EWCA Civ 145.

> *preference to reliance on the statutory obligations of a public authority should not be entitled to do so as a matter of right".*[180]

Claimants may also refer to the judgment of Nicholson LJ in *McMullen v Gibney and Bibney*[181] sitting in the High Court of Northern Ireland, which also held that the availability of a courtesy car to a claimant under a policy of insurance afforded no defence to a claim for hire of a replacement vehicle. The same results was reached in the High Court in Northern Ireland in *McCauley v Brennan and Coulter*,[182] in which the Court held that finding that the claimant should have invoked her own insurance was wrong in principle because it penalises the conscientious person who takes out comprehensive insurance in comparison to a person with cheaper third part insurance.[183] Further, the High Court in Northern Ireland held that on the facts, first, there was no evidence that the claimant could have afforded to pay the excess which would have applied if she had invoked her own insurance and, second, there was no evidence that her no claims bonus would have remained intact / been re-instated.[184]

As the law currently stands, these parallel lines of authority undoubtedly make it difficult for the Defendant to show that the Claimant failed to mitigate by failing to take advantage of a courtesy car from his own insurer or, more generally, failing to invoke their own insurance policy.

Nevertheless, in a credit hire context the point has not been definitively ruled out by the Court of Appeal. Indeed, in *Zurich Insurance Plc v Umerji*, when the Defendant sought to argue that the claimant should have replaced his vehicle at an early stage by claiming the pre-accident

---

180 Peters, para. 53

181 [1999] NIQB 1 (13 January 1999)

182 [2017] NIQB 41.

183 Ibid. para. 34.

184 Ibid. paras 36, 37.

value from his own insurer, the Court of Appeal did not dismiss the argument out of hand. Instead, it indicated that the issue was "an interesting one and plainly of some general importance". But in that case the issue had not been pursued at first instance and, accordingly, the Court of Appeal concluded that "this battle will have to be fought, if insurers are so inclined, on another field".[185] Defendants might take some encouragement from the fact that the Court of Appeal did not dismiss the attempt to distinguish *Bradburn* out of hand.

Ten years have now passed since the decision in *Umerji.* In that time, there have been some first instance decisions, such as *Rashid v Naylor*,[186] in which the Courts have found that the relatively small insurance excess, absence of evidence about impact on no claims bonus and size of the hire charges, justified a finding that the Claimant failed to mitigate his loss by failing to proceed through his own insurance. However, the point has not been taken at appellate level. There remains no binding authority on the issue in the specific context of credit hire.

If an insurer wished to accept the Court of Appeal's invitation to fight this battle on another field, it is suggested that the issue needs to be properly investigated. The point should be specifically pleaded in the Defence. The evidence needs to be obtained. The Court of Appeal in *Umerji* stated that "it would be necessary to consider the full circumstances, including the terms of the policy as regards excess and / or no claims bonus, before we could reach a view as to whether he [the claimant] had acted reasonably". That is likely to require disclosure of, at least, the relevant insurance policy terms and conditions. In relation to courtesy cars, the evidence would likely need to extend to the types of vehicle available and whether they were a reasonable substitute for the claimant's vehicle.

---

185 Zurich Insurance Plc v Umerji, para. 43.

186 Rashid v Naylor, Unreported, District Judge Branchflower, Barnsley County Court, 23 August 2018.

B. From Defendant's Insurer

Different issues arise where the Defendant offered to provide the Claimant with a replacement vehicle. After skirmishes in the County Courts, these issues were addressed by the Court of Appeal in two important cases: *Copley v Lawn* and *Sayce v TNT.*[187]

In *Copley*, the Defendant's Insurer had written to the Claimant to offer to provide her with a courtesy car. However the letter did not specify the cost to the Defendant of providing the courtesy car. The Court of Appeal held that in these circumstances there could be no failure to mitigate. The cost to the Defendant might have been greater than the cost of credit hire and, if it was, it could not be unreasonable for the Claimant to choose the cheaper option. Until the Claimant was informed of the cost, there could therefore be no failure to mitigate.

The ratio of *Copley* was discussed in detail in *Sayce v TNT*. In that subsequent case, a differently constituted Court of Appeal found that the ratio of *Copley* was that:-

> *"the claimant cannot be found to have acted unreasonably in refusing the defendant's offer unless he has been made aware that by doing so he would impose a greater burden on the defendant".*[188]

Defendants should also note that the Court of Appeal were critical of the drafting of the intervention letter. They remarked that it had *"an unpleasant threatening tone"* and that it was *"tempting"* to find that the claimant was entitled to *"ignore it completely"*.[189] Intervention letters must be carefully crafted to avoid this impression in future. Furthermore, both

---

187 Copley v Lawn; Sayce v TNT [2012] 1 WLR 1261.

188 Sayce, para. 20.

189 Copley, para. 9.

in *Copley* and in *Sayce* (per Pill LJ) the Court was particularly critical of the practice of Defendant Insurers cold-calling the Claimant.[190]

The Court of Appeal in *Copley* went on to consider what the position would have been, had the offer letter specified the cost to the insurer of providing the replacement vehicle. Here the conclusion was less clear. The Court of Appeal accepted that:-

> *if a defendant or his insurers does make an offer of a replacement car to an innocent claimant and he makes clear that he is going to pay less for such a car than the claimant is intending to pay (or is paying) for a car from a company such as Helphire, then (other things being equal) it may well be the case that a claimant should accept that lower cost replacement.*[191]

Defendants may argue that this suggests that, providing a simple alteration is made to the offer letter so that it specifies the cost, there is a failure to mitigate. Claimants may respond, however, that the Court of Appeal stopped short of saying that in those situations there would be a failure to mitigate. Instead it said that there "*may*" be a failure to mitigate "other things being equal". This must mean that, depending on the circumstances of the case, there might not be a failure to mitigate.

In *Copley*, the Court of Appeal did not discuss the question of reasonableness in any further detail. But the point arose again in *Sayce v TNT*. The procedural history of *Sayce* was deeply unusual, because in it HHJ Harris had declined to follow the Court of Appeal decision in *Copley*. Strictly, to dispose of the appeal it was sufficient to note that by the doctrine of precedent, the circuit Judge was bound to follow the Court of Appeal decision.[192] But one member of the Court of Appeal

190 Copley, para. 9 and Sayce, para. 45.

191 Copley, para. 22.

192 Sayce, paras 22 and 24.

went on to express views about whether it would be unreasonable for a Claimant to refuse an offer in these circumstances.

Lord Justice Pill, delivering a separate concurring opinion,[193] noted that in assessing the reasonableness of the Claimant's refusal of the Defendant's offer, the following might be relevant considerations on the facts:-

- Whether the Claimant is given a reasonable time to consider their position;
- Whether the insurance cover to be provided accords with the victim's existing insurance arrangements in terms of additional drivers or unusual drivers;
- Whether the victim prefers to deal with a company in which they have confidence rather than the defendant's insurer.

These sorts of considerations led Lord Justice Pill to remark that in the offer letter the Defendant *"may need to descend to particulars"*. This suggests that even where the Defendant offers to provide a vehicle and specifies the cost, there is ample scope for the Claimant to argue that it was nevertheless reasonable to refuse the offer on the facts of particular cases. Nor are the Claimant's arguments necessarily limited to those itemised by Pill LJ. For example, the Claimant might wish to challenge whether the vehicle provided by the Defendant was really an equivalent vehicle. Defendants may take some comfort from the fact that the other two Court of Appeal judges in *Sayce* did not associate themselves with this reasoning.

193 Sayce, paras 46-48.

The Court of Appeal returned to the reasoning in *Copley* on a further occasion in *Manton Hire & Sales Ltd.*[194] In the context of the very different facts of that case, the Court observed that Copley was *"an unusual case"* because where a motorist is seeking an alternative vehicle *"time is of the essence in that the motorist will often if not usually need to make arrangements for a replacement vehicle as a matter of urgency"*. In that context, the Court of Appeal suggested that the Defendant may realistically have *"only one chance"* to make an intervention offer.[195] That suggests that in the assessment of reasonableness in a credit hire case, the timing of the offer is likely to be a critical factor.

There have been numerous first instance decisions considering the extent to which it was reasonable for a claimant to refuse a specific offer of a replacement vehicle from the defendant. For example, in *Powell v Palani*[196] it was argued that the defendant's offer letter was deficient in that it failed to provide the claimant with all the information necessary to make a reasonable comparison, including by failing to set out the full terms and conditions and insurance provisions. HHJ McKenna held that the real issue was whether the contents of the letter were objectively sufficient to enable the claimant to make a realistic comparison between the cost of hire to the defendant and the cost of credit hire. Despite the issues raised by the claimant, he held that on the facts the letter was sufficient. In so finding, he held that the fact that the intervention letter arrived after the claimant had commenced hiring was "neither here nor there".

The next question which arises is whether the Claimant is entitled to recover anything by way of damages, if he has unreasonably refused the

194 Manton Hire & Sales Ltd v Ash Manor Cheese Company Ltd, [2013] EWCA Civ 548.

195 Ibid., para. 38.

196 Unreported, Birmingham County Court, 5 September 2016.

offer of a vehicle from the Defendant. In *Copley*, the Court of Appeal concluded that:

> *"if a claimant does unreasonably reject or ignore a defendant's offer of a replacement car, the claimant is entitled to recover at least the cost which the defendant can show he would reasonably have incurred; he does not forfeit his damages claim altogether"*[197]

In other words, the Claimant should recover the amount that it would have cost the Defendant to provide the courtesy vehicle.

This conclusion has proved controversial. It provoked HHJ Harris to depart from the Court of Appeal's decision in *Sayce*. Even though the Court of Appeal in *Sayce* found that HHJ Harris was bound to follow *Copley*, the majority (Moore-Bick LJ with Aitkens LJ agreeing) were critical of the Court of Appeal's reasoning. A plain reading of Moore-Bick LJ's judgment is enough to identify his doubts:-

> *"I can understand why some find it difficult to see why the claimant should be entitled to recover anything...I respectfully question whether the analogy with the offer of money is sound [which the Court in Copley had relied on]...I would respectfully doubt whether Strutt v Whitnell supports the conclusion for which it was cited... I confess that I also have difficulty with the conclusion that a claimant who has unreasonably refused an offer from the defendant of a free car can recover "at least the cost which the defendant can show he [i.e. the defendant] would reasonably have incurred" (paragraph 32). That, it seems to me, reflects the approach taken in the first part of the judgment, namely that one must look at the matter from the defendant's point of view, but it is not an approach that is reflected in the earlier authorities. Nor, with respect, do I think that it is one that is easy to reconcile with the principle relating to avoidable loss to be*

[197] Copley, para. 32.

derived from the leading cases and summarised in McGregor on Damages 18th ed., paragraphs 7-004 and 7-014"[198]

It is difficult to recall another Court of Appeal decision which has been so openly critical of the reasoning of another (not much) earlier Court of Appeal decision, without actually departing from it. In *Sayce* permission to appeal to the Supreme Court was refused, in part because an appeal could only be academic for the result of that case. But this does not mean the point is forever closed. The divisions in the Court of Appeal suggest that there is an opportunity for Defendants to run this point, perhaps all the way to the Supreme Court.

It is worth noting that this is a point of general importance not limited to credit hire cases: for example, would it be unreasonable for a Claimant in a personal injury case to arrange their own physiotherapy rather than use a physiotherapist paid by the Defendant? This suggests that clarification would benefit the law of damages as a whole.

One further oddity in the decision in *Copley* is that the Court of Appeal considered *"the extent to which (if at all) it is right to take account of the fact that both parties are insured"*.[199] The Court noted that at first instance the Judges had conflated the position of the Claimants and their respective insurers and solicitors. The Court held that *"in most cases that will be the right approach"*.[200]

If this is correct, then it is open to Defendants in all mitigation cases to argue that the Court should not consider the position of the Claimant in isolation but should consider *"the combined position of the claimants and their advisers"*. This might enable Defendants to argue for a more exacting standard – what is reasonable for a lay person might be less reasonable for an insurer / solicitor well versed in the duty to mitigate. However, it

198 Sayce, paras 27 – 28.

199 Copley, para. 12.

200 Copley, para. 16.

should be noted that in *W v Veolia* the High Court doubted that *Copley* intended such a result: *"If the court had intended to make as fundamental a change to the law of mitigation ... the matter would have been addressed explicitly and at a greater length."*[201]

Thus to summarise the section, the present state of the law is that:-

- if the Defendant offers the Claimant a courtesy vehicle without stating the cost of the vehicle to the Defendant, it is not unreasonable for the Claimant to refuse it;

- if the Defendant offers the Claimant a courtesy vehicle and does state the cost of the vehicle to the Defendant, it might be unreasonable for the Claimant to refuse it, depending on the facts;

- if such refusal was unreasonable, the Claimant would still be entitled to recover the cost to the Defendant of providing the replacement.

---

201 W v Veolia, [2012] 1 All ER Comm 667 para. 39.

CHAPTER NINE

LIKE FOR LIKE

Is a Claimant who drives a particular vehicle entitled to hire the same or an equivalent vehicle? Or should he, in mitigation of his loss, accept a lesser vehicle? The question often arises particularly in respect of Claimants who drive prestige vehicles, where the cost of hiring an equivalent may be significantly more expensive than the cost of hiring a standard vehicle.

Different cases have again reached inconsistent results on this point. Like for like was allowed or the principle assumed or accepted in: *Watson Norie Ltd v Shaw;*[202] *Mattocks v Mann;*[203] H L *Motorworks v Alwabi;*[204] *Daily Office Cleaning Contractors v Shefford;*[205] *Williams v Hoggins;*[206] *Vaughan Transport Systems v Fackrell*[207] and more recently *Brain v Yorkshire Rider Ltd.*[208] However cases in which like for like hiring was held to be unreasonable include: *Lyne v Cawley*[209] and *Gowen v Owens Radio and TV.*[210]

---

202 [1967] 111 Sol Jo 117.

203 [1993] RTR 13.

204 [1977] RTR 276

205 [1977] RTR 361.

206 [1996] CLY 2148.

207 [1997] CLY 1810.

208 Unreported, HHJ Grenfell, 26 March 2007.

209 [1995] CLY 1624.

210 [1995] CLY 1631.

In *H L Motorworks v Alwabi*, a Rolls Royce was the vehicle damaged. Cairns LJ held that:

> *"On the face of it, the customer was entitled to have, during the 11 days for which he was deprived of his Rolls Royce, another Rolls Royce to take its place. If it could have been shown that the amount of use he wished to make of the car in those 11 days was very small or that some other car would have been equally suitable for his purpose, then it may well be that the plaintiff company should not have met his full claim, or, if they did, would not have been entitled to pass on the claim to the defendant. But those matters, I apprehend, would be for the defendant to establish"*

In *Burdis v Livsey*, the Court of Appeal concluded on this issue at paragraph 133: *"if a need for a particular replacement car is established, then the cost incurred of hiring that car is recoverable."* Defendants may say that this appears to place the burden of proof on the Claimant, at least to establish a *prima facie* case of need for a particular vehicle. Claimants may point to the very low threshold for establishing need set out by Lord Mustill in *Giles v Thompson* (cited at the start of this chapter).

In *Bent (no2)*, the Court of Appeal summarised the earlier authorities:-

> *"The injured party cannot claim reimbursement for expenditure that is unreasonable. If the defendant can show that the cost that was incurred was more than was reasonable, either by proving that the claimant had no use for a replacement car in part or at all, or <u>because the car hired was bigger or better than was reasonable in the circumstances</u>, the amount expended on the hire must be reduced to the amount that would have been needed to hire the equivalent to the damaged car."*[211]

[211] Bent no2, para. 32.

In *Chatterton v AXA Corporate Solutions*,[212] having reviewed the authorities, HHJ Rawlings concluded that the Claimant "is entitled to recover hire costs of a car to fulfil the reasonable transport needs of [the Claimant] and his family".[213] On the facts of that case, no doubt influenced by the answers given by the Claimant in cross-examination, the Court concluded that his reasonable needs would have been met by a standard class vehicle rather than a Mercedes / BMW.

The opposite result was reached in *Gow v NFU Mutual Insurance*,[214] in which whilst acknowledging the difficulty of the issue, HHJ Bailey concluded that the Claimant had established a personal need for a like for like replacement for his Mclaren supercar. The Court summed up: "I have no doubt, having seen him in the witness box, that when Mr Gow sits in his Mclaren and drives about, even if it is only to visit a public house, he feels very much better in himself. I leave it at that. He does, in my judgment, establish need."[215]

The result appears to be that the choice of replacement vehicle is a question of reasonableness, to be determined on the facts of any given case.

An interesting issue arises where the Claimant's vehicle is a very old prestige vehicle with correspondingly low value and he hires a new prestige vehicle. The Defendant may argue that it was unreasonable for such a Claimant to hire what is in reality a very much more expensive vehicle. There is some support for this in the ABI General Terms of Agreement which suggests that *"Where the vehicle is over 6 years old it is*

---

212 Chatterton v AXA Corporate Solutions, Unreported, Stoke on Trent County Court, 4 August 2016.

213 Ibid., para. 34.

214 Gow v NFU Mutual Insurance, Unreported, Central London County Court, 24 May 2016.

215 Ibid., para. 33.

the exception, rather than the rule, that a similar prestige replacement is required".[216] However, as set out in Chapter Four in relation to rates, the Courts are unlikely to take account of the General Terms of Agreement in hostile litigation. Instead the point is likely to depend on the facts of the case. Defendants intending to run this argument should note that in order to stand any chance of success they would need to provide evidence of the cost of hiring a vehicle that the Defendant suggests is a real equivalent.

Beyond this, when the courts are called upon to adjudicate on rates evidence they will often have to determine what represents an equivalent vehicle and evidence may well be led on this issue, as set out in the Chapter on Rates Evidence above.

Finally, it is worth noting that if the car that was damaged was a sports car but in fact the Claimant only hired an ordinary car, he can only recover the rate charged for the ordinary car not the notional cost of hiring an equivalent vehicle. In *Burdis v Livsey,* one of the Claimants had his sports car damaged in an accident. He only hired a saloon as a replacement which was cheaper than a sports car would have been. The Court of Appeal held that:

> *"In the present case the loss suffered by Mr Dennard was the cost he had to pay for hire of the Vectra, not the amount which he might have paid for the hire of another car. A person who has no need for a replacement car because, for instance, he is abroad during the repair cannot recover the cost of hiring a replacement which he never incurs (see Giles v Thompson at 167D). Similarly, a person who does not incur the cost of hiring a sports car cannot recover more than the cost actually incurred."*[217]

---

216 Associated of British Insurers General Terms of Agreement, para 4.5.

217 Burdis v Livsey, para. 133.

CHAPTER TEN

PERIOD OF HIRE

Defendants often argue that the period of hire was unreasonable and that they should not be responsible for paying for the whole of that period. Much depends on the reason why the period of hire was prolonged.

A. Delay by Garage in Repairing the Claimant's car

Experience suggests that this is one of the most common problems in credit hire cases. Imagine, by way of example, that, in spite of an expert report from an engineer indicating that repairs to the Claimant's vehicle should take no more than three days, repairs actually take thirty days, throughout which the Claimant hired a replacement vehicle. Should he be able to recover hire charges for a period of 30 days or only for 3 days?

In *Mattocks v Mann,*[218] the Court of Appeal had to consider a case in which there had been a delay in repairing the Claimant's car. Bedlam LJ giving the leading judgment held that:

> *"For a supervening cause or a failure to mitigate to relieve a Defendant of a period of hire there must, in my judgment, be a finding of some conduct on her [Mrs Mattocks] part or on the part of someone for whom she is in law responsible, or indeed of a third party, which can truly be said to be an independent cause of loss of her car for that period."*

In *Mattocks*, this led the Court of Appeal to allow the Claimant to recover hire charges during periods of time where: (1) the garage had not yet sent the car to the repair shop; (2) the repairs took longer than expected; and

---

218 Mattocks v Mann, [1973] RTR 13.

(3) the garage used its *lien* to refuse to return the vehicle for four months after repairs were completed until it was paid for the repairs.

In part, these conclusions were reached because there was no evidence that the Claimant had caused the delay in sending the car to the repair shop: *"the plaintiff had put the car with reputable and well known repairers. She was not, in my view, to be criticised because they were over-worked"*. In relation to the delay in repairs, the Court noted that *"there was no evidence... that the car could have been more speedily repaired elsewhere"* and was prepared to take into account that parts need to be obtained.

In *Burdis v Livsey*, the Court of Appeal expressly approved the earlier decision in *Mattocks.*[219] The Court of Appeal concluded at paragraph 121:

> *"The defendants' actions damaged the cars of Mrs Clark and Mr Dennard. They should pay the loss caused by their actions. The actual loss incurred involved hire of replacement cars for 10 days in the case of Mrs Clark and 12 days in the case of Mr Dennard. They both appear to have acted reasonably in placing the cars in the hands of respectable repairers and there were no supervening events. Further delays of that order were foreseeable. The extra loss caused by the delay in the repair must fall on the tortfeasor as there was no failure to mitigate. On the findings of fact in those cases the cost of hire should not have been reduced.'*

Thus where the Claimant's car takes an unexpectedly long time to repair, provided that the car was entrusted to an apparently reasonable repairer, the Defendant will remain liable for the whole hire period unless the Defendant can point to a <u>supervening event which was an independent cause of the loss of use of the car for that period</u>. Examples of such a supervening event might arise where the garage negligently causes further

[219] See also a privy council decision Candlewood Navigation Corporation Ltd v Mitsui O.S.K. Lines Ltd [1986] 1 AC 1.

damage to the car whilst it is being repaired, which delays the completion of repairs. But it also means that in many more common situations, for instance where there is a delay in the garage obtaining parts, the Defendant is likely to remain liable.

This places Defendants in a difficult position. Experience suggests that there are very many credit hire cases in which the duration of repairs turns out to be very much longer than the initial estimate. Often the reason for the delay is unclear. On the Court of Appeal's analysis, there is often no proper basis for a reduction in the period of hire in these cases. The Court of Appeal's solution to the potential unfairness that this creates was to suggest: *'The insurers of the defendants should seek a contribution from the repairers for any unjustified length of repair.'*[220] As we will see, it is in fact open to serious doubt whether the Defendant can claim a contribution from the repairer. It is suggested that this might place some doubt on the correctness of the Court of Appeal's decision as a whole, because it leaves the Defendant with so little protection in cases where there is a delay in carrying out repairs.

One interesting case, in which the Court found a way around this problem was *Chatterton v AXA Corporate Solutions*. In that case, the Court held that contrary to the Claimant's engineering evidence the Claimant's Ford Transit van was driveable and roadworthy. He therefore had no need for a replacement vehicle until arrangements had been made for repairs to commence, which reduced the hire period to a mere 6 days. In dealing with engineering evidence which had suggested it was unroadworthy, the Court held that the engineer's action in wrongly assessing that the vehicle was unroadworthy broke the chain of causation between the Defendant's negligence and the hire charges.[221]

It should also be noted that it is unlikely ever to be sufficient for the Defendant to assert without evidence that repairs should have been

220 Burdis v Livsey, para. 121.

221 Chatterton v AXA Corporate Solutions, paras 15-23.

completed more rapidly. In *Morgan-Rowe v Woodgate*, the Defendant's suggestion that repairs should have been completed in two weeks was criticised by the High Court as having been plucked from the air, or having no coherent basis.[222]

B. Claiming a Contribution from the Garage

Section 1(1) of the Civil Liability (Contribution) Act 1978 provides as follows:

> *"Subject to the following provisions of this section, any person liable in respect of any damage suffered by another person may recover contribution from any other person liable in respect of the same damage (whether jointly or otherwise)."*

In order to claim a contribution from another defendant pursuant to this section, it is thus a pre-requisite that both defendants are liable in respect of *the same damage*.

In *Mason v TNT*,[223] concerning a contribution claim against an insurer, HHJ Harris asked whether the insurer's potential breach of contract was "the same damage". He held that the Defendant had negligently damaged the Claimant's car. The Insurer had, possibly, breached the contract of insurance. In reliance on *Royal Brompton Hospital v Hammond*[224] he concluded that this was not the same damage:-

> *"The insurer has no responsibility at all for causing the diminution of the value of the claimant's car, nor for the need for a replacement vehicle while repairs are carried out. This was the loss or damage which the defendant caused. All that could be said against the third party is*

[222] Morgan-Rowe v Woodgate, [2023] EWHC 2375 para. 63.

[223] Mason v TNT, Unreported, HHJ Harris, 13 March 2009.

[224] Royal Brompton Hospital v Hammond, [2002] 1 WLR 1397.

> *that it failed to provide some benefits which, to an extent, would have alleviated the position in which the plaintiff found herself..."*

Although that case related to a claim for contribution against an insurer, the same logic would apply to a claim for contribution against a garage. It remains possible for Defendants to argue that *Mason v TNT* represents an overly narrow reading of the words "the same damage" or that it is inconsistent with the Court of Appeal's intention in *Burdis v Livsey*. But at least at first instance, courts are likely to find the decision in *Mason* highly persuasive and this may lead to claims for contribution being struck out altogether.

Should Defendants be able to surmount this hurdle, it would be necessary to consider whether the Claimant would have a viable claim against the garage. Where the Claimant contracted directly with the garage, the position is likely to be more straightforward. But even where the contractual arrangements were not directly between the garage and the Claimant, the Courts may be persuaded to imply a duty of care between them.

In these cases, the duty the garage owes to the Claimant is inevitably fact sensitive. However in *Charnock v Liverpool Corporation,*[225] the Court of Appeal held that where the owner of a car took it to a garage for repair, on the basis that his insurers would pay the cost of the repairs pursuant to an estimate which they had accepted, the proper inference was that there was a contract between the car owner and garage to repair the car at a price acceptable to the insurers within a reasonable time and also a contract between the garage and the insurers. Accordingly, they went on, there was a contract between the car owner and the garage to repair the car within a reasonable time. This suggests that the court is likely to imply a term between Claimant and garage that repairs be completed within reasonable time.

---

[225] Charnock v Liverpool Corp, [1968] 1 WLR 1498.

Having established that there was an express or implied contractual term requiring repairs to be effected in a reasonable time, the next question is how high the standard of care should be. Does the garage have to act in the same manner as a reasonable body of professional garages, by analogy with the medical negligence case law? Is the garage required to complete repairs within reasonable time or with reasonable expedition? The difference is that reasonable time simply refers to the passage of time whereas expedition puts the focus onto the garage's actions. There are no clear answers to these questions yet. In *Charnock* the court applied the standard of the "average competent repairer." It is clear however that there is not an implied term that the repairs will be completed in accordance with the time estimate: this would not be commercially realistic.

Whether or not repairs have been completed within reasonable time / with reasonable expedition is a question of fact which will depend on the circumstances of the case.

C. Claiming a Contribution from the Claimant's Insurer

Claiming a contribution from the Claimant's Insurer is likely to be very difficult.

As set out above, Defendants face a preliminary hurdle in showing that the Insurer is liable for the same damage. As set out above, current authority suggests that it is not; *Mason v TNT* itself was a case concerning a claim for contribution against an insurer.

In any event, the Defendant would face additional challenges in claiming a contribution from the Claimant's insurer. To succeed, the Defendant would need to show that the Claimant could successfully claim damages against their own insurer. This would entail:

- showing that there was an express / implied term in the Claimant's insurance contract stating that the insurer will act with reasonable expedition;

- showing that there is an action for consequential losses as a result of breaching such a term;

- showing on the facts that the insurer breached the term and that the breach caused the Claimant loss.

In the absence of an express term stating that the insurer will handle claims efficiently and in default will be liable for consequential losses (and we are not aware of any insurance contracts with such an express term), the Defendant can only argue that there is an implied term in the insurance contract that the insurer will act with reasonable expedition.

Different cases have reached different results in relation to whether such an implied term exists in an insurance contract. In *Insurance Corporation of the Channel Islands v McHugh (No 1)*,[226] Mance J held that an insurer does not owe an implied duty to conduct negotiations, assess the amount due or make payment within a reasonable time. He considered that such a term could not be implied either as a matter of business efficacy or as a matter of mutual intention. However, the opposite result was reached in *Mason v TNT*, where HHJ Harris said (obiter) that:

> *"I would however make clear my view that where the third party insurer enters into a contractual obligation to repair the car, and it proceeds to get these repairs carried out, in my judgment, it cannot sensibly assert that it was under no obligation to get the work done within a reasonable time... An implied term that the work would be*

---

226 [1997] LRLR 94.

> *done with a reasonable time or as soon as reasonably practicable is clearly necessary to give efficacy to the contract."*[227]

Furthermore, the present position is that an insured cannot recover damages for consequential losses arising out of late payment of an insurance claim. The reason is that the insurer is liable to indemnify the insured from the moment of loss. It is therefore liable in damages from that moment. The only remedy for late payment of damages is interest, because it is not possible to recover further damages for losses arising out of the late payment of damages. Where an insurer delays paying a claim, the only remedy available to the insured is interest. Relevant caselaw includes *Sprung v Royal Insurance* among others.[228]

It is also not possible to claim damages for inconvenience or distress arising out of late payment of insurance claims. The reasons are, first, that an insurance contract is not considered a contract to secure peace of mind and, second, that the only remedy for late payment is interest.[229]

Thus the law at present stands against the Defendant. It would take a House of Lords decision or Parliament to reform the law. However, there are signs that change might be forthcoming. The Court of Appeal in *Mandrake Holding Ltd v Countrywide Assurance Group Plc*[230] indicated that the House of Lords might revisit the law in this area. Similarly concerns have been expressed in a 2006 Law Commission report and in academic articles about the state of the law in this area.

There may also be a specific clause in the insurance policy excluding liability for consequential loss. Depending on the precise wording of the

227 Mason v TNT, para. 26.

228 [1999] Lloyds Rep IR 111 followed in Tonkin v UK Insurance Ltd [2006] EWHC 1120 TCC.

229 See, for instance, Ventouris v Mountain [1992] 2 Lloyds Rep 281.

230 Mandrake Holding Ltd v Countrywide Assurance Group Plc, [2005] EWCA civ 840.

exclusion clause, this might operate to limit liability for breach of any implied term.

If the Defendant succeeds in establishing that there was such an implied term in the Claimant's insurance policy, it would then have to establish that the insurer breached that term and that the breach caused the Claimant increased loss. This will inevitably be fact sensitive. It is unlikely that every administrative delay would be held to be a breach of contract: the courts would be sensitive to commercial realities. Clearly the Defendant's argument becomes more attractive the more severe the delay. Further there is a practical difficulty for Defendants in that all the evidence about the alleged delay would be held by the Claimant's insurer.

D. Delay in Replacing or Starting Repairs to the Claimant's vehicle

Issues relating to the period of hire may also arise either where the Claimant's vehicle is written off in the accident or where the Claimant delays in instructing a garage to start repairs to his vehicle (this is different from (a) above because the delay is on the part of the Claimant himself). In these situations, one issue is often whether the Claimant can afford to replace / repair his vehicle. Claimants often hire a vehicle until the Defendant Insurer refunds them the pre-accident value of the vehicle to enable them to purchase a new vehicle or pays the cost of repairs. If this results in an unduly long period of hire (more than 12 months is not unknown), is there likely to be a failure to mitigate?

These issues assume particular importance in circumstances where the pre-accident value of the Claimant's vehicle is relatively low, but the hire charges are high because the hire has persisted for a prolonged period.

These issues have been explored in two recent Court of Appeal cases. In *Zurich Insurance Plc v Umerji*, the Claimant's vehicle which was damaged in the accident was a Mercedes worth around £8,000. The accident occurred in October 2010. The Mercedes was not driveable. In early November 2010, the Claimant received an engineer's report suggesting that it was a write off. He did not receive a cheque for the pre-accident value of the vehicle from the Defendant until November 2012. In the interim, he had hired a replacement vehicle on credit for 591 days at a total cost of roughly £95,000. He argued that he could not have afforded to replace his vehicle until the Defendant paid him its pre-accident value.[231]

As explained above, the Court of Appeal began by holding that a debarring order in relation to impecuniosity applied just as much in relation to period of hire as it did in relation to rates. That meant that the Claimant was debarred from asserting that he could not have afforded to replace his vehicle.[232]

The Court of Appeal held:-

> *"the Claimant was indeed debarred from asserting that he could not afford to buy a replacement vehicle. It follows that he should only have been entitled to recover hire charges up to the date when he should reasonably have done so."*[233]

On the facts, the Court of Appeal concluded that it was reasonable for the Claimant to wait until his vehicle had been assessed by an engineer to see if repairs were practicable AND to wait until the Defendant "had had the opportunity to inspect it and say whether they agreed". In Umerji, the Defendant did not indicate whether it intended to inspect and the Claimant disposed of the vehicle in mid February 2011. The Court of Appeal held that *"it was reasonable for the Claimant to wait until that date before deciding to go ahead and buy a replacement. He could have bought a replacement vehicle within a fortnight thereafter"*.[234]

---

231 See the facts summarised in Umerji, paras 1-2.

232 Umerji, paras 37-39.

233 Ibid., para. 39.

234 Ibid., para. 40.

On its face, *Umerji* is thus a strong endorsement of the principle that a pecunious Claimant cannot reasonably continue to run up hire charges until paid the pre-accident value by an Insurer.

Claimants may note, however, that the Court of Appeal did not hold that the Claimant should have replaced his own vehicle immediately or even within fourteen days of receipt of his engineering evidence. Instead, he was allowed to wait until the Defendant had a chance to clarify its position. That resulted in hire charges being allowed from 20 October 2010 – 8 March 2011, a period of some four and a half months which is not insubstantial.

That in turn suggests that the Defendant should clarify its position at an early stage. If the Defendant had written to the Claimant to indicate that (1) liability was disputed and so no payment will be made for pre-accident value and (2) the Defendant had no intention of inspecting the vehicle, the period of hire permitted in *Umerji* might have been significantly shorter.

Logically, the same result should apply to cases in which the Claimant delays in instructing a garage to repair his vehicle. Indeed, HHJ Gregory reached an analogous result in *R S Fleet Installations Ltd*, holding that *"in permitting the matter to drift…in failing to take steps either to repair the car or have it replaced I am satisfied that a company of the size and scale with the assets of RS Fleet Installations Ltd failed to mitigate its loss."*[235]

That, of course, leaves open the position of the impecunious Claimant. The law cannot expect the Claimant to do the impossible and so, if a Claimant really could not afford to repair or replace the vehicle, it may be that there is no failure to mitigate. However, just because a Claimant could not afford to repair / replace the vehicle at the start of the hire period does not mean that he remained so throughout. In *Opoku v*

[235] RS Fleet Installations Ltd v Southern Rock Insurance Company Ltd, HHJ Gregory, Walsall County Court, 4 May 2014 at para. 14.

Tintas,[236] the Claimant sought to recover credit hire charges of roughly £130,000 incurred over a period of almost two years on the basis that he could not have afforded to pay for repairs, which were estimated to cost roughly £3,400. It was held at first instance that he was indeed impecunious in relation to hire charges. But, the Court held that a point came when he should nevertheless have paid for repairs. The Claimant appealed on the basis that this was inconsistent with the finding in relation to impecuniosity.

The Court of Appeal began by noting that "in the context of credit hire claims such as this, the courts emphasise the need for careful and proper control of the claims by the application of the doctrine of mitigation".[237]

The Court continued that there was no necessary inconsistency in the decision: "it does not, however, follow that because a person is not able to pay a conventional hire rate for similar cars to be used as minicabs for an open-ended period that it was unreasonable for him to fund a total cost of some £3,200 for the repair of the car."[238]

The Court of Appeal accepted that the Judge was entitled to find that – considering all of the evidence before her – over an eight-month period, the Claimant could have saved enough to pay for the repairs.[239]

It is also interesting that the Court of Appeal made the obvious point in assessing the reasonableness of the Claimant's actions "this was not the case of a person who was being asked to put himself in a debt position where the alternative is not to be in debt, or not to increase his debt. It is a balance between the debt of £5,000 a month [the credit hire charges]

---

236 [2013] EWCA Civ 1299.

237 Opoku, para. 13(2).

238 Ibid., para. 23.

239 Ibid., paras 28-30.

and the alternative of funding £3,400 on a one-off basis to repair the car".[240]

Defendants may rely on this case to argue, particularly in cases with a very long period of hire, that the reasonable course of action for a Claimant is to save money over time to pay for repairs or a replacement vehicle. Claimants may take some comfort from the fact that a considerable period of hire was still allowed on the facts of *Opoku*.

In Irving v Morgan Sindall Ltd,[241] in relation to an issue of impecuniosity, the High Court noted that the first instance Judge had based his findings on an assumption that the claimant could have bought a replacement car immediately. That finding was untenable because it had taken a fortnight before her own vehicle was written off. The High Court held that, even if pecunious, the claimant would have been entitled to hire a replacement vehicle at basic hire rates during this period. The cost of basic hire added to the capital cost of the replacement vehicle suggested that the sum that the claimant needed to raise was far in excess of the figure on which the trial Judge based his calculations.

It is noted that the High Court was specifically concerned with impecuniosity in relation to the issue of rates in that decision.[242] It is respectfully submitted that in relation to the period of hire, it must remain open to Defendants to argue that the Claimant ought reasonably to have hired on credit terms (and hence not laid out any money) whilst saving for the cost of repairing / replacing their own vehicle. In *Opoku v Tintas Ltd* in particular, there is no suggestion in the Court of Appeal's conclusions (or argument) that the cost of hire needed to be brought into account in assessing whether the claimant would have been able to afford to replace his vehicle.

---

240 Ibid., para. 31.

241 [2018] EWHC 1147, at para. 35 in particular.

242 See paras 27 – 28.

At the end of these recent authorities, it is worth highlighting that much still depends on the specific facts of the case. Defendants should seek to establish the cost of repairing / replacing the Claimant's vehicle and whether the Claimant had that money readily available or could have saved it. Claimants might explore why there was a delay in receiving money from the Insurer and whether the Insurer's position was clearly communicated; it is hardly attractive for the Insurer to argue that the Claimant has acted unreasonably when the delay is entirely of their own making.

As a practical point, it is often unattractive for Defendants simply to suggest that something unreasonable must have happened because the hire charges exceed the pre-accident value; there is no golden ratio at which the hire charges become unreasonable. For instance, in *Motor Insurers' Bureau v Houston*, having found that the trial judge was not wrong to accept the Claimant's evidence that he could not afford to buy a replacement vehicle, the disparity between the hire charges and the pre-accident value of the vehicle did not assist the Defendant.[243] Nor is it simply a case of identifying a reasonable period of hire in the abstract; it is a question of determining on the facts at what stage (if at all) it became unreasonable for the Claimant to continue hiring. It is more attractive for Defendants to try to identify a moment at which it became unreasonable for the Claimant to continue hiring. For example, it might be argued that once the Claimant received a letter from the Defendant denying liability, he must have realised that the Defendant would not be sending the cheque for pre-accident value any time soon and hence should have reconsidered the hire at that point.

A further practical point is that it in many circumstances it will be advantageous for Defendants to pay the pre-accident value of the Claimant's vehicle at an early stage. A principled refusal to pay often

243 Motor Insurers' Bureau v Houston, paras. 45, 49.

appears less attractive months down the line when the Insurer is facing a substantial potential bill for hire charges.

CHAPTER ELEVEN

SELF-EMPLOYED CLAIMANTS AND BUSINESSES

A separate issue of reasonableness can arise in relation to self-employed Claimants who use their vehicle for their business. Suppose that the Claimant's business makes a profit of £1,000 per month. Suppose further that the Claimant hires a replacement vehicle for work purposes at a cost of £2,000 per month. If the Claimant were to pay the hire charges himself, that would mean that his business would be running at a loss of £1,000 per month. Defendants may argue that this is simply not reasonable; it is certainly "uneconomic". As the disparity in the figures grows, the Defendants' argument becomes stronger.

This led one distinguished textbook to conclude that in relation to a profit earning chattel *"if, for example, the cost of hiring exceeds the profit which could have been earned, only the latter may be recovered".*[244]

The clearest authority for this proposition was the old House of Lords decision in *the Steamship Valeria*, in which Lord Buckmaster held that *"What has to be considered is what would this vessel have earned for the period of the seven days that she was incapacitated owing to the accident; and that amount is the true measure of the damage which the vessel who was to blame is called upon to pay, and it can only be ascertained by considering what she had earned under similar conditions".*[245] That decision was

---

[244] Clark and Lindsell on Torts 22nd edition 28-121.

[245] Commissioners for Executing the Office of Lord High Admiral of the UK v Owners of the Steamship Valeria, [1922] 2 AC 242 at 247-248.

heavily based on the factual context of commercial freight which pertained in that case.

Defendants relied on this to argue that wherever the loss of profit is lower than the hire charges, only loss of profit should be recovered. Defendants have had some success in this argument in credit hire cases (at least at first instance). Thus in *Singh v Aqua Descaling Ltd,*[246] the court held that:

> *"It is obvious, and I so find, that the cost of hiring exceeded by far the profit which could have been earned; consequently, only the loss of profit can be recovered... and then only for that period reasonably required to achieve a replacement and 'restore' the profit. In this case I am prepared to award six week's loss of net profit"*

Other cases which reached the same result include *A Line Taxis v Ward*[247] and *Ali v Spirit Motor Transport Ltd*[248] (however the latter decision was appealed by the Claimant and compromised by the Defendant before the appeal was heard).

The matter is now governed by Hussain v EUI Limited.[249] An appeal reached the High Court on facts where the hire charges over an 18-day period were almost equal to the claimant taxi driver's declared annual

246 Singh v Aqua Descaling Ltd, Unreported, HHJ Oliver Jones QC, 18 February 2008 at paragraph 9.2.

247 A Line Taxis v Ward, Unreported, Chesterfield County Court, Wall DJ, 2 May 2014.

248 Ali v Spirit Motor Transport Ltd, Unreported, Leeds County Court, HHJ Saffman, 24 January 2014.

249 Hussain v EUI Ltd, [2019] EWHC 2647.

income.[250] The Court clearly had in mind that the same principles would apply to chauffeurs, hauliers and delivery drivers.[251]

The principles were set out by the Court in paragraph 16. Importantly, at paragraph 16.5 the High Court stated the general rule that "where the cost of hire significantly exceeds the avoided loss of profit, the court will ordinarily limit damages to the lost profit". Clearly, however, if the difference is more marginal, the Court would not "count the pennies".

However, the High Court recognised three exceptions to this general rule. First, businesses may sometimes have to run at a loss in order to retain key customers or contracts.[252] Examples include a chauffeur not letting down a regular client or a self-employed taxi driver risking being dropped by a taxi company.

This aspect of the decision is clearly consistent with established principles of mitigation. McGregor notes that "a claimant need not prejudice his commercial reputation".[253] If a small business would be unable to service its clients without a vehicle, it may be difficult for a Defendant to show that hiring a vehicle was unreasonable. Further, "a claimant need not act so as to injure innocent persons".[254] Thus where the Claimant is a company providing taxis for sub-contracted drivers to use, it is arguable that it is reasonable for it to hire a replacement vehicle because the alternative is effectively to put the innocent driver out of work.

In such cases, the Court will not expect a Claimant to have weighed the different costs too precisely:

---

250 Ibid., para. 4.

251 Ibid., para. 1.

252 Ibid., para. 16.6(a).

253 McGregor on damages 7-087.

254 McGregor on Damages 7-086.

> *"the claimant is really saying that, but for his or her actions in hiring a replacement vehicle, the true loss of profit would not have been limited simply to the pro rata loss calculated on the basis of the period of closure but that future trading would itself have been compromised. Again, claimants are not required to weigh these factors precisely, and a claimant who reasonably incurs what at first might appear to be disproportionate hire costs in order to avoid a real risk of greater loss, will usually be entitled to recover such hire costs from the tortfeasor"*[255]

The second exception arises where a professional driver proves that they use their vehicle for personal purposes as well as business. In such cases, the High Court reasoned that reasonable hire charges exceeding loss of profits may be recovered "in the event that a private motorist would have been entitled to recover such costs".[256]

This leaves open the question how such a loss should be calculated. After all, the cost of hiring a replacement vehicle for business purposes is likely to exceed the cost of hiring an equivalent for purely personal use. In *Ali v Spirit Motor Transport Ltd*, the Court tried to resolve this point by awarding loss of profit plus general damages of £15 per day for personal loss of use, but it is open to serious argument whether this mix and match approach is really sustainable.[257]

The third exception is that it may be reasonable for a self-employed driver to hire a vehicle even at a cost exceeding loss of profits, because he simply cannot afford not to work.[258] A self-employed claimant cannot be left without income, relying on the hope that they will be compensated by a future loss of earnings claim.

---

255 Hussain v EUI Ltd, para. 16.6(a).

256 Ibid., para. 16.6(b).

257 Ali v Spirit Motor Transport Ltd, para. 22.

258 Hussain v EUI Ltd, para. 16.6(c).

The High Court noted that the issues raised by the third exception are the same as the issues that the Court is used to dealing with in relation to impecuniosity.[259] Accordingly, a claimant who intends to rely on this exception, must comply with the pleading and disclosure requirements in relation to impecuniosity. The Court will not accept an assertion that the claimant could not afford not to work without evidence.

On the facts of *Hussain*, the Claimant was restricted to loss of profit, because he was debarred from relying on impecuniosity and he had failed to prove the need for the car for personal use (the family had a second car).

The exceptions stated in Hussain, however, are potentially very broad. If proper attention is given to pleading and proving potential long-term consequences for the business, personal use or impecuniosity, there is likely to be significant scope for Claimants to argue that they fall within these exceptions.

259 Ibid, para. 17.

PART FOUR

ENFORCEABILITY

CHAPTER TWELVE

INTRODUCTION TO ENFORCEABILITY

A. Introduction

The next chapters are devoted to the issue whether a particular credit hire agreement is enforceable in the light of various statutory and common law issues, which in particular dictate the form of consumer credit agreements.

It is necessary to begin this Part with a health warning. At the time of writing, there are few viable enforceability challenges in credit hire litigation. These issues have a natural life cycle. First, perhaps prompted by new legislation, one insurer begins to argue that particular hire agreements are unenforceable in a few cases. Before long the issue becomes widely known and is litigated, initially at least, in a significant number of low value cases in the County Courts (characteristically with mixed results). Finally, one or more test cases are selected and pursued through the higher courts. Whilst this process is ongoing, the hire companies will, if necessary, amend their agreements and procedures so as to seek to comply with the legislation. Once all the hire companies have successfully amended their agreements or all challenges to enforceability have been rejected by the Courts, the issue will cease to be argued.

As we write, many of the issues based on consumer protection legislation are at the end of this life cycle. Arguments based on the Consumer Credit Acts were prevalent in the 1990s and 2000s, but have been dormant now for many years. After a short period of great activity, arguments based on the Cancellation of Contracts made in a Consumer's Home or Workplace Regulations 2008 ("the Cancellation Regulations") have also faded away and the Regulations themselves have been replaced so that they do not apply to new contracts.

It might therefore be wondered whether the following chapters are still necessary. Our view is that they are. First, in the arena of consumer protection and consumer credit, there is often new legislation. When novel issues arise under new legislation, the Courts are likely to be guided by the approach taken by the higher courts in relation to earlier similar legislation. Many of the arguments surrounding the 2008 Cancellation Regulations were shaped by the earlier disputes about the Consumer Credit Act. As a result, the sections on the Consumer Credit Act and the Cancellation Regulations remain important as case studies to understand the likely arguments should relevant issues arise in the future.

Second, Chapter Fifteen, in particular, remains current and relevant. Common law arguments about the formation or enforceability of credit hire agreements remain, although they have been weakened considerably by recent decisions. Since such arguments are drawn from the general law of contract, rather than any specific statutory regime, they are not subject to repeal or amendment, and it remains necessary for a lawyer working in credit hire to be familiar with them.

The following chapters are thus designed to help the practitioner to understand historic enforceability issues and the issues of principle which underlie them, and also to provide a framework which might be applied to analysing any new enforceability issues in the future.

Since the primary purpose of these chapters is to understand the historic litigation and the principles which were applied, we have not sought to update every reference to a statute or statutory instrument. In particular, where an older case uses the language of a particular statutory provision, we have kept that language so that the case is understandable, even if in some cases the statutory provision has been repealed or amended. We have flagged some of these amendments in the text. However, readers should take care to check which statutory provisions are current before citing them in argument.

We will therefore address:-

- Does enforceability of the credit hire agreement matter? (Chapter Twelve)
- Enforceability Issues under the Consumer Credit Acts (Chapter Thirteen)
- Enforceability Issues under the Cancellation Regulations 2008 (Chapter Fourteen)
- Other Enforceability Issues (Chapter Fifteen)

Does Enforceability of the Credit Hire Agreement Matter?

Before considering the intricate issues that can arise from considering whether a particular agreement is enforceable, it is worth pausing to ask a logically prior question: why does it matter that the hire agreement is technically unenforceable?

The discussion that follows is informed by the common facts which arise in all these cases. The Claimant enters into a credit hire agreement, as a result of which the Claimant is provided with a replacement vehicle for a number of days. The agreement turns out to be technically unenforceable. The Defendant Insurer raises the unenforceability of the agreement as a defence to a claim by the Claimant for the hire charges.

Claimants may argue that, regardless of enforceability, the Claimant's car was still damaged in an accident that was the Defendant's fault. He still lost the use of his vehicle. The Claimant still needed and, in fact, obtained a replacement vehicle. The individual Claimant, usually, does not wish to challenge enforceability themselves.[260] Why in these circumstances

[260] It is usually not advisable for the Claimant to challenge enforceability, since the hire agreement usually contains a clause requiring the Claimant

should the Defendant Insurer take the benefit of legislation which was only intended to protect the Claimant? Why can the Claimant not simply claim general damages for loss of use, even where a particular agreement is not enforceable?

We will look first at the resolution of this issue in *Dimond v Lovell.* Second, at the attempts by the hire companies to avoid the result in *Dimond v Lovell* through offering undertakings or subrogation. Third, at whether human rights arguments may assist the hire companies.

B. The Decision in Dimond v Lovell

The Claimant in *Dimond v Lovell* argued that it did not matter whether the credit hire agreement between the Claimant and the hire company was unenforceable. It was argued that (a) if the agreement was unenforceable, the claimant would be unjustly enriched and (b) that the enforceability of the hire agreement was *res inter alios acta* (literally thing done between / among others). We will deal with these arguments in turn.

a. Unjust enrichment

The Claimant's first argument was that if the hire agreement was unenforceable then Mrs Dimond would have had the benefit of a replacement vehicle at no cost to herself. She would therefore have been unjustly enriched at the hire company's expense.

Lord Hoffmann addressed this point robustly:

> *"The real difficulty, as it seems to me, is that to treat Mrs. Dimond as having been unjustly enriched would be inconsistent with the purpose of section 61(1). Parliament intended that if a consumer credit*

---

to cooperate with the hire company in pursuing the claim against the Defendant.

> *agreement was improperly executed, then subject to the enforcement powers of the court, the debtor should not have to pay. This meant that Parliament contemplated that he might be enriched and I do not see how it is open to the court to say that this consequence is unjust and should be reversed by a remedy at common law: compare Orakpo v. Manson Investments Ltd. [1978] A.C. 95."*[261]

Lord Hobhouse also rejected the Claimant's argument:

> *"Again I agree with your Lordships that there is no basis for implying an obligation of the hirer to pay contrary to the statute. Nor is there any basis for the application of some restitutionary principle. The contemplation of the parties was that the hirer should not in fact pay out of her own pocket for the hiring of the car. In the present case she has not been unjustly enriched; her position is precisely that which was intended."*[262]

Thus the House of Lords relied on the terms of the relevant legislation to reject the unjust enrichment argument. By enacting the legislation, Parliament had decided that, in order to protect consumers, in certain circumstances an agreement could not be enforced. The Court could not subvert this intention by allowing the hire company to enforce the agreement through the back door by a claim in restitution.

b. Res inter alios acta

The second line of the Claimant's argument was to assert that it did not matter to the success of her claim against the Defendant whether she was liable to pay for the hire.

After reviewing the authorities, Lord Hoffmann stated that:

---

261 Dimond, at p 398.

262 Dimond, at p405 – 406.

> *"since high water the tide has retreated. The courts have realised that a general principle of res inter alios acta which assumes that damages will be paid by "the wrongdoer" out of his own pocket is not in accordance with reality. The truth is that virtually all compensation is paid directly out of public or insurance funds and that through these channels the burden of compensation is spread across the whole community through an intricate series of economic links. Often, therefore, the sources of "third party benefits" will not in reality be third parties at all. Their cost will also be borne by the community through taxation or increased prices for goods and services."*[263]

He then quoted Lord Bridge in *Hunt v Severs,*[264] as Scott V-C had done in the Court of Appeal, and also referred to the fact that for voluntary carers the Claimant "can sue only if he claims as trustee for the person who provided the services". He then concluded:

> *"This case is of course far away from the gratuitous provision of services (usually by a relative) which was considered suitable for recovery as trustee in Hunt v. Severs [1994] 2 A.C. 350. If Mrs. Dimond is allowed to sue Mr. Lovell as trustee for 1st Automotive, the effect will be to confer legal rights upon 1st Automotive by virtue of an agreement which the Act of 1974 has declared to be unenforceable. This would be contrary to the intention of the Act. The only way, therefore, in which Mrs. Dimond could recover damages for the notional cost of hiring a car which she has actually had for free is if your Lordships were willing to create another exception to the rule against double recovery. I can see no basis for doing so. The policy of the Act of 1974 is to penalise 1st Automotive for not entering into a properly executed agreement. A consequence is often to confer a benefit upon the debtor, but that is a consequence rather than the primary purpose. There is no reason of policy why the law should insist that Mrs. Dimond should be able to retain that benefit and make a double recovery rather than that*

263 Dimond, p399.

264 Hunt v Severs, [1994] 2 AC 350.

> *it should reduce the liability of Mr. Lovell's insurers."*[265] *(emphasis added)*

Lord Hobhouse made a careful analysis of the basis for loss of use claims and in particular for the claim for hire and stated that whilst "Each case depends upon its own facts", "loss of use of the chattel in question is, in principle, a loss for which compensation should be paid". However, he went on:

> *"one of the relevant principles is that compensation is not paid for an avoided loss. So, if the plaintiff has been able to avoid suffering a particular head of loss by a process which is not too remote (as is insurance), the plaintiff will not be entitled to recover in respect of that avoided loss."*[266]

It should be noted that the approaches of Lords Hoffmann and Hobhouse are not identical. Lord Hoffmann laid emphasis on the breach of the relevant legislation. In similar terms to his rejection of the unjust enrichment argument, he concluded that where a statute has rendered an agreement unenforceable the common law should not step in and render it enforceable again. But he also relied on the risk of double recovery – if the damages were awarded to the Claimant, she could not be compelled to pay the hire charges to the hire company and so she would recover for her loss twice. Lord Hobhouse's approach was broader and simply emphasised the principle of compensatory loss coupled with remoteness. This distinction has some practical significance, since Claimants may argue that Lord Hoffmann's approach only applies to agreements which are rendered unenforceable by reason of breach of an absolute provision of consumer protection legislation and is tied to situations where there is a risk of double recovery. It would not necessarily apply to common law

265 Dimond, p400.

266 Dimond, p406

enforceability arguments for example. Defendants may, however, rely on the broader approach taken by Lord Hobhouse.

The result of *Dimond* was thus that the unenforceability of the hire agreement did bar the Claimant from recovering hire charges.

C. Attempts to Avoid the Rule in Dimond v Lovell

Since the decision in Dimond, Claimants have tried various different approaches in order to avoid the conclusion that hire charges are not recoverable.

The Claimant in *Burdis v Livsey* offered an undertaking that they would pay over to the hire company whatever was recovered in damages. This was an attempt to remove the risk of double recovery.

The Court of Appeal was unimpressed:

> *"We think the short answer to these submissions is that double recovery is a bar to the analysis and it is not overcome by the undertaking. Even though the contractual obligations of the claimant to pay Helphire for hire and repairs subsist if the credit agreements are unenforceable Helphire have no enforceable right to recover these amounts. The claimant has not paid and cannot be required to pay them so that if he recovers from the defendant there will be double recovery. The undertaking given to the court is truly collateral and could not be said to be the consequence of the defendant's tort. It is to be noted that the Court of Appeal was not tempted by a similar undertaking offered in Dimond"*[267]

[267] Burdis v Livsey, paragraph 58.

In *Bee v Jenson*, the Defendant took issue with the fact that the hire charges had been paid direct by the Claimant's insurer and were not a liability owed by the Claimant himself. The Court of Appeal held that

> *"it does not follow from the fact that Mr Bee was not liable for the hire charges of the replacement car that he cannot recover damages for the deprivation of his use of his car...in so doing he may in legal jargon be recovering general damages rather than special damages, but there is no significance in that"*[268]

This dicta has been relied on by Claimants to argue that hire charges may still be recoverable by way of general damages, even in the face of an unenforceable agreement. At least in the case of consumer protection legislation where unenforceability is absolute, this reliance appears misplaced because it would run contrary to the House of Lords decision in *Dimond* itself.

In *Chen Wei v Cambridge Power and Light Ltd*, the Court resolved the conflict between the two decisions in this way: "*there is, however, a material difference between recovering general damages for an admitted injury and recovering special damages in respect of an alleged debt that is positively unenforceable under recent policy-based legislation*".[269] In that case the Court found that, following *Dimond*, no general or special damages were recoverable.[270] The Court of Appeal reached the same result in *Salat v Barutis*.[271]

In *Wei*, the Claimant tried to find a further way around *Dimond* by arguing that the court should not make findings about the agreement,

---

268 Bee v Jenson, [2007] EWCA Civ 923, at para 15.

269 Wei v Cambridge Power and Light, Unreported. HHJ Moloney QC, 10 September 2010, para 21a.

270 Ibid., para 25 – 26.

271 Salat v Barutis (full reference below), para. 23.

because one party to the agreement (the hire company) was not a party to the action. This too was rejected, with the Court holding that

> *"provided an issue involving a third party contract is relevant in the RTA case...there is no reason in principle why the fact that the credit hire company is not actually a party should debar the RTA court from dealing with the issue and making findings...A related point, which I do consider valid, is that the RTA court should exercise a proper caution about making such contractual findings".*[272]

In relation to the 2008 Cancellation Regulations, Claimants have also sought to argue that they had 'affirmed' the contract by bringing the proceedings. The foundation for that argument is a statement by the Advocate General in the European case of *Martin v EDP Editores* that it is for the consumer to decide whether to maintain a contract which was apparently unenforceable.[273] However, in *Salat v Barutis* the Court of Appeal confirmed that *"Whether the Regulations, properly understood, allow a consumer to affirm a contract that would otherwise be unenforceable against him so as to render it enforceable depends on the intention of the legislation."*[274] The Court was inclined to find that the Regulations did not permit affirmation, but did not need to decide the issue because "in order for any affirmation to occur it would be necessary at least for the consumer to know that the contract was unenforceable and, in that knowledge, to express in unequivocal terms his willingness to be bound".[275] On the facts, the Claimant could not establish the factual basis for an affirmation, because there was no evidence that he took any positive action after becoming aware that the agreement was not enforceable.

---

272 Ibid., para. 2.

273 Martin v EDP Editores SL, [2009] ECR 1-11939.

274 Salat v Barutis, [2013] EWCA Civ 1499, para. 22.

275 Ibid.

We should also draw attention to one other possible attempt to distinguish *Dimond.* In *McGuffick v Royal Bank of Scotland,*[276] the High Court accepted that a creditor could continue to report the debtor's outstanding amount to credit reference agencies, even though the loan agreement was unenforceable pursuant to the Consumer Credit Act (at least in circumstances where the unenforceability of the agreement could be remedied by the creditor). That reasoning was approved and extended to cover irredeemably unenforceable agreements by the Court of Appeal in *Grace v Black Horse Ltd.*[277] This may allow Claimants to argue that even though an agreement is unenforceable, if they do not pay the hire charges they may still be exposed to adverse consequences which were not known at the time of *Dimond.* Claimants may potentially argue that they should not be exposed to the risk of these consequences, at the instance of the tortfeasor. This argument has yet to be ruled on.

D. Subrogation / Already Paid

In more recent cases, the Claimant finessed their argument further. Instead of simply relying on an undertaking to pay the charges, which as we have seen failed in *Burdis v Livsey,* Claimants began to arrange for the hire charges to be paid by an insurance company and to argue that, having already been paid, no enforceability issue could arise.

In *W v Veolia Environmental Services (UK) Plc,*[278] the claimant argued that regardless of the enforceability of the agreement, the hire charges had in fact been paid out by an insurance policy. The Claimant argued that the fact that the hire charges had already been paid meant that there was

[276] McGuffick v Royal Bank of Scotland, [2010] 1 All ER 634.

[277] Grace and other v Black Horse Ltd, [2014] EWCA civ 1413, para. 33.

[278] W v Veolia Environmental Services (UK) Plc, [2011] EWHC 2020, HHJ Mackie QC, 27 July 2011.

no possibility of double recovery and hence the rationale for disallowing the claim for hire charges in *Dimond* should not apply.

In that case, at the same time as signing the hire agreements, the Claimant had signed a separate agreement to take out an insurance policy in respect of the hire charges. When the Defendant argued that the hire agreement was unenforceable, in what was freely admitted to be a *"litigation tactic"*, the hire company arranged for the insurer to pay the hire charges and to bring a subrogated claim for the loss.

In spite of the *"informality"* of the insurance arrangements, HHJ Mackie QC sitting in the Mercantile division of the High Court, accepted that there was a valid insurance policy in place and that it had indeed paid out on the claim.[279] This is a vital step in the Claimant's argument – in order to succeed on similar arguments in the future, Claimants would need to provide at least the policy documentation provided in *W v Veolia.*

The Court accepted that the rationale of the decision in *Dimond* was to avoid the prospect of double recovery and consequently held that:-

> *"where a claimant has already paid the hire charges there is no risk of double recovery. The risk of a windfall to a claimant who obtains payment from the defendant but then declines to pay the hire car provider on legal grounds falls away..."*[280]

The Court therefore concluded that the Claimant could recover the hire charges, subject only to the question of whether it was reasonable for the insurer to have paid them. But this mitigation argument proved unsuccessful for the Defendant:-

279 Ibid., para. 22.

280 Ibid., para. 37.

> *"a claimant who pays a charge for goods or services which he has enjoyed is not failing to mitigate even if it is likely or even probable that he will not have to pay if he takes the matter to court."*[281]

A further peculiarity was that, despite indemnity being limited to £100,000 the insurer in fact paid out £138,000. The Court observed that "cheerful, prompt and knowing overpayments of claims by insurers is unheard of...I will not treat anything above £100,000 as being a good faith payment of a claim made under the policy."[282] But this did not affect the result of the case, because on the facts the Court was able to treat the additional £38,000 as arising from a second enforceable contract.

The result was that through the subrogated claim, the Claimant was able to recover damages for the hire charges, even though the hire agreement was unenforceable.

Although *W v Veolia* was not appealed, the Court of Appeal had to consider that decision in the subsequent case of *Sobrany v UAB Transtira.*[283] That was another case in which subrogation was in issue. The Claimant had hired two vehicles for consecutive periods (having returned the first because it had previously been used by a smoker). Although he had only pleaded reliance on a policy of insurance, his oral evidence was that there were two policies. At first instance, the Court effectively held that since he had only pleaded reliance on one policy, he could only recover as a subrogated claim the hire charges which related to the first of the two policies.

---

281 Ibid., para. 39. The cases referred to in support of this proposition are King v Victoria Insurance Co [1896] AC 250; London v Scottish Building Society v Stone [1983] 1 WLR 1242 and Forde v Birmingham CC [2009] 1 WLR 2732

282 W v Veolia, para 40.

283 Sobrany v UAB Transtira, [2016] EWCA Civ 28.

The Court of Appeal cited the decision in *W v Veolia* with approval several times. In so doing, it emphasised that the reason that a claimant cannot recover damages where the hire agreement is unenforceable is to prevent double recovery; *"to give him damages for services which he has received but for which he has not had to pay would mean that he recovered damages for a loss for which he had already been compensated by the provision of a free vehicle"*.[284]

Indeed, the only point on which the Court of Appeal disagreed with the High Court was in relation to the payment by the Insurer of more than the £100,000 policy limit. Whereas the High Court in *W v Veolia* had indicated that a payment of more than £100,000 would not be a good faith payment under the policy, the Court of Appeal observed that "it would still be a payment of the hire charges which the insured was bound to repay if it obtained damages: so there would be no double recovery".[285]

The outcome in *Sobrany* was that the Court of Appeal allowed recovery of the hire charges in full. It concluded that there were two policies, that the insurer had paid out under both and that there could be no question of double recovery since the claimant would hold any damages recovered on trust for the insurer.

The result of these cases is thus that where a credit hire agreement appears to be unenforceable, it is open to claimants to activate any insurance policy available under the hire arrangements to pursue the hire charges by way of a subrogated claim.

A number of criticisms might be made of this result. The effect is that by waving the magic wand of subrogation / payment, the Claimant is able to convert an agreement that Parliament has decided should be unenforceable, into one which can be enforced. Defendants may argue that as a matter of policy this outcome simply cannot be correct. A related

[284] Ibid. para. 5.

[285] Ibid. para. 46.

point is that it should be possible to tell immediately after the signature of the agreement whether the agreement will be enforceable, rather than it becoming enforceable at a later time.[286]

Moreover, these decisions appear to be inconsistent with obiter dicta in *Burdis v Livsey*, where the Court of Appeal had considered and rejected the argument that Dr Sen (one of the claimants in that case) could take advantage of payments made by insurers on his behalf. In that case the Court had indicated that recovery would still amount to double recovery.[287] HHJ Mackie in *W v Veolia* was critical of this analysis, commenting that "the court does not explain why once payment has been made there would still be double recovery". In any event, *W v Veolia* and *Sobrany* now provide binding authority on the issue.

E. Human Rights Issues

The effect of the Consumer Credit Act 1974, as originally drafted, was that contracts become automatically unenforceable for relatively minor technical breaches. It has been argued on behalf of the hire companies that this infringes their human rights. Two arguments may arise. First, that rendering an agreement automatically unenforceable deprives the Courts of any discretion and hence remove the hire companies' right to a fair hearing under Article 6 of the European Convention on Human Rights. Second and more promising, that rendering an agreement unenforceable is a disproportionate interference with the hire companies' property rights under Article 1 of the First Protocol to the European Convention.

The human rights arguments were argued before the House of Lords in *Wilson v Secretary of State for Trade and Industry.*[288] Mrs Wilson had

---

[286] This was rejected at para 27 of the judgement in W v Veolia.

[287] See Burdis, para. 56 – 58.

[288] Wilson v Secretary of State for Trade and Industry, [2003] UKHL 40.

pawned her BMW convertible for six months in return for £5,000. She did not repay the loan. Instead she commenced proceedings in the Kingston-upon-Thames County Court arguing that the agreement was unenforceable as it did not comply with the prescribed terms. The pawnbroker relied on the above human rights issues. From modest beginnings, the case snowballed. There were interventions from the Attorney General on behalf of the Secretary of State for Trade and Industry, the Speaker of the House of Commons, four motor insurers and the Finance and Leasing Association.

The House of Lords held that the Human Rights Act 1998 did not apply to Mrs Wilson's contract. The reason was that her cause of action accrued before section 3(1) of the Human Rights Act 1998 came into force. This meant that the House of Lords did not need to go on to address the remaining human rights arguments. However, the House of Lords did go on to address them in detail. Whilst their speeches on this issue are strictly obiter, they are likely to be highly persuasive.

Article 6(1)

Article 6(1) guarantees everyone the right to a fair expeditious and public trial of disputes about their civil rights. It includes the implied right of access to the courts. It is not a means of creating new civil rights: it only means that existing civil rights have to be capable of being submitted to a Judge for adjudication.[289]

Lord Nicholls held at paragraph 35 that *"the crucial question…is whether, as a matter of substance, the relevant provision of national law has the effect of preventing an issue which ought to be decided by a court from being so decided"*.

He analysed the creditor's complaint as being that: "section 127(3) of the Consumer Credit Act has the effect that a regulated agreement is not

289 Fayed v UK (1994) 18 EHRR 393.

enforceable unless a document containing all the prescribed terms is signed by the debtor". In his view this did not engage article 6(1). The reason is that it is:

> *"a restriction on the rights that a creditor acquires under a regulated agreement. It does not bar access to a court to decide whether the case is caught by the restriction. It does bar a court from exercising any discretion over whether to make an enforcement order. But in taking that power away from the court the legislature was not encroaching on territory which ought properly to be the province of the courts in a democratic society."*[290]

The other four members of the House of Lords agreed that article 6(1) was simply not engaged by this case.

Article 1 of the First Protocol

The issues raised by article 1 of the First Protocol provoked more debate in the House of Lords. It provides:-

> *"every natural and legal person is entitled to the peaceful enjoyment of his possessions. No-one shall be deprived of his possessions except in the public interest and subject to the conditions provided for by law…the preceding provisions shall not, however, in any way impair the right of a State to enforce such laws as it deems necessary to control the use of property in accordance with the general interest."*

The majority of the House of Lords rejected the creditor's arguments for two reasons. First they thought that article 1 of the First Protocol was not engaged. Second they thought if it was engaged, the Consumer Credit Act was proportionate and reasonable.

290 Wilson, para. 36.

In relation to whether article 1 was engaged, Lord Hope held at paragraph 109 that article 1 of the First Protocol was not engaged. His reason was that the lender never had an absolute or unqualified right to enforce the agreement or property rights. Article 1 could not be used to confer absolute rights, where they did not previously exist.

Lord Scott at paragraph 168 thought that Article 1 *"is directed to interference with existing possessions or property rights."* Section 127(3) prevented the lender from ever having the right to enforce the agreement. Accordingly article 1 was not engaged.

Lord Nicholls on the other hand thought that article 1 of the First Protocol was engaged. He considered that the effect of the relevant provisions in the Consumer Credit Act was a statutory deprivation of the lender's rights of property rather than a mere delimitation of the extent of those rights. Quite simply, *"the lender's right were extinguished in favour of the borrower by legislation for which the state is responsible".*

It is suggested that Lord Nicholls is correct; there is nothing in the wording of Protocol One to indicate that its protection is limited to absolute or unqualified property rights.

On the second point however all their Lordship agreed: the provisions in the Consumer Credit Act did not violate article 1 Protocol 1.

Lord Nicholls stated at paragraph 68 that inherent in article 1 is the need to hold a fair balance between the public interest and the fundamental rights of creditors. It was common ground that article 1 pursued a legitimate aim: protecting vulnerable persons from exploitation. Therefore the point turned on whether the means employed were proportionate to the legitimate aim.

At paragraphs 74 – 78, Lord Nicholls concluded that the means employed were proportionate. He thought that it was open to Parliament to make compliance with formalities a prerequisite to the enforceability of certain contracts. He noted *that "money lending transactions as a class give rise to significant social problems"*. A uniform solution applied across the board may be the most appropriate was to deal with the problem: a tailor-made solution considering the facts of each case may fail to protect the vulnerable. Further, in relation to proportionality, he noted that the Act only applied (at that time) to agreements for less than £25,000. Accordingly he held that section 127(3) was compatible with article 1 of the First Protocol. Lord Hope expressed agreement with Lord Nicholls on this point.

Lord Scott similarly held at paragraph 169 that the provision in the Consumer Credit Act could not be characterised as disproportionate. The reason is that all legal systems have attempted to control money lending transactions. The control measures reflect the vulnerability of those members of the public who need to borrow.

Lord Hobhouse agreed that the Consumer Credit Act did not beyond the measures which are justifiable under that Article.[291] He thought the enforceability provisions a legitimate exercise in consumer protection, because without effective sanction the rules would be flouted. He too noted the low value of cases to which the Act then applied.

Although the human rights arguments failed in *Wilson*, and there may potentially be less need to resort to them in the future due to the subrogation issue and the reform of unenforceability introduced by the Consumer Credit Act 2006, this does not meant that human rights arguments will always fail in this context. In particular, Claimants may note that the reasons for finding that the measures introduced by s127(3) were proportionate included (1) the perceived social evil of moneylending and (2) the low value of transactions affected.[292] These factors might not apply to other Regulations.

---

291 Ibid., para. 138.

292 Note in this regard that when the 2006 Act removed the financial limitation, it removed s127(3) and automatic unenforceability at the

Thus in the cases arising from the Cancellation of Contracts made in a Consumer's Home or Place of Work Regulations 2008, the claimants again sought to argue that the inflexible automatic unenforceability provisions in those Regulations were disproportionate. Here the Claimant's argument was stronger, because the Regulations did not relate to money lending and did relate to transactions of any value. However, here too, the Claimants arguments were rejected. Although in *W v Veolia Environmental Services (UK) Plc*,[293] the point was rendered academic by the Court's decision on subrogation, the Court suggested that the human rights argument did not assist the Claimant: *"Whatever arguments might be made on a different set of facts I see nothing disproportionate or unlawful in the circumstances of this case, given that the unenforceability would arise only from a failure by Accident Exchange to provide notice to the consumer as clearly required by the Regulations".*[294]

The point was argued more fully in *Salat v Barutis*, but the Court of Appeal held that the case could not properly be distinguished from *Wilson v First County Trust* and therefore there was no violation of Article 1 Protocol 1.[295] It added that the hire company, being presumed to understand the Regulations, could have had no expectation of being able to enforce the contract and so no issue of proportionality arose. The Court of Appeal also considered the argument that the Regulations were disproportionate because they contained no exception for small businesses. However, the Court did not need to deal in detail with the argument because the hire company was not a small business - "we are

---

same time.

293 W v Veolia Environmental Services (UK) Plc, [2011] EWHC 2020, HHJ Mackie QC.

294 Ibid., para. 53.

295 Salat v Barutis, para. 27.

not concerned with cases of the kind to which [the claimant] referred and prefer to express no opinion on them."[296]

It follows that although Claimants have tried to avoid the strict application of *Dimond v Lovell* in a variety of ways, most have failed. Claimants may consider that, in cases where insurance arrangements are in place, arranging for the insurer to pay the hire charges as in *W v Veolia* offers the best chance of recovering the hire charges. As we have seen, other arguments such as affirmation or human rights issues have not been wholly ruled out by the Courts – but thus far no cases have offered a sufficient factual basis for the Courts to distinguish *Dimond*.

[296] Ibid., para. 28.

CHAPTER THIRTEEN

ENFORCEABILITY ISSUES: THE CONSUMER CREDIT ACTS

A. Introduction

The purpose of this chapter is to discuss the enforceability of credit hire agreements under the Consumer Credit Act 1974 as amended by the Consumer Credit Act 2006. As such, the health warning given in the introduction to this Part applies particularly to this Chapter. *Dimond* and the following line of cases were decided prior to the Consumer Credit Act 2006 and other more recent statutory developments. We have kept the language and references used in *Dimond*, in order to help to explain that seminal case. Whilst we have sought to indicate in the text where provisions have subsequently been amended, given the limited significance of these issues in contemporary credit hire litigation, these updates have not been a focus of this revised edition.

We will deal with the issues in this way:-

1. Is a credit hire agreement regulated by the Consumer Credit Acts?

2. If so, what do the Acts require?

3. What becomes of an improperly executed regulated agreement?

However, we should remind the reader that the heyday of these arguments was in the 1990s. Most credit hire agreements have now been amended so as to avoid the worst effects of the Acts, and the 2006 Act itself draws much of the venom of the earlier statute. As a result, the most important issues for practitioners are likely to be (1) the provisions regarding exemptions from the Acts and (2) the effects of unenforceability. This chapter has not been materially amended since the previous edition of this book (2016); we are not aware of any significant cases on these issues in the intervening years that would justify substantial updating to the text.

Since many of these issues turn on the interpretation of clauses in credit hire agreements, it is worth beginning with some general observations on contractual interpretation.

Defendants may preface their submissions in this respect by stating that if there is any doubt or ambiguity as to construction, the construction most preferable to the consumer, i.e. the Claimant, rather than the credit hire company should apply. In other words the *contra preferentum* rule should be applied. Thus in *Ketley v Gilbert*[297] Brooke LJ recognised, obiter, that:

> *"if there had been any doubt in the interpretation of the agreement that doubt would have been resolved in favour of [the claimant] as the hirer, so as to render the agreement unenforceable."*

Claimants may counter that contracts should be interpreted as far as possible to give effect to their commercial purpose (in this case to provide the Claimant with a car and for the Claimant to claim back the cost of that car from the tortfeasor). In order to fulfil this commercial purpose the contract would have to be enforceable. Reference may also be made to the rule of construction that it is better for a thing to have effect than to be made void. For example, in *Mills v Dunham,*[298] it was stated:

---

297 Ketley v Gilbert, (2001) 1 WLR 986.

298 Mills v Dunham, [1891] 1 Ch 576 at 590.

"It is a settled canon of construction that where a clause is ambiguous a construction which will make it valid is to be preferred to one which will make it void."

B. Is a Credit Hire Agreement Regulated?

In this section we will consider:

a) Whether the agreement provides credit?

b) The correct classification of credit hire agreements under the 1974 Act

c) Exemptions from the regime of the 1974 act.

a) Does the Agreement provide Credit?

In *Dimond v Lovell* in both the Court of Appeal and the House of Lords, the Claimant argued that the credit hire agreement in question did not in fact provide credit.

This apparently unattractive argument was encouraged by the drafting of the Act itself. Section 9 defines "credit" as follows:

"(1) In this Act "credit" includes a cash loan, and any other form of financial accommodation."

This is not necessarily a helpful definition, since it does not state what "credit" means, instead it merely indicates that cash loans and financial accommodation are included within the definition.

Perhaps a more helpful definition of credit is that provided by Professor Goode:-

"credit [is] extended whenever the contract provides for the debtor to pay, or gives him the option to pay, later than the time at which

> *payment would otherwise have been earned under the express or implied terms of the contract."*[299]

In *Dimond*, the Claimant argued that the services provided to Mrs. Dimond were not only the use of the car but also the pursuit of her claim. These obligations should be treated as forming part of an entire contract in which 1st Automotive could not recover any part of the consideration until it had not only allowed Mrs. Dimond the use of the car but also brought the claim for damages to a conclusion. Only at this point would 1st Automotive become entitled to payment and therefore the provision for "credit" was not really credit at all. Payment was thus not postponed, they argued, until later than the time at which payment would otherwise have been earned.

The House of Lords unanimously held that the agreement provided credit for two reasons. First, the agreement stated on its face that it provided credit. Second, payment was in fact delayed until later than it would otherwise have been earned.

On the first issue, according to Lord Hoffmann the agreement in question provided:-

> *"1st Automotive "allow[s] the hirer credit on the hire charges" this arrangement is described as a "credit facility" and if there is a breach of condition 5(iii) the "credit allowed" may be terminated."*[300]

The clear and repeated references in the contract to "credit" were according to Lord Hoffmann "*unpromising material for an argument*".

Lord Hobhouse made a similar point:-

> *"Here the terms of the agreement are explicit. The lessor is extending credit to the hirer. It is described as a "credit facility" and the allowance*

299 Goode, Consumer Credit Legislation, loose leaf ed., vol 1, para. 443.

300 Dimond v Lovell, p394.

of credit and its termination are specifically referred to. Under these circumstances there can be no escape from the answer which your Lordships have given."[301]

Second, Lord Hoffmann considered that the agreement did allow for the deferral of payment:

"Th[e claimant's] argument depends upon construing the contract as imposing upon 1st Automotive a duty to Mrs. Dimond to pursue the claim and treating the performance of that duty as forming part of an entire contract which also included the provision of the vehicle."[302]

He went on:

"The only obligation of 1st Automotive under the agreement was to provide the vehicle. In the absence of credit, it would have been entitled to payment during or at the end of the hire. All the provisions about the pursuit of the claim were express or implied conditions that deferred the right to recover the hire and therefore constituted a granting of credit. In addition, of course, the pursuit of the claim by 1st Automotive on behalf of Mrs. Dimond may have given rise to further obligations to her, such as the obligation to indemnify her against a liability for costs which Lord Mustill mentions in Giles v. Thompson [1994] 1 A.C. 142, 163."

By implication, Lords Browne-Wilkinson, Nicholls and Saville agreed with the analysis of Lord Hoffmann on this point.

Lord Hobhouse agreed that on the facts there was a deferral of payment:

"Where the transaction is a relatively simple consumer transaction little sophistication is required. The car has been hired, used and returned. No payment of the hire charges is stipulated for at that time. Payment

301 Ibid., p405.

302 Ibid., p395.

> *is postponed until the hirer has been put in funds: "the lessor will allow the hirer credit on the hire charges". But neither the lessor nor the hirer is under an obligation to procure that the hirer is put in funds. The lessor has no obligation; the hirer's obligation is simply to co-operate. As is illustrated by the present case, the accident hire company itself in the contractual document characterised what it was doing as the providing a credit facility. It was clearly right to do so."*[303]

However he also expressed doubt about the definition of credit propounded by Professor Goode, and suggested a rather narrower definition.

> *"The test formulated by Professor Goode adopted by the Vice Chancellor in the Court of Appeal [1999] 3 W.L.R. 561, 572 will not always be a satisfactory one to apply. Many commercial agreements contain provisions which could be said to postpone (or advance) the time at which payment has to be made. Frequently, there will be reasons for this other than the provision of credit. Payment may be postponed as security for the performance of some other obligation by the creditor. Payments may be made in advance of performance in order to tie the paying party into the commercial venture. Payment provisions may like any other aspect of the transaction be part of its commercial structure for the division of risk, for the provision of security or simply the distribution of the commercial interest in the outcome of the transaction."*

It therefore seems to be clear that an ordinary credit hire agreement will be understood as providing credit. However Claimants may argue that this result is not inevitable. First, in *Dimond*, one of the terms in the written agreement expressly provided for payment to be deferred and other terms expressly referred to "credit". This made it easy for the House of Lords to decide that credit was provided. Not all credit hire agreements are so transparent. Where an agreement does not include a term deferring

303 Ibid., p405.

payment, it may be more difficult for Defendants to argue that any credit is provided at all. Claimants might argue that the fact that an agreement has not been enforced might be a gratuitous indulgence or a forbearance on the part of the credit hire company and not a contractual deferment of debt. Second, in *Dimond*, the agreement did not oblige the credit hire company to pursue the Claimant's claim nor suggest that this was part of an "entire agreement". It might remain open to Claimants to argue that there was no deferral of payment, where such terms are included in the contract.

b) The Correct Classification of the Credit Hire Agreements

Sections 8 – 14 of the Consumer Credit Act 1974 go on to divide credit agreements into different categories. It is therefore necessary to consider briefly which categories credit hire agreements fall into.

In *Dimond*, the categorisation of the agreements was addressed in most detail by the Court of Appeal. Scott V–C concluded:

> "*In my judgment the 1st Automotive agreement was a personal credit agreement (section 8(1)), a consumer credit agreement (section 8(2)), an agreement for a fixed sum credit facility (section 10(1)(b)), a restricted-use credit agreement under section 11(1)(a) and a debtor-creditor-supplier agreement under section 12(a)*"[304]

In the House of Lords, none of the speeches explicitly analyse exactly what sort of agreement it was. However, Lord Hoffmann referred to paragraph 3(1)(a) of the Consumer Credit (Exempt Agreements) Order 1989 which only applies to fixed sum debtor-credit-supplier agreements. This suggests that he agreed with the Court of Appeal that the agreement was a fixed-sum debtor-creditor-supplier agreement.

---

304 Dimond v Lovell, CA decision, para. 69. This was the conclusion of a detailed discussion which extended over paras 27 – 69.

Is it also a consumer hire agreement?

An issue which sometimes arises in practice is whether a particular agreement is also a consumer hire agreement as defined by section 15 of the Act. It is advantageous for Defendants to argue that the agreement is a consumer hire agreement because the exemption provisions in paragraph 3(1) of the 1989 Order do not apply to consumer hire agreements.

There appears to be nothing to prevent a particular agreement being both a consumer credit agreement and a consumer hire agreement. The Court of Appeal in *Dimond* concluded that:-

> *"[I] am not persuaded that the two regimes would necessarily be incompatible. If certain prescribed requirements have to be included in regulated agreements for the hire of goods and other requirements have to be included in regulated agreements that provide credit, then agreements that both provide for the hire of goods and allow credit for payment of the hire charges may have to include both sets of requirements. If any genuine case of incompatibility were to arise, the Act provides the remedy via an application under section 60(3) for a waiver or variation of the requirements [see below]."*[305]

The definition of consumer hire agreement is contained within section 15, which provides:-

> *(1) A consumer hire agreement is an agreement made by a person with an individual (the "hirer") for the bailment . . . of goods to the hirer, being an agreement which –*
>
> > *(a) is not a hire-purchase agreement and*
> >
> > *(b) is capable of subsisting for more than three months, and*

[305] Ibid., para. 67.

(c) [...][306]

The critical issue is the meaning of *"capable of subsisting for more than three months"*. Although Defendants have argued that this phrase applies to the duration of the agreement, in *Burdis v Livsey* the Court of Appeal concluded that it applied to the bailment of the car:-

> *"Although sub-section (1)(b) could have been more clearly drafted we agree with the judge's construction. Section 15 is directed at the long-term bailment of goods which are not the subject of hire purchase agreements. Sub-section (1)(b) is intended to refer to the period of such bailment and not to any other obligations which might be assumed under the agreement. Sub-section (1)(c) is merely intended to limit the application of the section to agreements of a certain size. It does not extend the type of agreement to which the section is intended to refer.*
>
> *Some support for this construction can be derived from the surrounding sections of the Act. Section 15 appears as one of six sections which closely define different categories of regulated agreements. Section 18 to which we will return contemplates that one must look at any agreement to see whether any part of it falls within one of these defined categories, in which case that part must be treated separately. This suggests that the intention was to confine the different categories of agreement. The construction contended for by the insurers gives a much wider definition of a consumer hire agreement than we think Parliament intended."*[307]

The result is that provided that the hire agreement includes a clause limiting the duration of bailment under the agreement to a period less

---

306 The 1974 Act included at subsection (c) a clause limiting the definition to agreements where the payments do not exceed £15,000. This financial limitation was removed by the Consumer Credit Act 2006 and no longer applies.

307 Burdis v Livsey, paras 48 – 49.

than three months, the agreement is unlikely to be a consumer hire agreement.

It remains possible for Defendants to argue that the clause limiting the duration of the bailment is a sham, particularly where the hire period in fact lasts more than three months, or multiple hire agreements are signed in respect of the same rental vehicle. But as set out below arguments based on sham are unlikely to succeed in this context. Where the hire period under a single agreement exceeds three months, Claimants may well argue that the contract itself was not capable of subsisting for more than three months, but the Claimant is in breach of a term of that contract.

Section 18: multiple agreements

In *Dimond*, the Claimant also argued in the alternative that the credit hire agreement provided for two things: the provision of a hire vehicle and the provision of credit. It should therefore be treated as a multiple agreement within the meaning of section 18 of the Act. The conclusion that the Claimant hoped to reach was that only the credit part of the agreement would be unenforceable, leaving the hire company able to enforce the hire part of the agreement.

In response to this argument, Lord Hoffmann stated:

> "*The difficulty I have with this argument is that it seems to sever the provisions that create the debt (hiring the car) from the provisions that allow credit for payment of the debt. Whatever a multiple agreement may be, one cannot divide up a contract in that way. The creation of the debt and the terms on which it is payable must form parts of the same agreement. The truth of the matter is that I accept that the hiring agreement was a single contract. But I do not accept Mr. Wingate-Saul's submission as to what that contract was. He argues that it involved multiple obligations on the part of 1st Automotive that had to be performed over a period starting when the car was hired and ending when the damages were recovered. I consider, on the contrary, that the only primary obligation of 1st Automotive was to provide the*

> *car. The rest of the agreement dealt with the conditions upon which it would be entitled to recover the hire. To such an agreement section 18 has, of course, no relevance."*[308]

A similar argument was also dismissed by the Court of Appeal in *Burdis.* There, the Claimant argued that the obligation to pay the hire company was free standing from the clauses concerning credit. Therefore, they argued, even if the credit provisions are unenforceable the Claimant will still be obliged to pay the hire company. The Court of Appeal concluded: *"we do not think it is possible to regard these terms as having a free standing life of their own. They are simply part of the terms on which credit is granted."*[309]

<u>*Act only applies to Individuals*</u>

Both section 8 and section 15 of the Act clearly state that they apply where the debtor or hirer is an "individual". Section 189 of the Act states that "individual" "includes a partnership or other unincorporated body of persons not consisting entirely of bodies corporate". The Act does not therefore protect any form of corporate entity.

Claimants might go further and argue that since the title of the Act only refers to "Consumer", the Act should only apply to consumers, either as defined under European law or perhaps pursuant to the Unfair Contract Terms Act 1977. Therefore, for example, a mini-cab driver who is self-employed and who hires a cab after an accident would not be covered by the Act even though he would come within the definition of individual.

---

308 Dimond v Lovell, p396.

309 Burdis v Livsey, para. 60.

c) Does the Agreement fall within an Exemption?

Section 16 of the 1974 Act empowered the Secretary of State to make Regulations exempting certain types of agreement from the Act (and hence from the rigours of enforceability).

The current relevant exemption is contained in paragraph 60F(2) of the Financial Services and Markets Act 2000 (Regulated Activities) Order 2001 (as amended). However, at the time when the enforceability of agreements under the Consumer Credit Act 1974 was being tested, the equivalent exemption was found in the Consumer Credit (Exempt Agreements) Order 1989. The following text and cases set out the text of the 1989 Order and the jurisprudence on its interpretation.

The Consumer Credit (Exempt Agreements) Order 1989 ("the Exemption Order") paragraph 3(1), as amended by Regulation 66 of the Consumer Credit (EU Directive) Regulations 2010 provided:

> *"The Act shall not regulate a consumer credit agreement which is an agreement of one of the following descriptions, that is to say – (a) a debtor-creditor-supplier agreement being either – (i) an agreement for fixed-sum credit under which- (aa) the total number of payments to be made by the debtor does not exceed four, (bb) those payments are required to be made within a period not exceeding 12 months beginning with the date of the agreement and (cc) the credit is provided without interest and without any other charges."* (emphasis added)

The amendment, which entered into force on 1 February 2011, added the requirement at (cc) that in order to qualify for an exemption an agreement must not provide for interest on the credit. The result is that, since most credit hire agreements provide for the payment of interest, they do not fall within the exemption and thus must be treated as regulated agreements.

Much litigation has concerned whether specific agreements comply with what are now conditions (aa) and (bb). We will summarise this litigation below, although it is worth repeating that much of this discussion is now academic since credit hire agreements are likely to fall foul of (cc).

In order to fall within conditions (aa) and (bb) of the exemption, credit hire agreements must satisfy five conditions. The agreement must be:

1. for fixed-sum credit,
2. under which the total number of payments to be made by the debtor does not exceed four and
3. those payments are required to be made
4. within a period
5. not exceeding 12 months beginning with the date of the agreement.

i. Fixed-sum credit

Some have attempted to argue that a credit hire agreement does not provide fixed-sum credit within the meaning of section 10 of the Act where there has been no price entered on the agreement.

This argument is misguided. Section 10 defines running account credit as "*a facility under a personal credit agreement whereby the debtor is enabled to receive from time to time (whether in his own person, or by another person) from the creditor or a third party cash, goods and services (or any of them) to an amount or value such that, taking into account payments made by or to the credit of the debtor, the credit limit (if any) is not at any time exceeded*". It then defines fixed sum credit as *"any other facility"*. Thus under the, admittedly odd, definition in the Act anything which is not running account credit falls within the definition of fixed sum credit.

As Scott V-C approached the question in the Court of Appeal in Dimond: "*It seems clear to me that 1st Automotive's agreement does not allow its customers "running account credit" as described in section 10(1)(a). It follows that... it allows fixed sum credit as described in section 10(1)(b)."*[310]

ii. Four Payments

Defendants may argue that unless the agreement expressly limits the number of payments to four or less it is not exempt.

However, in *Burdis v Livsey*, the Court of Appeal held that:

> *"This issue is simply one of construction of the agreements concerned. Looking at the credit hire agreement the principal obligation is contained in condition 3, the first sentence of which says when the credit period is to expire and continues "at that point you will be liable to pay". This is a one payment requirement."*[311]

Thus where the agreement is silent as to the number of payments, it is likely to be interpreted as a one payment requirement. This result was consistent with the decisions of HHJ Harris in *Seddon v Tekin*[312] and in *Burdis* itself.

iii. Required

If the agreement leaves a discretion as to whether payment will be enforced within twelve months, Defendants may argue that this does not <u>require</u> payment as set down in the Order. Such arguments may be strengthened where payment has not in fact been enforced within that time.

---

310 Dimond v Lovell, CA decision, para. 27.

311 Burdis v Livsey, para. 52.

312 Seddon v Tekin and Dowsett v Clifford, HHJ Harris, Oxford County Court, 25 August 2001.

An authoritative analysis of these arguments was carried out in *Seddon v Tekin*, in which HHJ Harris analysed a clause which provided that, "The credit period extended by this agreement shall expire in any event 51 weeks from the date of the agreement. At the expiry of the credit period you shall then become liable to pay the hire charges in full."

He held that this came within the Exemption Order and stated:

> *"In my judgment the hypothetical reasonable person reading the stipulation, "You shall then become liable to pay in full" would understand that to mean that he was required to pay then and not that he may be asked to pay thereafter.*

This approach also accords with the nature of credit. In the Court of Appeal in *Dimond v Lovell*, the Vice Chancellor referred to *Grant v Watton* [1999] STC 330 and cited Pumphrey J where he said: *"Credit is granted when payment is not demanded until the time later than the supply of services or goods to which the payment relates. Credit is the deferring of a payment of a sum which in the absence of an agreement would be immediately payable"*, and said that he entirely agreed with this. Thus at the end of the 51 or 26 weeks credit expires and the charges are immediately due and due without further demand or particularisation. The hirer, if he does not know what they are can always ask.

iv. Within

Defendants may also argue that the wording of the agreement does not fall within the exemption because payment was not required "within" the prescribed twelve months.

This issue came before the Court of Appeal in the case of *Ketley v Gilbert.*[313] The question for the court was whether the clause requiring charges to be paid "on the expiry of 12 months starting with the date of this agreement", satisfied the wording of the 1989 Order. The Court of

---

313 Ketley v Gilbert, [2001] 1 WLR 986.

Appeal held that an agreement permitting the final payment to be made "on expiry" of that period permitted the final payment to be made after the 12-month period had expired. Payment was not required to be made within a period "not exceeding 12 months" which was necessary if exemption was to be afforded to the agreement pursuant to the 1989 Order.

Where payment falls due on the anniversary of the agreement, Defendants may argue that it is not therefore due "within" the twelve months stipulated in the Order.[314]

In other cases, whilst an agreement may make it clear that a credit period comes to an end before the expiration of twelve months, it may also be argued that a reasonable time to actually pay the debt would be implied for the Claimant after that date. Thus in *Ketley v Gilbert,* Brooke LJ states:

> *"If the words of the agreement could be flexibly interpreted to permit payment a reasonable time after the expiry of 12 months (since it could not reasonably by expected that the hirer would make payment on the stroke of midnight), such payment was not required to be made within a period not exceeding 12 months, as was necessary if exemption was to be afforded to this agreement pursuant to the 1989 order."*[315]

However, Claimants may argue that if the credit period comes to an end, the clear implication is that payment is then due. Thus in *Burdis v Livsey,* it was argued that once a person becomes liable to pay, he has a reasonable time before he is actually required to pay the money hence taking payment beyond the twelve months. The Court of Appeal rejected this argument: *"liable" may mean "bound or obliged by law" in which sense*

[314] cf further Zoan v Rouamba unreported 21/1/2000.

[315] Ketley v Gilbert, para. 26.

condition 14 [the relevant provision] would obviously require payment at the end of the credit period or "obliged if asked."[316]

v. Twelve Months

This is the most technical of all the arguments surrounding the exemption clauses. If an agreement requires payment within twelve months "after" or "from" or "of" the date of the agreement, Defendants may argue that this does not come within the exact wording of the Order since it allows credit for one day more than that permitted by the Order.

In *Zoan v Rouamba,*[317] the Court of Appeal reviewed the authorities on time limits and concluded:

> *"Where, under some legislative provision, an act is required to be done within a fixed period of time "beginning with" or "from" a specified day it is a question of construction whether the specified day itself is to be included in, or excluded from, that period. Where the period within which the act is to be done is expressed to be a number of days, months or years from or after a specified day, the courts have held, consistently since Young v Higgon (1840) 6 M&W 49, that the specified day is excluded from the period; that is to say, that the period commences on the day after the specified day.... Where, however, the period within which the act is to be done is expressed to be a period beginning with a specified day, then it has been held, with equal consistency over the past forty years or thereabouts, that the legislature (or the relevant rule making body, as the case may be) has shown a clear intention that the specified day must be included in the period."*[318]

This led the Court of Appeal to uphold the trial Judge's finding that *"it was "obvious", from the use of the expression "beginning with the date of the*

[316] Burdis v Livsey, para. 55 upholding HHJ Harris QC.

[317] Zoan v Rouamba, Unreported, Court of Appeal, 20 January 2000.

[318] Ibid., paras 23 – 24.

agreement" in paragraph 3(1)(a)(i) of the 1989 Order, that the period of twelve months prescribed by that paragraph included the date of the agreement."[319]

The result in that case was the phrase in the contract requiring payment "twelve months after the date of this agreement", permitted payment to be made one day after the twelve-month period had expired for the purposes of the Exemption Order. The agreement therefore fell outside the scope of the exemption, and was regulated and ultimately unenforceable.

The Current Exemption

As explained above, the 1989 Order has been repealed and the equivalent exemption is now found in paragraph 60F(2) of the Financial Services and Markets Act 2000 (Regulated Activities) Order 2001 (as amended), which provides:-

A credit agreement is an exempt agreement if—

(a) the agreement is a borrower-lender-supplier agreement for fixed-sum credit, other than a green deal plan,

(b) the number of payments to be made by the borrower is not more than twelve,

(c) those payments are required to be made within a period of 12 months or less (beginning on the date of the agreement),

(d) the credit is—

(i) secured on land, or

[319] Ibid., para. 25.

(ii) provided without interest or other charges.

Aside from the updated language in (a), there are three potentially significant differences between the provisions. First, the number of payments permitted within the exemption has risen from four to twelve. Second, the period within which payment is required is "within a period of 12 months or less" instead of "within a period not exceeding 12 months", which might arguably make some difference to the highly technical reasoning in some of the above cases. Third, any agreement which charges interest cannot fall within the exemption.

Is the exemption clause a Sham or Pretence?

Defendant insurers have attempted to argue that the clauses drafted to bring credit hire agreements within the wording of the exemption order are a sham or a pretence.

These arguments were rejected by the Court of Appeal in *Burdis v Livsey*. The Court of Appeal adopted the narrow definition of sham propounded by Lord Justice Diplock (as he then was) in Snook v West Riding Investments Ltd:

> *"for acts or documents to be a sham...all the parties thereto must have a common intention that the acts or documents are not to create the legal rights and obligations which they give the appearance of creating".*[320]

The credit hire agreement could not come within this narrow definition of a sham because in credit hire cases there is rarely any evidence of deceit or improper motive on the part of the Claimants. The Court of Appeal were content to quote from the judgment below of Judge Harris QC in the Oxford County Court:

[320] [1967] 2 QB 786 at 802.

> *"There was no suggestion ... that any of the claimants who entered into their credit or insurance agreements had any improper motive whatsoever .... There is no evidence that they had any intention to avoid, legitimately or illegitimately, the application of the consumer credit legislation."*[321]

However the courts remain alert to agreements that are shams in the wider sense that the agreements do not do what they say on the packet. For example in *Antoniades v Villiers*[322] the House of Lords refused to give effect to an agreement which called itself a licence and reserved a right of occupation to the landlord. The reserved right was never intended to be exercised. It was a pretence to avoid the provisions of the Rent Acts.

In *Burdis* the Court of Appeal noted that:

> *"in this type of case the courts have made it clear that they will look at the scheme as a whole if there is more than one transaction and subsequent conduct in order to determine its effect and validity....In the instant case the court is concerned with consumer protection legislation. It is not possible to contract out of the provisions which regulate some transactions but the Act says that other transactions are exempt. There is therefore nothing wrong with entering or attempting to enter into such a transaction. Either it is exempt or it is regulated and the courts must decide which."*[323]

The point was that the court simply had to decide whether the agreement in question meets the requirements of an exempt agreement or not. Guidance was taken from Lord Hoffmann's words in *Norglen Ltd v Reeds Rains Prudential Ltd:*[324]

---

321 Burdis v Livsey, para. 31.

322 Antoniades v Villiers, [1990] 1 AC 417.

323 Burdis v Livsey, paras 32-33.

324 Norglen Ltd v Reeds Rains Prudential Ltd, [1999] 2 AC 1.

> *"The question is simply whether upon its true construction, the statute applies to the transaction. Tax avoidance schemes are perhaps the best example. They either work ... or they do not.... If they do not work, the reason .... is simply that upon the true construction of the statute, the transaction which was designed to avoid the charge to tax actually comes within it. It is not that the statute has a penumbral spirit which strikes down devices or stratagems designed to avoid its terms or exploit its loopholes."*

The Court considered that on their face the credit hire agreements were exempt from the Act. The Defendant argued that the court should infer that there was no limit to the credit period because the insurance arrangement was a pretence and was not pursued by the hire company in practice. This failed on the facts. Judge Harris had found as a fact at first instance that there were payments from the insurer to the hire company which had the effect of discharging the Claimants' debts. The source of the insurer's funds was irrelevant. There is nothing unusual about the circular flow of funds around a group of companies. Accordingly the Court of Appeal upheld the Judge's decision that there was no sham or pretence on these facts. For completeness, we quote from paragraphs 39 and 44 of the judgment:

> *"These points [relating to the insurance arrangements] were obviously considered by the judge who, as we have said, referred to the scheme as a whole as being sloppily executed and to the insurance arrangement as being artificial. But the documents do show an intention to create genuine insurance arrangements. The underwriting agreement contains many of the terms one would expect to find in such an agreement and there was an assumption of risk by underwriters. Subject to the point about the policy wording, which was obviously a mistake, a claimant would have a valid claim under the policy for the cost of hire and repairs if no payment was made by Angel. In effect the risk assumed by underwriters was of the solvency of the Helphire Group. There is nothing wrong or unusual with insurance arrangements which have this effect...*

> *"We have so far considered the insurers' main attack on the scheme. The fact that customers who did not claim on the insurance were not pursued was not considered in any detail by the Judge. But just because the scheme was, as he said, "sloppily enforced" does not lead to the conclusion that the credit hire and repair agreements were intended to have some meaning contrary to their express terms. Commercial parties may, and often do, choose not to enforce their strict legal rights without intending to create or demonstrate some different state of affairs. Other matters relied on by the insurers about the way in which the Helphire scheme was run do not in our judgment advance their case. Looked at from the claimants' point of view there was no pretence. They got exactly what they bargained for: car repair and hire at little or no cost. It might be said that it is only the insurers' attack on these schemes which has raised the spectre of long term credit because in the ordinary way claims of this kind are settled within weeks of the accident."*

In a different context arguments of sham / pretence were also rejected in *Corbett v Gaskin*[325] and *Barker v First West Yorkshire.*[326]

This does not necessarily mean that the issue of pretence / sham is dead. The decision was based on factual findings about how the particular companies and their contracts operated. There may be room for Defendant insurers to argue sham / pretence if on the facts of a different scheme, with a different contractual or corporate set up, no payments are being made by the nominal insurer.

It might also be open to Defendant insurers to argue that the exemption clause is an unfair term within the meaning of the Unfair Terms in Consumer Contracts Regulations 1999.[327]

---

325 Corbett v Gaskin, HHJ Harris QC, unreported, 31 August 2007.

326 Barker v First West Yorkshire, Unreported 13 September 2007.

327 These Regulations are explored in more detail in Chapter 7.

C. What Do the Consumer Credit Acts Require?

Assuming that the Defendant is able to show that the credit hire agreement is regulated by the Acts, the next question to consider is what exactly the agreement must do in order to comply with the Acts.

We set out below the position as at the time of *Dimond*, in order to explain that case. The precise requirements of the Acts have varied over time.

Section 60(1) of the Act requires the Secretary of State to "make regulations as to the form and content of documents embodying regulated agreements . . ."

Sub-section (2) says that:

> *Regulations under subsection (1) may in particular:–*
>
> > *(a) require specified information to be included in the prescribed manner in documents, and other specified material to be excluded;*
> >
> > *(b) contain requirements to ensure that specified information is clearly brought to the attention of the debtor or hirer, and that one part of a document is not given insufficient or excessive prominence compared with another.*

Section 61 introduces the concept of a regulated agreement being "properly executed". It provides, under sub-section (1), that an agreement is not "properly executed" unless:

> *(a) a document in the prescribed form itself containing all the prescribed terms and conforming to regulations under section 60(1) is signed in the prescribed manner both by the debtor or hirer and by or on behalf of the creditor or owner, and*
>
> *(b) the document embodies all the terms of the agreement, other than implied terms, and*

. . . . .

The prescribed terms and prescribed form were set out in the Consumer Credit (Agreements) Regulations 1983 ("the 1983 Regulations").

Paragraph 2 of the 1983 Regulations deals with the form and content of regulated consumer credit agreements and, by sub-paragraph (1), requires them to contain the information set out in column 2 of Schedule 1 of the 1983 Regulations. Where information about financial particulars could not be exactly ascertained, sub-paragraph (2) permitted "estimated information based on such assumptions as the creditor may reasonably make in all the circumstances of the case . . ." to be included.

Paragraph 6(1) of the 1983 Regulations requires that:

> *"The terms specified in column 2 of Schedule 6 . . . in relation to the type of regulated agreement referred to in column 1 . . . are hereby prescribed for the purposes of section 61(1)(a) . . . and of section 127(3) . . ."*

Schedule 6 paragraphs 1 and 5 provide that a debtor-creditor-supplier agreement must contain the following prescribed terms:-

> *"(a) a term stating the amount of credit; [paragraph 1] and a term stating how the debtor is to discharge his obligations under the agreement to make the repayments, which may be expressed by reference to a combination of any one of the following-*
>
> > *(i) number of repayments;*
> >
> > *(ii) amount of repayments;*
> >
> > *(iii) frequency and timing of repayments;*
> >
> > *(iv) dates of repayment;*

> *(v) the manner in which any of the above may be determined; or in any other way, and any power of the creditor to vary what is payable."* *[Paragraph 5]*

The prescribed term for regulated consumer hire agreements is in paragraph 6 of Schedule 6 and consists of the following:

> *"A term stating how the hirer is to discharge his obligations under the agreement to pay the hire payments, which may be expressed by reference to a combination of any of the following– (a) number of payments; (b) amount of payments; (c) frequency and timing of payments; (d) dates of payments; (e) the manner in which any of the above may be determined; or in any other way, and any power of the owner to vary what is payable."*

<u>*A term stating the amount of credit*</u>

Whilst the interpretation of many of the prescribed terms is straightforward, some difficulty has arisen over the meaning of "a term stating the amount of credit".

In the Court of Appeal in *Dimond*, the Claimant argued that it would not have been possible to have included the prescribed term. i.e., the amount of credit, since the length of the hire period would not be known. Scott V–C disagreed:

> *"But the daily rate of hire would be known and an estimate of the period of hire could be obtained from the garage that was repairing the damaged vehicle. In these circumstances paragraph 2(2) of the 1983 Regulations would, as I have read it, apply and would have allowed 1st Automotive to insert an estimate of the amount of credit with an indication of the assumptions on which the estimate was made. I do*

> *not accept that 1st Automotive could not have complied with the Regulations."*[328]

This statement remains the best judicial guidance on the point. However, Defendants may argue that it is wrong to suggest that an estimate may be applied to Schedule 6 since paragraph 2(2) of the 1983 Regulations allows estimates to be made only for those particulars set out in paragraphs 9 to 11 of Schedule 1 and not for those required by Schedule 6.

Claimants may potentially argue that entering the price of the hire at the time was enough. If there is a three-month clause, they can argue that that is the maximum period of hire and therefore the amount of credit can be worked out.

However, Defendants can argue that Scott V–C's comments suggest that the agreement needs to go further and in fact an estimate of the period of hire also needs to be included. Credit hire companies will therefore be able to argue that they have included the "amount of credit" if they have included the daily rate and the estimated time of hire. Even if such an estimate of the period of hire is included, Defendants will be able to argue that this is inadequate if the estimate does not actually end up being accurate as to the actual period of hire.

It is likely that the prescribed terms must be included in the agreement itself, rather than any collateral agreement in writing or orally. Paragraph 1296 of Consumer Credit, edited by Professor Goode, states:

> *"Schedule 6 to the agreements regulations sets out the terms prescribed by s 61(1)(a) of the Act, that is, terms which are required to be contained in the executed agreement itself and not merely in some other document embodied in it by cross-reference."*

---

[328] Dimond v Lovell, CA Decision, para. 71.

D. What Becomes of an Improperly Executed Regulated Agreement?

The final question that must be addressed is, assuming that the credit hire agreement is a regulated, what is the result of failing to include the prescribed terms or prescribed forms?

Section 65 of the Act provides that:

> *"(1) An improperly-executed regulated agreement is enforceable against the debtor or hirer on an order of the court only."*

At the time when *Dimond* was decided, section 127(3) of the Act required a court to dismiss an application for an enforcement order under section 65(1) *"unless a document (whether or not in the prescribed form and complying with regulations under section 60(1)) itself containing all the prescribed terms of the agreement was signed by the debtor or hirer (whether or not in the prescribed manner)".*

This informed the decision in Dimond that that the hire agreement, not containing the prescribed terms, was automatically unenforceable and hence that the hire charges could not be recovered. It also created what was sometimes analysed as a two-tiered system, where failure to comply with the prescribed terms led to automatic unenforceability whereas failure to comply with the prescribed form led to possible unenforceability, subject to an enforcement order from the Court.

However, with effect from 6 April 2007, section 127(3) has been repealed by the Consumer Credit Act 2006.

Now in respect of all improperly executed credit agreements, enforceability is governed by section 127(1):

> *"the court shall dismiss the application [for an enforcement order] if, but only if, it considers it just to do so having regard to (i) prejudice caused to any person by the contravention in question, and the degree of culpability for it"*

In considering whether to grant the enforcement order the court may "reduce or discharge" any part of the sum payable to compensate for prejudice suffered by the debtor (Section 127(2)). Further the court retains the powers in section 135 and 136 to make the enforcement order conditional, suspend the operation of any term of the order and amend any term of any agreement as a consequence of making the order.

There is little guidance on what principles would be applied with regard to an enforcement order. The notes to the Act provide some help but not with respect to the particular example of credit hire.

The result is clear: an improperly executed regulated agreement is no longer automatically unenforceable. Rather it remains potentially enforceable by order of the Court. The question remains what effect this has on the recoverability of hire charges.

Claimants may argue that they should recover the full amount on the basis that there is a potential liability. A similar argument succeeded in cases including *Hatfield v Hiscock.*[329]

On the other hand, Defendants may argue that the proper approach is for the court to assess the probability of an enforcement order being granted in the future. If the probability of enforcement is less than 50%, then it may be argued that the Claimant has not proved his claim. This approach was adopted in *Aggett v Aston Rothbury Factors Limited*[330] in which the Judge stated (obiter):

---

[329] Hatfield v Hiscock, [1998] CCLR 68; [1998] 6 CL 88. See also Marchant and Marchant v Brown, unreported, 2/8/1999 (HHJ Poulton), Knott v Stott, unreported, 29/9/1999, Jones v Lindon, unreported, 26/7/1999, Pitt-Miller v Patel, HHJ Marr-Johnson, Mayor's & City County Court, 24 July 2001 and Wood v Gell, HHJ Poulton, Canterbury County Court, 27 July 2001.

[330] Aggett v Aston Rothbury Factors Ltd, HHJ Overend, Exeter County Court, 6 July 2001.

"the prospect of a court granting the s.65 order would not be high where – as here – the evidence was that the claimant would not have entered into the transaction if he had appreciated that he might have had to pay the full amount of the hire charges in the sums finally claimed by Crash Care, and that he was committing himself to them by signing the hire agreements. Had there been compliance with the provisions of the Statute, then it is likely that this Claimant would not have entered into the agreements. In those circumstances, I find that the chances of a court making a section 65 order low....

It seems to me that on the state of the evidence before the Court the prospects of Crash Care being able to recover the credit hire charges from the claimant are negligible...For those additional reasons, I find for the Defendant in relation to the sole issue before the Court, namely the recoverability of the hire charges."

These issues have not been tested under the Consumer Credit Act 2006. It remains unclear exactly what approach the Court would adopt. The issue is therefore open to be tested in the future.

CHAPTER FOURTEEN

CANCELLATION OF CONTRACTS

A. Introduction

The Cancellation of Contracts made in a Consumer's Home or Place of Work Regulations etc 2008 ("the Cancellation Regulations") came into force on 1 October 2008.[331] They gave further effect to the Doorstep Selling Directive,[332] and were enabled by the Consumers, Estate Agents and Redress Act 2007. In short they provided that, where the Regulations apply, the trader must give to the consumer a notice of their right to cancel the agreement. If this cancellation notice is not given, the Regulations provide that the agreement "shall not enforceable against the consumer".[333]

These Regulations provoked a flurry of litigation, particularly in the credit hire context.[334] It transpired that some credit hire companies had not provided a cancellation notice at all, and in other cases Defendants subjected the drafting of the cancellation notice to detailed scrutiny to test whether it complied with the Regulations. We can now stand back and summarise the results of these skirmishes.

---

331 Regulation 1, Cancellation Regulations 2008.

332 Council Directive 85/577/EEC

333 Regulation 7(6).

334 Though of course their application is broader and all tradesmen including plumbers, electricians and others were potentially affected by the Regulations.

However, we should start by acknowledging that the 2008 Cancellation Regulations were repealed and replaced by the Consumer Contracts (Information, Cancellation and Additional Charges) Regulations 2013. The 2008 Regulations do not apply to credit hire agreements made after 13 June 2014. The new regulations do provide that the trader must provide the consumer with specified information including about cancellation. But the consequences of failing to comply are largely criminal and there is no automatic unenforceability provision. As a result, the new regulations do not assist Defendants in credit hire cases.

The material in this Chapter thus only directly concerns agreements made on or before 12 June 2014. For later agreements, this chapter is only relevant insofar as it sets out general principles or identifies the general approach to enforceability issues.

For those readers who are most interested in the already paid / subrogation issues or the human rights issues that arose under these Regulations, we refer back to the discussion in Chapter Four.

B. When Did the Cancellation Regulations Apply?

Regulation 5 provided:-

> *"these Regulations apply to a contract, including a consumer credit agreement, between a consumer and a trader which is for the supply of goods or services to the consumer by a trader and which is made-*
>
> *(a) During a visit by the trader to the consumer's home or place of work, or to the home of another individual;*
>
> *(b) During an excursion organised by the trader away from his business premises; or*
>
> *(c) After an offer made by the consumer during such a visit or excursion."*

A credit hire agreement is plainly a contract for the supply of services by a trader.

The first condition which must be met for the Cancellation Regulations to apply to a particular credit hire agreement is that the Claimant must be a *"consumer"*.

Consumer was defined as *"a natural person who in making a contract to which these Regulations apply is acting for purposes which can be regarded as outside his trade or profession"*.[335]

The reference to a *"natural person"* plainly excludes corporations. However, the issue sometimes arises whether a self-employed taxi driver or an individual who uses their vehicle for the purposes of their profession falls within the definition of a consumer.

Defendants may argue that in applying the Unfair Contract Terms Act 1977,[336] the Courts have held that where a business makes a contract of a kind which is not a regular part of its business, it may act as a consumer.[337] Under this expansive definition, a potentially broad category of individuals would fall within the scope of the Regulations.

However, since the Regulations originate in European legislation, Claimants may respond that it is necessary to look at the narrower definition of *"consumer"* which the European Court of Justice has adopted in similar cases. Thus in *Di Pinto*, concerning the definition of

335 Regulation 2(1).

336 Section 12, by which a person is a consumer if "he neither makes the contract in the course of a business nor holds himself out as doing so".

337 R & B Custom Brokers Ltd v United Dominions Trust Ltd [1988] 1 WLR 321, in which the Court of Appeal distinguished between transactions which are "integral parts of the businesses" (not acting as a consumer) and those which are not.

consumer under the doorstep selling directive, the Court observed that the wording of the definition:

> *"does not make it possible, with regard to acts performed in the context of such a trade or profession, to draw a distinction between normal acts and those which are exceptional in nature."*[338]

In that case, the European Court concluded that acts which are preparatory to the sale of a business fall outside the definition of a consumer. In so doing the Court seemed to limit the definition of a consumer to contracts for *"family or personal requirements"*. In the later case of *Benincasa v Dentalkit Srl*, the Court was even more prescriptive:-

> *"only contracts concluded for the purpose of satisfying an individual's own needs in terms of private consumption come under the provisions designed to protect the consumer… The specific protection sought to be afforded by those provisions is unwarranted in the case of contracts for the purpose of trade or professional activity."*[339]

Further, dealing specifically with contracts with a dual purpose, both business and personal, the European Court has held: *"the benefit of those provisions cannot, as a matter of principle, be relied on by a person who concludes a contract for a purpose which is partly concerned with his trade or profession and is therefore only partly outside it. It would be otherwise only if the link between the contract and the trade or profession of the person concerned was so slight as to be marginal"*[340]

Claimants may rely on these European authorities to argue that wherever a contract is partly connected to an individual's trade or profession, he is not a consumer for the purposes of these Regulations. Defendants may argue that this narrow definition of consumer produces odd results.

338 Di Pinto [1991] ECR 1-1189 at 15.

339 Benincasa v Dentalkit Srl, [1997] ECR 1-3767 at 17.

340 Gruber v Bay Wa, Case C-464/01 at para. 39.

Would the individual who buys a car for domestic and personal reasons but also sometimes uses the vehicle to commute to work, really not be treated as a consumer?

Assuming that the Claimant was a consumer, the Regulations are triggered primarily if the contract was made during a visit by the trader to the consumer's home or place of work. In *Chen Wei v Cambridge Power and Light*, the Court was faced with facts typical of a credit hire case. The Claimant had at least one initial telephone conversation with the hire company. Then the hire vehicle was delivered to his home address, at which point he saw the contractual documents for the first time and signed them.

At first instance it was held that the contract was made when the Claimant signed the agreements and hence the Regulations applied. On appeal, the Claimant sought to argue that the agreement had been made in the course of the earlier telephone call. HHJ Moloney QC rejected this argument for two reasons. First, he held that "*the question whether a contract has been sufficiently agreed in the course of telephone conversations, or whether those discussions were merely preliminaries to the making of a written contract at the consumer's home, is one of mixed fact and law for the trial Judge no sufficient reasons were put before me to overturn the fact elements in that finding.*"[341] Second, the written agreement contained an entire agreement clause which the Court held "*has the effect of revoking any prior oral agreement.*"

This suggests that in contracts containing an entire agreements clause, there is likely to be little scope for dispute; the contract is made when the written agreement is signed. In other cases, it may be open to Claimants to argue that the contract was made during the preceding telephone call,

[341] Wei v Cambridge Power and Light, Unreported, 10 September 2010 at para. 11.

provided that the evidence about that call is sufficiently cogent to demonstrate that a concluded agreement was reached.[342]

In *W v Veolia Environmental Services Ltd*, the Claimant sought to avoid the conclusion that the Regulations applied in similar circumstances, by arguing that the Regulations were never intended to apply to mere delivery of a pre-arranged service. This argument had a strong foundation in the *travaux preparatoire*[343] and certain principles of statutory interpretation.[344] But these arguments were rejected. The Court concluded, obiter:-

> *Parliament has chosen to make the Regulations pursuant to the relevant European Directive and to do so in a particular way following the lengthy consultations to which [counsel for the claimant] has drawn attention…They are not ambiguous…There is no warrant to give these Regulations a meaning beyond that conveyed naturally by the words used"*[345]

Many of these arguments were dealt with briefly by the Court of Appeal in *Salat v Barutis*. The Court rejected the submission that the agreement was made in the initial telephone call as being "at odds with both

342 It may be worth noting that in practice the claimant may need to rely on more than simply the Claimant's evidence in this regard. Experience shows that individuals are unlikely to recall the detail of the initial telephone call in sufficient detail. Evidence may therefore need to be led of any log / record of the telephone call, or from the hire company itself.

343 cf the explanatory note to the Consumers Estate Agents and Redress Act 2007, the OFT report Doorstep Selling (May 2004) and Government Papers entitled Doorstep Selling and Cold Calling. Claimants may argue that these are entirely directed at the perceived evil of high pressure doorstep selling

344 See Bennion on Statutory Interpretation, in particular that provisions which impose criminal sanctions should not be expansively construed.

345 38 W v Veolia, para. 51.

commercial common sense and everyday experience, as well as unsupported on the evidence".[346] The Court rejected the further submission that the word "made" encompasses all the exchanges between the contractual parties, holding that "a contract is made for the purposes of regulation 5 when and where it is concluded".[347]

The underlying reasoning of the Court of Appeal in *Salat,* and the High Court in *W v Veolia,* is simply that the wording of the Regulations was unambiguous and did not allow for more than one interpretation. As a result, there was little scope for argument about the construction of the agreements.[348]

Where the agreement is signed at the repairing garage or elsewhere, however, the Regulations appear not to apply. Defendants have sought to argue that where the hire company arranges for the Claimant to collect the vehicle and sign the agreements in a third location, this is an excursion within the meaning of paragraph 5(b). This argument has met little success. There are two obstacles to this line of argument. First, whilst the statute gives no definition of *"excursion"* it is difficult to see that it applies in this context. The Regulations appear to be directed against time share selling. Moreover the natural meaning of excursion implies a pre-arranged journey to a particular location and back, arranged by the trader. However here, the consumer is free to get to the garage any way they choose and to leave in any direction. Second, given the variety of companies involved in credit hire and repair, it may be difficult to show that the excursion was organised by the credit hire organisation itself.[349]

346 Salat v Barutis, para. 14.

347 Ibid., para. 18.

348 Ibid., para. 19.

349 These difficulties were fatal to the Defendant's position in Osmond v Gammon, HHJ Hughes QC Winchester County Court

Finally, we should note that the Regulations applied in *Wei* and *W* because the written agreement was passed to the Claimant on delivery and signed by him in the presence of the delivery driver. It would be possible for hire companies (and other traders) to avoid the application of these Regulations by amending their standard procedures so that, for example, the written agreement is sent to Claimants through the post or is executed online.[350]

C. Exemptions from the Cancellation Regulations

Regulation 6 provides that the Regulations do not apply to certain contracts including: *"a cancellable agreement"* and "*a consumer credit agreement which may be cancelled by the consumer in accordance with the terms of the agreement conferring upon him similar rights as if the agreement were a cancellable agreement*".[351]

A "cancellable agreement" refers to a consumer credit agreement regulated by the Consumer Credit Act 1974 which may be cancelled by the debtor or hirer by virtue of Section 67 of that Act.[352]

350 Of course this would not avoid regulation altogether, it is just that a different set of Regulations would likely apply. For instance the Consumer Protection (Distance Selling) Regulations may well apply. They require the supplier to provide the consumer with certain information prior to and after the conclusion of the contract, and also provide for a cooling-off period within which the contract can be cancelled. But they make no provision for unenforceability. Instead Regulation 26 obliges an enforcement authority to look into complaints.

351 Regulation 6(1)(b) and (c).

352 Regulation 2(1) provides that "cancellable agreement has the same meaning as in section 189(1) of the 1974 Act. Section 189(1) in turn defines cancellable agreement by reference to s67.

To summarise the relevant provisions of the 1974 Act, section 67 provides that a *regulated agreement may be cancelled by the debtor or hirer in accordance with this Part"*. In the case of such agreements, section 64 provides that the creditor must give the debtor a notice of cancellation rights, in the prescribed form, indicating how and when the right to cancel is exercisable. In default, a cancellable agreement is not properly executed and hence may not be enforced without an order of the Court.[353] Section 68 allows the debtor to cancel the agreement primarily by the end of the fifth day following the day on which he was notified of the cancellation right.[354]

In order to show that a particular hire agreement was exempt from the Cancellation Regulations therefore, the claimant would need to show either (1) that the agreement was a cancellable agreement or (2) that the cancellation rights specified in the contract are similar to those in a cancellable agreement.

In relation to the first possibility, there are likely to be two difficulties for the claimant in arguing that the hire agreement is a cancellable agreement. First, in order to argue that the agreement is a cancellable agreement, the claimant would need to show that it is a regulated agreement (ie not an exempt agreement). This is problematic because many hire agreements specify that they are not intended to be regulated agreements and because in principle many hire companies may be reluctant to argue that their agreements are regulated, as this may expose them to enforceability issues. Second, the cancellation requirements under the Act are hardly any less stringent than under the Regulations, so there is little advantage in advocating that one applies over the other.

However, where a hire agreement contains a cancellation notice which does not quite meet the requirements of the 2008 Regulations (hence

353 See section 65(1) in particular.

354 See section 68(a) and note that a longer period of fourteen days applies in certain circumstances.

would be unenforceable if the Regulations applied), it might be open to the claimant to argue that the cancellation rights that he was provided with were similar rights to those required of a cancellable agreement.

Of course it is unlikely to be enough for claimants to simply assert that the rights provided were similar. Rather the claimant would need to forensically analyse the rights accorded to consumers in the case of cancellable agreements, and compare them to the rights he was given. In the main this would seem to require a cooling off period of five days, and also the rule that where the agreement is cancelled the debtor ceases to be liable to pay any money.[355] However, the exemption only requires the rights to be "similar" and not "identical". This allows the claimant to argue that so long as some form of cancellation notice has been provided which does not obviously disadvantage the consumer, the strictures of the Regulations can be avoided. This argument has not been tested in the higher courts.

D. What Did the Regulations require?

Where the Regulations apply, the consumer has the right to cancel the contract within the cancellation period.[356] The cancellation period is defined by Regulation 2(1) as a period of seven days starting with the date of receipt of a cancellation notice.

Moreover, the trader is required to give to the consumer a notice explaining the consumer's right to cancel the contract.[357]

The Regulations prescribe the form and content of the cancellation notice. These requirements include that the notice must be dated, it must indicate the consumer's right to cancel the contract and it must contain

355 Section 70(1)(b).

356 Regulation 7(1).

357 Regulation 7(2).

both the information set out in Schedule 4 to the Regulations and a detachable slip for the consumer to return, in the form set out also in Schedule 4.[358] If the trader elects to incorporate the notice into the agreement, it must *"be set out in a separate box"* with a prescribed heading.[359]

Furthermore, Regulation 7(4) provides that where the contract is in writing, the cancellation notice must be *"incorporated in the same document"*. In a number of cases, the Defendant argued that where the cancellation notice was provided on a separate sheet of paper it was not incorporated in the same document.[360]

Resolution of this issue is likely to depend on a careful analysis of the contractual documentation in question. The cases indicate that the following points are likely to be relevant: whether the notice and the agreement were given to the consumer at the same time; whether the notice refers to the agreement; whether the agreement refers to the notice; whether they bear the same reference number.

The meaning of "give to the consumer" was considered by the High Court in *All Property Claims Limited v Pang and ITC Compliance Ltd.*[361] That was not a credit hire case. The contract in question was made at the consumer's home. The Court found as a fact that the signed contract,

---

358 Regulation 7(3).

359 Regulation 7(5).

360 The Claimant succeeded in Lawford v Pacey, HHJ Coltart, 26 August 2010, Orley v Viewpoint Housing, HHJ Armstrong 7 December 2010, Fay x AXA HHJ Walton 25 February 2011, Larcombe v Arnold Clark HHJ Cotter QC, 28 February 2011 and Trimble v AXA HHJ Harris QC 12 May 2011; but the Defendant was successful in Guerrero v Nykoo HHJ Vosper QC 25 October 2010 and Rennie v Vasey HHJ Taylor 7 February 2011.

361 All Property Claims Ltd v Pand and ITC Compliance Ltd, [2015] EWHC 2198.

including the cancellation notice, was put inside a presentation folder. The company representative used the presentation folder as a clipboard during the meeting with the consumer. He then, in a genuine mistake, put the folder in his briefcase and took it away with him. Later that day, the company emailed the consumer to say that a scanned copy would be sent to him and the originals put in the post. The Court concluded, with reluctance, that *"I cannot see how on any sensible reading of the word 'give' it was given to him on the occasion when the agreement was signed … because he never took it and after a brief period in fact it was removed from his home".*[362] Thus, in order to "give" the cancellation notice to the consumer, it needs to be physically handed over rather than taken away by the trader.

E. What are the consequences of failing to comply?

Regulation 7(6) provides that:

> *"a contract to which these Regulations apply shall not be enforceable against the consumer unless the trader has given the consumer a notice of the right to cancel and the information required in accordance with this Regulation"*

This appears to mean that where no cancellation notice is provided, the agreement becomes automatically and irredeemably unenforceable.

In order to avoid this stark conclusion, the Claimant in *Wei* argued that by accepting the hire vehicle and brining a claim to recover the hire charges, he had affirmed the contract. He argued that the wording of Regulation 7(6) deliberately preserved the possibility of a consumer deciding not to cancel the agreement. He relied in this regard on *Martin v EDP Editores*[363] in which paragraph 76 of the Advocate General's

362 Ibid. para. 44.

363 (2010) 2 CMLR 27.

opinion indicates *"he [the consumer] must also have the possibility of deciding for himself whether or not he will maintain in force the contract"*. The Claimant argued that this suggested that it was possible for a contract to be maintained under the relevant EU Directive even though there was no cancellation notice.

HHJ Moloney QC rejected this submission. He concluded that based on the drafting of the 2008 Regulations if the Claimant did not seek to take a point on the Regulations, it would be the court's duty to take the point itself. Further he held that it is not open to the Claimant to argue that he affirmed the contract by any conduct prior to the time when he was actually informed of his right to cancel.[364] In *W*, the Court indicated that it would have rejected the Claimant's position for the same reasons given by HHJ Moloney QC.[365] The Claimant also failed on these issues in *Salat v Barutis* at Court of Appeal level.

In the above case of *All Property Claims Ltd*, the High Court also found that the agreement was irredeemably unenforceable. The High Court was clearly unhappy with that conclusion, describing the Defence as a *"wholly unmeritorious technical defence but one which must succeed."* Nevertheless, the High Court accepted that the agreement was automatically unenforceable. There was no discretion to allow enforcement. There was no room for waiver / estoppel. Nor could there be any claim in unjust enrichment, because that would run contrary to the public policy expressed in *Dimond v Lovell*.[366]

Where a cancellation notice is provided, but it does not comply with the prescribed language of Regulation 7 or Schedule 4, it would appear that the contract is also unenforceable. However Claimants might argue that on a literal reading, provided that a cancellation notice has been provided

---

364 Chen Wei, paras 18 and 19.

365 W v Veolia, paragraph 38.

366 All Property Claims Ltd, paras 44-45.

which includes *"the information required"* (but does not comply with all the formalities) Regulation 7(6) would not be triggered.

Further in such circumstances there might be scope for the Claimant to argue that the hire company had substantially complied with the Regulations and hence the sanction of unenforceability ought not to be required. However Defendants may respond that the Cancellation Regulations themselves provide that contracts are either enforceable or unenforceable. They do not make any provision for partial compliance. In the context of consumer protection, Defendants may argue that this absolute distinction is justified.

F. The Current Regulations

With effect from 13 June 2014, the Consumer Contracts (Information, Cancellation and Additional Charges) Regulations 2013 replaced the Consumer Protection (Distance Selling) Regulations 2000 and the 2008 Cancellation Regulations.

The new Regulations apply to distance contracts, off-premises contracts and on-premises contracts.[367] Different requirements apply to the different types of contracts, but each require the trader to provide specified information including about the consumer's cancellation rights.[368]

There is currently limited caselaw on the application of the Regulations and none in a credit hire context.

It is worth making two observations. First, the definition of consumer is "an individual acting for purposes which are wholly or mainly outside

367 Pursuant to the definitions section in Regulation 5, on-premises contracts are the residual category catching all contracts between a consumer and a trader which do not fall into either of the other categories.

368 See Regulations 9-14.

that individual's trade, business, craft or profession".[369] In some cases, that may give rise to disputes about whether a hire contract is entered into for purposes which are "mainly outside" the individual's trade. It is clear though that corporate claimants are excluded from the definition of consumer. Moreover, private hire vehicle drivers would be unlikely to be regarded as consumers where they hire a vehicle to use for their work.

Second, as mentioned in the previous chapter, the primary sanction for failing to comply with the Regulations, at least as regards notice of the right to cancel, is criminal.[370] Failing to provide the required information is a summary offence, capable of attracting a fine not exceeding level 5 of the standard scale.[371] There is no provision rendering a non-compliant agreement automatically unenforceable. Accordingly, raising these issues is unlikely to benefit the Defendant.

---

369 Regulation 4.

370 Regulation 19(1).

371 Regulation 19(2).

CHAPTER FIFTEEN

OTHER ENFORCEABILITY ISSUES

In this chapter, we address other issues related to enforceability which may arise in relation to credit hire agreements whether by statute or at common law.

Defendants should however bear in mind that many of these arguments share a common weakness. As set out in Chapter Twelve above, it is not enough for the Defendant (who is not a party to the credit hire contract) to identify some legal flaw with the contract. Rather the Defendant needs to show that the agreement is not enforceable against the Claimant. At the heart of the issue is the risk of double recovery. If the credit hire agreement is clearly unenforceable, then there is a risk of double recovery because the Claimant could keep any damages received in relation to the credit hire for himself. If, however, the alleged defect does not render the agreement irredeemably unenforceable, the risk of double recovery fades away. Since many of the above issues would (at best) render the hire agreement voidable at the Claimant's instance, the Defendant is unlikely to be able to show that the agreement is irredeemably unenforceable. Outside the context of consumer protection legislation, arguments founded on restitution are also likely to carry greater weight. The result is that it is more difficult for the Defendant to establish that the hire charges cannot be recovered through these avenues.

In this chapter, we will start by addressing common law points about the enforceability of the agreement and these are addressed particularly in sections (a) to (c) below. We will then briefly mention two other statutory issues, which may be relevant in the credit hire context but which have not convincingly been tested in credit hire litigation.

A. Signature of the Hire Agreement

i) No Signature

If there is no signed hire agreement, then questions naturally arise as to whether the contract was properly formed. In particular, the Defendant may be able to argue that the Claimant never actually agreed to hire a vehicle, never intended to enter legal relations with the hire company or entered into an unenforceable oral consumer credit agreement.

Claimants should not lose sight of the practical difficulties inherent in such cases. Courts are used to seeing standard form signed agreements. In the absence of such basic documentation, the Courts are unlikely to be well disposed to the Claim. It follows that if there is no signed agreement, Claimants would do well to anticipate the potential difficulty and explain the nature of any oral agreement in the witness statements. As an example of a Court's approach, in *Cook v Mulsanne Insurance Company Ltd*, where the Claimant had failed to produce any invoices for the hire charges and had disclosed parts of signed agreements which were internally inconsistent (including as to the daily rate charged) and inconsistent with the witness statement, the claim was dismissed because the Claimant could not prove what loss (if any) he had sustained.[372]

Nevertheless, the absence of a signature need not be decisive. In considering a late signature case, HHJ Freedman observed that the conclusion below that there was never an agreement was *"astonishing"* because *"looking at the matter in its commercial context [...] it is inconceivable, in my judgment, that any hire company would allow a vehicle to be kept and used by a hirer [...] in excess of three weeks without having any contractual protection in force"*.[373] In many cases, commercial

[372] Cook v Mulsanne Insurance Company Ltd, Birmingham County Court, 1 September 2025, HHJ Kelly.

[373] Armstrong v Hussain, Newcastle County Court, unreported, 29 May 2015 at para. 9.

common sense will be a powerful argument against the conclusion that there was in reality no contract. HHJ Freedman later added *"it is not necessary to cite authority for the proposition that there can be a contract in place without a signature appearing on a document"*.[374]

Claimants may also consider arguing that absence of an agreement is not fatal to the claim. They might argue by analogy with *Bee v Jenson* that they can still advance a claim for general damages for loss of use, in the same sum as the hire charges. Additionally, Claimants might argue that they remain vulnerable to claim from the hire company founded in restitution. It does not appear from the judgment that these arguments were advanced in *Cook v Mulsanne Insurance Company Ltd.*

ii) Late Signature

A different situation arises where the Claimant did not sign the hire agreement at the time, but did sign it at a later date. Here Defendants have argued that there was no consideration for entering into the written hire agreement, because past consideration is no consideration, and hence the written agreement is invalid.

In *Carson v Tazaki Foods Ltd,*[375] the Claimant spoke with the hire company on the telephone. She then received a hire car for three days. The hire documents were sent to her in the post at the time of hire, but she did not actually sign the papers until months later. It was held that the Claimant entered into a contract with the hire company orally by telephone and that the terms of that contract were identical to the subsequent written terms. The best evidence of the terms of agreement was the signed written documents, even where that signature was late. Hence there was an enforceable agreement.

---

374 Ibid., para. 18.

375 Carson v Tazaki Foods Ltd, Central London County Court, HHJ Mackie QC, unreported, 25 August 2005.

A similar though not identical result was reached in *Borley v Reed,*[376] in which the Court held that during the preliminary telephone call, the Claimant agreed to use the hire company subject to the detailed terms and conditions which would be sent to her later. As a result, the content of the telephone call did not constitute a concluded oral agreement. The Court described this arrangement as commonplace. Again, this constituted an enforceable agreement.

In both cases, the Courts expressed concern about the viability of the Defendant's arguments. Thus in *Borley v Reed*, the Judge said *"I do not understand why the law should contemplate with equanimity the determined attempt on the part of the tortfeasor's insurers to meddle in that sensible and beneficial arrangement [the hire agreement]"*. In *Carson v Tazaki Foods Ltd*, whilst the Judge accepted that close analysis of contract was a feature of credit hire litigation, he went on to comment that the evidential burden on the Claimant would be light in such cases and it would be very difficult for Defendants to succeed on such points. Defendants should therefore be cautious about such arguments.

To those cases, we should now add *Armstrong v Hussain* in which HHJ Freedman found that after an initial telephone conversation with his Solicitor, a hire car and the terms and conditions were delivered to the Claimant. He delayed in signing and returning them, until the day after the hire period ended. The Court held that "once he has the terms and conditions and he is not taking exception to them and he continues to keep and drive the car, then on any view of the matter, there is a concluded agreement and it matters not that he does not sign the agreement until a day after the hire period".[377]

That said, the Defendant succeeded on a similar argument in *Company Call Centre Technology Ltd v Sheehan.*[378] In that case the Claimant

---

376 Borley v Reed, HHJ Hughes QC, unreported, 20 October 2005.

377 Armstrong v Hussain, para. 17.

378 HHJ Worster, unreported, 26 February 2009.

company hired a replacement vehicle from 19 March 2007 to 3 April 2007. The hire agreement was signed by a representative of the company on 12 August 2007, and the oral evidence suggested that the written agreement was only received by the company shortly before it was signed. In those circumstances, on appeal the Court refused to accept that the trial Judge was wrong to find that there was no agreement to pay the hire charges.

There were two factual distinctions which go some way towards explaining the result in this case. First, there was no evidence about an initial oral discussion between Claimant and hire company.[379] Second, unlike in *Carson* and *Armstrong*, there was no evidence that the Claimant had the terms and conditions available to it whilst the hire was ongoing. That is significant because the Claimant would not therefore be aware of the contractual terms until after the hire vehicle had been returned.

However, we also note that on appeal the Court in *Company Call Centre* did not have to deal with issues of novation or of restitution, since those were not raised at all at first instance. This suggests that even where the facts are closer to *Company Call Centre* than to *Carson* and *Borley*, the Claimant should be prepared to argue that there remains a claim in restitution or founded in novation.

iii) <u>Signed by a different person</u>

A situation which frequently arises in the County Courts is that the hire agreement turns out to have been signed by a different person from the owner of the damaged vehicle and / or the named Claimant. It is not uncommon for cases to be dismissed on the basis that the claim should have been brought by the signatory / the owner.

---

379 This highlights the importance of putting forwards the best evidence. Given that the Claimant was a company it may be that there was an earlier oral agreement, but that the witness (who later signed the written agreement) was not able to speak to it.

Nevertheless, it is suggested that cases should not automatically be dismissed on this basis. Rather it depends on the evidence about the formation of the agreement. In very many of these cases, the person who signed the agreement is a family member, who has been specifically instructed by the Claimant to sign the agreement on the Claimant's behalf. This often happens where, for example, the hire car has to be delivered whilst the Claimant is out at work. In these circumstances, the Claimant can readily argue that the agreement was signed on his authority by a family member acting as his agent.

Again, where this is likely to be an issue, the Claimant would do well to anticipate the problem and address it in witness statements. In the absence of proper evidence, it is more difficult for the Court to conclude that there was an agency arrangement in place.

iv) Bailment

A related issue arises from the law of bailment. Suppose an individual lawfully borrows a friend's car and has a no-fault accident in it. Can that individual bring a claim for the cost of hire charges (and indeed repair charges), or must the claim for hire charges be brought by the owner of the car?

Although the early shipping cases were not entirely clear on the point, the present position is that the bailee of property can sue in tort in respect of damage to the bailed goods.[380] This left only the question whether the bailee could sue in respect of the bailor's loss of use or only for repairs and his personal loss of use. In *Richards v Thomas*[381] HHJ Price QC held that the bailee can recover "all losses arising from damage to a chattel whilst in his hands". The Supreme Court recently confirmed that a bailee

[380] O'Sullivan v Williams [1992] 3 All ER 385, relying on the Winkfield (1902) Probate 42.

[381] [1997] CLY 1777.

in possession can sue a stranger whose negligence results in damage to the property.[382] A claim for hire charges by the bailee was therefore allowed.

Assuming that this approach is correct in principle, it nevertheless creates certain practical problems. First, if the bailee is effectively claiming loss of use on behalf of the owner – and especially if the hire agreement was signed by the owner, then evidence about need, impecuniosity and mitigation should presumably relate to the owner. Claimants would need to ensure that that evidence is available. If the bailee is left to attempt to answer questions about the owner's need and financial position, the result is likely to be unedifying.

A number of the above issues were discussed in *Mungall v West Oxfordshire District Council*.[383] That was a case in which the damaged vehicle was leased to a company. The director of the company gave the vehicle to his son to use, although his son had no other connection to the company and paid nothing for it. The father entered into a credit hire agreement, signed by the son as his agent, but the use of the hired vehicle was exclusively the son's. Both had sought to recover the hire charges at first instance.

HHJ Harris QC put the problem pithily: the father had no need for a replacement vehicle (he had not lost the use of the damaged vehicle which he had not owned, leased or driven). The son did lose the use of the vehicle, but he was not responsible for the hire charges and hence before and after the accident he remained "the happy recipient of a free car".[384]

The Court held that the son could not claim as special damages the money spent on a replacement car which he had not paid or contracted

382 Armstead v Royal Sun Alliance, [2024] UKSC 6, para. 21.

383 Oxford County Court, HHJ Harris QC, 3 November 2014.

384 Ibid., para. 4.

to pay.[385] In reliance on *Bee v Jensen*, however, the son, as the regular driver of the vehicle, did have a claim for general damages for loss of use and that claim could be measured by the reasonable cost of hiring a replacement vehicle.[386]

Although the Claimants succeeded in *Mungall*, the case exposes the analytical difficulties which can arise in pursuing such a claim. As a result, hire companies may observe that this case would have been more straightforward had the credit hire agreement been made with the son himself or, perhaps, with the company. The complications only arose because the credit hire agreement was with the father, who was the person with the least interest in the vehicle on the facts.

HHJ Harris QC raised in passing a further potential difficulty – whether a negligent driver who damages another vehicle actually owes a duty of care to someone who is not the owner of the other vehicle but who has use of that vehicle.[387] He described the issue as "potentially complex" and it presumably turns on the limits of duty of care according to the well-known principles in cases like *Caparo v Dickman*.[388] But, at least in cases where the primary user of the vehicle happens not to be the owner, it is thought that no issue should arise; there would be a significant gap in the law if such a person was left without a remedy.

B. Oral Assurances / Representations

One of the most common issues which can arise from cross-examination of the claimant, is that the claimant suggests that they were told that they would never have to pay for the hire car or, at least, that no payment will

385 Ibid., para. 19.

386 Ibid., para. 22.

387 Ibid., para. 16.

388 [1990] 2 WLR 358.

be due until after the litigation has come to an end (which may be longer than the prescribed twelve months for consumer credit purposes). What legal effect might these assurances have?

The starting point is that where the Claimant has signed a written hire agreement, he is likely to be bound by what he signed. As a matter of contract law, oral assurances would not ordinarily be relevant pursuant to the 'parol evidence rule'. However, there have been a number of modern cases which have whittled away at the parol evidence rule on various grounds. Oral assurances may be relied on in support of the arguments set out below.

We should note at the outset that, however unattractive the oral evidence of the Claimant may appear, recent High Court decisions in *Irving v Morgan Sindall Plc* and *Parker v Skyfire Insurance Company Ltd* [2024] EWHC 1060 have made arguments based on oral assurances and alleged misrepresentation very difficult for the Defendant to sustain.

Collateral contracts

Depending on the facts, it may also be argued that the main credit hire agreement was entered into by the Claimant only in consideration of a promise by the credit hire company that they would never enforce the agreement against him. In such a case, it could be argued that a collateral contract has arisen. Therefore, the Claimant cannot rely on a term in the main contract suggesting that he has a liability if it is contradicted by a term in the collateral contract suggesting that in reality he does not.[389]

Defendants should be aware that very clear oral evidence in cross-examination is likely to be needed in order to provide the foundation for such an argument. Arguments that appear attractive during the cut and

[389] See cases such as City and Westminster Properties (1934) Ltd v Mudd [1959] 1 Ch 129 and Lord Denning MR in J. Evans & Son (Portsmouth) Limited v Andrea Merzario Limited (above).

thrust of trial, may appear less convincing when the transcript is analysed in the cold light of appeal proceedings.

As an example of this issue, in *Morris v MCE Insurance Company Ltd*, led by certain answers in cross-examination, the trial Judge had concluded that "there is no enforceable contract" and "the agreement he had was in reality an oral reassuring arrangement whereby a car would be provided to him for his general use without charge".[390] On appeal, HHJ Gosnell noted passages in the transcript in which the Claimant had said "everything was sort of sold to me as it would be recovered from the other – the other party"; "I wasn't specifically told I would never have to pay them, no"; "I was told that the – the costs would be recovered from the other party's insurance". But, in the face of a signed written agreement, on any analysis those answers fall far short of showing that there was a collateral warranty or that there was no agreement. HHJ Gosnell duly accepted the Claimant's argument that "the Claimant has signed an agreement. He is bound by his signature as long as he understands, in general terms, that he's signing a contract, even if he may not understand its full terms in advance". He also accepted that if the Claimant had been assured that there were no circumstances in which he could be required to make payment, that could amount to a collateral warranty but "I have got to say I don't think the evidence in this case was that strong to make that contention anyway".[391]

Further, Claimants and credit hire companies may argue that there was never any legal intention to enter into a collateral contract. Further, credit hire companies may claim that any such suggestion was mere sales talk and did not amount to a legal representation. Finally, it should be noted that in at least one of the cases in *Giles v Thompson*, publicity materials

---

[390] Morris v MCE Insurance Company Ltd, Unreported, Leeds County Couty, HHJ Gosnell, 23 July 2018. See paras 5 & 6.

[391] Ibid. para. 14.

had suggested that the car would be free but this did not lead the Court to dismiss the claim.[392]

Contingent Liability

An issue which has arisen in this context is whether the Claimant can recover damages in circumstances where, on a true understanding of the agreement, the Claimant's liability to pay the charges under the credit hire agreement was contingent upon her recovering damages in her claim against the Defendant. That may be the correct understanding of the written terms and conditions, or it might arise from an oral representation amounting to a collateral warranty.

That issue was addressed directly by the High Court in *Irving v Morgan Sindall Plc*.[393] In that case, the oral evidence included the following answers: "I believed at the time that of course there would be charges but those charges would be recovered from the third party insurer with like the accident not being my fault"; "I was always told it was a no win. No fee. That, I didn't honestly, I don't remember being told what would happen if I didn't win, what would happen with the charges if I'm honest". The Claimant was then asked directly by the trial Judge "as regards the hire charges, you did not think you were going to have to pay for these" and the answer was "I didn't no". At first instance, the hire charges were dismissed on the basis that the Claimant had not proved that she was obliged to pay the hire charges.

On appeal, Turner J held that the oral evidence was not to the effect that the provision of the hire car was free but that "it was expected that the charges would be paid by the insurer".[394] Turner J then identified the

392 Giles v Thompson, [1993] 3 All ER 321, 364H–365B. However Lord Mustill did suggest that this practice should be changed.

393 Irving v Morgan Sindall Plc, [2018] EWHC 1147. This case was discussed earlier in relation to impecuniosity.

394 Ibid. para. 13.

principle underlying the enforceability cases as the risk of double recovery. He then held that:

> *"there can be no suggestion of double recovery on the facts of the present appeal. On no interpretation of the assurances given to the claimant on behalf of the credit hire company could she have been under the impression that she would be entitled to keep any sums recovered in respect of the hire charges to herself".*[395]

The High Court also cited with approval to the earlier High Court decision in *Wakeling v Harrington* [2007] EWCH 1184 in which Mann J observed "a liability owing from A to B can exist notwithstanding that B has agreed not to enforce it directly against A."

As a result, Turner J held that the assurances given to the claimant, even taken at their highest, were not such as to compromise her claim for credit hire against the Defendant. This is clear authority for the proposition that a contingent liability (i.e. the claimant only expects to pay the hire charges if the defendant insurer pays them to her) is sufficient.

In *Morris v MCE Insurance Company Ltd*, HHJ Gosnell found that the contingent liability issue had been "laid to rest" by the decision in Irving. As an additional reason for allowing the appeal in that case, he held that if the trial Judge's factual findings had been correct, the claimant was still entitled to succeed on the credit hire claim because there was no question of double recovery and a contingent liability is still a liability.[396]

As a result of those cases, the collateral warranty line of argument is only likely to be worth pursuing for the Defendant in those cases in which the Claimant says that they understood the vehicle to be entirely free and that they would not have to pay for it in any circumstances.

---

395 Ibid. para. 22.

396 See Morris v MCE Insurance Company Ltd, paras 15 and 17.

Estoppel

The oral assurance may create an estoppel preventing the hire company from relying on provisions which contradict it.[397] However, estoppel is usually thought of as a shield rather than a sword: the Claimant could use estoppel to defend a claim brought by the hire company but could not base a claim on it. This limits the usefulness of estoppel to Defendant insurers, though estoppel may well be relevant should a hire company ever try to enforce the agreement against a Claimant.

Misrepresentation

An oral assurance may amount to a misrepresentation making the contract voidable.[398]

This is likely to be hard to prove since the Defendant would need to establish that a positive misrepresentation was made (as opposed to mere sales talk) and that this induced the Claimant to enter into the contract.[399]

In any event, Claimants may argue that the effect of a misrepresentative is that the agreement is voidable and not void. It therefore remains enforceable by a Court, until the Claimant elects to void it. A liability

397 See City and Westminster Properties (1934) Ltd.

398 See L'Estrange v Graucob [1934] 2 KB 394, Couchman v Hill [1947] 1 KB 554, Thomas Witter Limited v TBP Industries Limited [1996] 2 All ER 573, Bleakley v Grimway [1998] 2 CL 125, Rendle v Hicks [1998] 2 CL 126 and Pinder v Martin [1998] 11 CL 160. See also the case of County NatWest Bank Ltd v Barton and Others [1999] Times, 29 July (on fraudulent misrepresentation) and the case of EA Grimstead & Son Limited v McGarrigan, Court of Appeal, [1999] Lawtel 27 October (in the context of entire agreement clauses).

399 It is worth recalling again that in Giles v Thompson the suggestion in publicity that the hire car was free did not prevent the Claimant recovering.

therefore remains for which it can be argued the Claimant should be compensated by the Defendant. Defendants may say that in any event, a failure to rescind the contract would be a failure to mitigate, though this argument is likely to weak because (as set out above) a Claimant does not have to take the risk of uncertain litigation against a third party[400] nor the risk of being sued by a third party.

There have been few reported cases addressing this issue in a credit hire context. In *Kadir v Thompson*,[401] the claimant, who was described as "very clear, consistent and convincing", had said that on two occasions he was told by employees of the car hire company that he had no contractual liability to pay the hire charges. At first instance, the Court found that this was a fraudulent misrepresentation which had induced the Claimant to enter the contract. As a result, the Court found that the agreement was voidable and that the Claimant "will seek to void the contract".

On appeal, the Court rejected the argument that fraudulent misrepresentation was not pleaded, accepting that a general pleading putting the Claimant to proof that the agreement was enforceable sufficed.[402]

The Court then turned to a more difficult question – whether the Judge had been right to dismiss the hire charges in circumstances where the finding appeared to be not that the agreement had been voided but that the claimant "will seek to void" it. The Claimant submitted that unless and until the contract was actually avoided, it remained a good and

---

400 See McGregor on Damages at paragraph 327, citing the dictum of Harman J in Pilkington v Wood [1953] Ch. 770 that, "the so-called duty to mitigate does not go so far as to oblige the injured party, even under an indemnity, to embark on a complicated and difficult piece of litigation against a third party".

401 Kadir v Thompson, Unreported, Central London County Court, HHJ Luba, 25 August 2016.

402 Ibid. para. 28.

enforceable contract. The Court held, however, that reading the judgment as a whole, the Judge had found that the Claimant had already rejected or avoided the contract. Holding that he had "made it very clear to the court that he does not accept any personal liability for the hire charges" was sufficient. On all of the evidence, that was a finding that the Court was entitled to make.[403]

However, the High Court considered the potential relevance of misrepresentation in the credit hire context in *Parker v Skyfire Insurance Company Ltd.* Anticipating an issue of misrepresentation, the Defendant in that case made a non-party disclosure application against the credit hire company, seeking disclosure of the call-recordings of conversations between the hire company and the Claimant. The critical issue on appeal was whether the conditions laid down in CPR 31.17(3) could be satisfied, specifically whether the disclosure of the recordings was "necessary in order to dispose fairly of the claim". If the misrepresentation argument would not make any difference to the outcome of the claim, disclosure of the recordings could not be necessary.

The High Court began by restating the general principle that "it unnecessary for a contracting party to have understood the true nature of the contract in order to be bound by it".[404]

The High Court then set out a helpful summary of some key principles about misrepresentation, which were not in dispute:-

i) The effect of a misrepresentation is only to render a contract voidable at the option of the innocent party. It is not thereby rendered automatically unenforceable.

ii) A voidable contract is valid unless and until it is avoided.

---

403 Ibid. paras 33-36.

404 Parker v Skyfire Insurance Company Ltd, [2024] EWHC 1060, para. 31.

iii) Avoidance requires the innocent party to take some step to rescind the contract.

iv) Rescission is not available unless it is possible to make restitutio in integrum.

v) A contract cannot be rescinded if it has been affirmed by the innocent party with full knowledge of the facts and of his or her right to avoid.

vi) Affirmation is not confined to an express declaration or statement but may be found in conduct.[405]

On the facts of the case, the High Court identified two obstacles to the Defendant succeeding on misrepresentation: affirmation and the impossibility of restitution. In relation to affirmation, the Court emphasised that affirmation can take place by conduct or even by lapse of time, it does not require the Claimant expressly to say that he is affirming the contract.[406] It is clear that the Court considered that the Claimant's actions in seeking to recover the hire charges from the Defendant in reliance on the contract and opposing the non-party disclosure application to be evidence of affirmation by conduct.[407] A decision by the Claimant to affirm the contract cannot be characterised as a failure to mitigate, because such a decision would expose the Claimant to potential litigation from the hire company.[408]

It was, however, the issue of restitution that the Court considered presented an "insuperable obstacle to avoidance of the contract".[409] The

[405] Ibid., para. 32.

[406] Ibid., para. 41.

[407] Ibid., para. 42.

[408] Ibid., para. 43.

[409] Ibid., para. 46.

Court noted that the Claimant had taken the benefit and use of the hire car during the period and held that, as a matter of law, a fully performed contract for services cannot be rescinded.[410]

The High Court stressed that this decision was fact-specific and that there may be other cases where there is no compelling evidence of affirmation and recission is not barred on the facts.[411] Nonetheless, the clear ruling on the possibility of recission would present an obstacle to the Defendant in all credit hire cases except perhaps those where the hire is ongoing.

As a result of *Parker v Skyfire Insurance Company Ltd*, it appears that *Kadir v Thompson* should be regarded as wrongly decided or as an exceptional case in which the Claimant's clear oral evidence showed that he avoided the contract.

Finally, it is worth noting that the Insurer's arguments in Parker were said to be founded on a concern about 'google-spoofing', the allegation apparently being that companies could pay to appear at the top of google search results, so suggesting to the claimant that they were connected to their own insurance company.[412] The High Court did not make any factual finding on the issue. It did, however, note that such concerns are "difficult for insurers to challenge in the context of Road Traffic Act proceedings" and that "it may well be that this can only be addressed by Parliament, the FCA or one of the other industry regulators".[413]

410 Ibid., para. 45.

411 Ibid., para. 48.

412 Ibid., paras. 57-58.

413 Ibid., paras. 60-61.

"Entire agreement" clauses

In this context, it is worth noting that many standard form credit hire agreements contain entire agreement clauses. These are clauses which state that the written agreement contains the whole agreement between the parties, and neither party will rely on any earlier oral representations.

The usual effect of such a clause is to prevent any party from relying on earlier oral representations in any subsequent litigation.[414] As a result, a properly drafted entire agreement clause takes the sting out of any argument based on an oral representation. However, Defendants may argue, depending upon the facts, that the entire agreement clause is unfair pursuant to the Consumer Rights Act 2015 or indicative of an Unfair Relationship.

The Claimant sought to rely upon an entire agreement clause in *Kadir v Thompson*. At first instance, the Court held that the entire agreement clause was an unfair term in a consumer contract and was therefore unenforceable. On appeal, the Court noted that whether or not the unfair contract terms point had been taken by Counsel, "the learned District Judge was obliged by European Union Law to herself take the point – even if it had not been raised between the parties – as the relevant regulations give effect to European Union directives that are directly binding in this country."[415] The Court held that "a provision which seeks to prevent a party to a contract from contending that they were induced to enter into it by fraudulent misrepresentation is one that is so one-sided as to be an unfair term".[416] Stated in those terms, the conclusion is perhaps too far-reaching – it would neuter entire agreements clauses in most circumstances. There was no detailed analysis of the definition of unfair terms in the appeal decision. However, it may well be that the

414 There is a detailed discussion of the point in EA Grimstead & Son Ltd v McGarrigan.

415 Kadir v Thompson, para. 38.

416 Ibid. para. 40.

factual position, which appears to have been set out starkly and visibly in the Claimant's oral evidence, was so clear that no detailed discussion was needed. As a result, if the Court has found that there the contract was induced by a fraudulent misrepresentation, the Claimant cannot count on the agreement being rescued by an entire agreements clause.

C. Minors

Where the Claimant is a minor,[417] the Defendant may argue that a hire agreement is not enforceable against him. For obvious reasons, it is relatively rare to find persons under the age of 18 hiring vehicles but the issue can arise in the context of low powered mopeds or similar vehicles.

Subject to exceptions, the only contracts which are generally binding on a minor are "contracts for necessaries",[418] other contracts in general being voidable unless or until the minor ratifies them after attaining the age of majority.

It is unclear whether a credit hire contract is a contract for necessaries. The concept of "necessaries" appears to stretch beyond the obvious needs for food, shelter and medicine to matters which have a real use beyond the ornamental or the convenient.[419] Thus Claimants may argue that wherever the Claimant is able to demonstrate need for a hire vehicle, the agreement is a contract for necessaries. Defendants may argue that the standard required in this context is more exacting, in order to protect the minor.

---

417 Eighteen is the age of capacity pursuant to the Family Law Reform Act 1969 section 1.

418 Aside from agreements related to apprenticeships or education

419 See Chitty on Contracts, 8-008 and examples given at 8-016

Plainly, the facts are likely to be significant. If a vehicle is required in order to travel to employment, apprenticeship or education, then the Claimant's position is strengthened.

Even if the hire agreement is not a contract for necessaries, it may still become binding on the Claimant if it is expressly or impliedly ratified once he reaches the age of majority.[420] Issuing proceedings against the Defendant might be construed as ratification of the credit hire agreement, provided of course that the Claimant is over eighteen. As above, the Defendant might argue that ratification in these circumstances would amount to a failure to mitigate.

D. Unfair Relationship

Section 140A of the Consumer Credit Act (as amended by the Consumer Credit Act 2006) provides that:

> *"the court may make an order under section 140B in connection with a credit agreement if it determines that the relationship between the creditor and the debtor arising out of the agreement (or the agreement taken with any related agreement) is unfair to the debtor because of one or more of the following:*
>
> > *(a) any of the terms of the agreement and any related agreement;*
> >
> > *(b) the way in which the creditor has exercised or enforced any of his rights under the agreement or any related agreement;*
> >
> > *(c) any other thing done (or not done) by, or on behalf of, the creditor (either before or after the making of the agreement or any related agreement)."*

420 See Chitty on Contracts, 8-043 – 8-045

This section replaced the provisions in the 1974 Act which prohibited "extortionate credit bargains". Although the old provisions were intended to protect consumers, they had limited impact because it was too difficult for consumers to prove that a particular bargain was "extortionate". It might therefore be expected that the new concept of an "unfair relationship" is designed to give the Court greater scope to protect vulnerable consumers.

The first question which must be determined under Section 140A is whether the relationship between creditor and debtor which arises out of the agreement is "unfair". In assessing this, the Court should "have regard to all matters it thinks are relevant" (section 140A(2)).

No further guidance on the definition of an 'unfair' relationship is given in the statute. It is suggested that the courts may draw guidance from the definition of unfair in the Unfair Terms in Consumer Contracts Regulations 1999 (see below).

The Supreme Court gave some consideration to the definition of an unfair relation in *Plevin v Paragon Personal Finance Ltd.*[421] Lord Sumption, with whom Lady Hale, Lord Carnwath, Lord Clarke and Lord Hodge agreed, describe the operation of s140A in these terms:

> *Section 140A is deliberately framed in wide terms with very little in the way of guidance about the criteria for its application, such as is to be found in other provisions of the Act conferring discretionary powers on the courts. It is not possible to state a precise or universal test for its application, which must depend on the court's judgment of all the relevant facts. Some general points may, however, be made. First, what must be unfair is the relationship between the debtor and the creditor. In a case like the present one, where the terms themselves are not intrinsically unfair, this will often be because the relationship is so one-sided as substantially to limit the debtor's ability to choose. Secondly,*

[421] Plevin v Paragon Personal Finance Ltd, [2014] UKSC 61.

> *although the court is concerned with hardship to the debtor, subsection 140A(2) envisages that matters relating to the creditor or the debtor may also be relevant. There may be features of the transaction which operate harshly against the debtor but it does not necessarily follow that the relationship is unfair. These features may be required in order to protect what the court regards as a legitimate interest of the creditor. Thirdly, the alleged unfairness must arise from one of the three categories of cause listed at sub paras (a) to (c). Fourthly, the great majority of relationships between commercial lenders and private borrowers are probably characterised by large differences of financial knowledge and expertise. It is an inherently unequal relationship. But it cannot have been Parliament's intention that the generality of such relationships should be liable to be reopened for that reason alone.*[422]

That contains a useful summary of the principles to be applied when considering the concept of an unfair relationship. The absence of any precise or universal test leaves much to depend on the facts and circumstances of an individual case. However, it is clear that the focus is on the fairness of the relationship between the creditor and the debtor. Further, in order to trigger section 140A the alleged unfairness must result from one of the three categories of cases specifically identified in the Act.

Interestingly, some further protection is given to the consumer by section 140B(9) which reverses the ordinary burden of proof, so that if a debtor alleges that a relationship is unfair, the burden of proof rests on the creditor to prove that it is not unfair.

Defendants may argue on the right facts that a credit hire agreement gives rise to an unfair relationship. For example it is frequently the case that the Claimant has not read or had explained to them the terms of the

---

[422] Ibid., para. 10.

agreement that they sign up to. All too often Claimants think that the hire car is free. This might render a relationship unfair.

If an agreement is found to be unfair, then the Court has the discretion to remedy the unfairness by exercising the wide-ranging powers set out in section 140B. These include the power to set aside any duties imposed on the debtor by the agreement (section 140B(1)(e)). Effectively this could render the contract unenforceable against the Claimant.

Defendants may argue that section 140A applies to all credit hire agreement, even those which are otherwise exempt from regulation. The basis for this argument is that section 140A applies simply to "credit agreements", whereas other sections in the legislation refer to "regulated agreements". The subtle point is that section 16 divides credit agreements into those which are regulated and those which are exempt. Most credit hire companies have managed to make their agreements exempt. However Defendants may potentially argue that by using the phrase credit agreement rather than regulated agreement, as used elsewhere in the statute, Parliament intends section 140A to apply to all credit agreements regardless of whether they are regulated or exempt.

The consequence if this argument succeeds is also unclear. *Dimond*, as noted above, only covered the situation where the agreement was automatically unenforceable. Claimants can argue that it just does not matter if an agreement is potentially unenforceable. According to section 140B(2) it is for the Claimant, as the debtor, to challenge the fairness of the relationship. The Defendant cannot force to the Claimant to take this challenge; after all, the Claimant is not obliged to enter uncertain litigation in order to mitigate their loss. Defendants can argue that Judges should determine for themselves whether the relationship is unfair and what the consequence is. Agreements cannot be half unfair: they are either fair or unfair and it only waits for the Court to determine which. Defendants running this argument may wish to consider whether to join the hire company as a party to the proceedings.

These arguments have never been tested in the Courts in a credit hire context.

E. Consumer Rights Act 2015

Previous editions of this work have considered the Unfair Terms in Consumer Contracts Regulations 1999 and, before that, the Unfair Contract Terms Act 1977. These are no longer in force. The relevant legislation is now the Consumer Rights Act 2015.

Unfair contract terms arguments have never featured regularly in credit hire cases. However, it might be possible for Defendants to argue that exemption clauses are unfair contract terms and thus are not binding.[423] After all, such clauses are designed to oust consumer protection legislation and therefore limit the rights of the consumer.

The relevant provisions of the Consumer Rights Act 2015 apply by section 61(1) to a "contract between a trader and a consumer".

Section 2(2) of the Act defines a trader as "a person acting for purposes relating to that person's trade, business, craft or profession, whether acting personally or through another person acting in the trader's name or on the trader's behalf."

Section 2(3) defines a consumer as "an individual acting for purposes that are wholly or mainly outside that individual's trade, business, craft or profession".

[423] In making this argument, the Defendant's ultimate goal is to persuade the Court that the agreement is regulated by the Consumer Credit Act and as a result unenforceable. The utility of such arguments is subject to the matters discussed in the previous chapters.

Credit hire companies are likely to be regarded as a 'trader'. Most claimants are also likely to be regarded as a 'consumer', though issues may arise in relation to those who use their vehicle for business purposes.

The Consumer Rights Act 2015 then sets out the test of unfairness in section 62:

> "(4) A term is unfair if, contrary to the requirement of good faith, it causes a significant imbalance in the parties' rights and obligations under the contract to the detriment of the consumer.
>
> (5) Whether a term is fair is to be determined—
>
> > (a) taking into account the nature of the subject matter of the contract, and
> >
> > (b) by reference to all the circumstances existing when the term was agreed and to all of the other terms of the contract or of any other contract on which it depends."

These provisions are very similar to those previous set out in Regulation 5(1) and 6(1) of the Unfair Terms in Consumer Contracts Regulations 1999. The earlier caselaw is therefore likely to remain persuasive.

In *Director General of Fair Trading v First National Bank Plc*[424] the House of Lords considered the meaning of the test for unfairness, as it arose in earlier legislation. It is worth setting out some passages from their speeches:

> *"The requirement of significant imbalance is met if a term is so weighted in favour of the supplier as to tilt the parties' rights and obligations under the contract significantly in his favour. This may be by the granting to the supplier of a beneficial option or discretion or*

---

[424] Director General of Fair Trading v First National Bank Plc, [2002] 1 AC 481.

> *power, or by the imposing on the consumer of a disadvantageous burden or risk or duty…*
>
> *The requirement of good faith in this context is one of fair and open dealing. Openness requires that the terms should be expressed fully, clearly and legibly, containing no concealed pitfalls or traps. Appropriate prominence should be given to terms which might operate disadvantageously to the customer. Fair dealing requires that a supplier should not, whether deliberately or unconsciously, take advantage of the consumer's necessity, indigence, lack of experience, unfamiliarity with the subject matter of the contract, weak bargaining position or any other factor listed in or analogous to those listed in Schedule 2 to the Regulations."*[425]
>
> *"There can be no one single test of this [unfairness]. It is obviously useful to assess the impact of an impugned term on the parties' rights and obligations by comparing the effect of the contract with the term and the effect it would have without it. But the inquiry cannot stop there. It may also be necessary to consider the effect of the inclusion of the term on the substance or core of the transaction; whether if it were drawn to his attention the consumer would be likely to be surprised by it; whether the term is a standard term, not merely in similar non-negotiable consumer contracts, but in commercial contracts freely negotiated between parties acting on level terms and at arms' length; and whether, in such cases, the party adversely affected by the inclusion of the term or his lawyer might reasonably be expected to object to its inclusion and press for its deletion. The list is not necessarily exhaustive; other approaches may sometimes be more appropriate."*[426]

Ultimately the question of whether or not a term is unfair is dependent on all the facts and circumstances of an individual case.

---

425 Ibid., per Lord Bingham at para 17.

426 Ibid., per Lord Millett at para 54.

If a term is found to be unfair, section 62(1) of the 2015 Act provides that "an unfair term of a consumer contract is not binding on the consumer". It would therefore be possible for a Defendant to argue, for example, that terms in a credit hire agreement exempting the agreement from regulation, are unfair and hence cannot bind the Claimant. The Claimant may, however, rely upon section 62(3) which provides that the consumer may rely on the relevant term "if the consumer chooses to".

In any event, the difficulties now inherent in running enforceability arguments for the Defendant have likely drawn the force out of these potential arguments. Even if an exemption clause is not binding, the agreement would not be irredeemably unenforceable.

To pursue such an attack, the Defendant is likely to need to join the credit hire company into the litigation to determine the specific issue of unfairness – which would, of course, have costs implications.

PART FIVE

OTHER ISSUES

CHAPTER SIXTEEN

MISCELLANEOUS

A. Introduction

The purpose of this chapter is to address a range of other issues which the practitioner will frequently encounter in dealing with credit hire claims, including procedural issues, claims for interest on credit hire charges and claims for engineer's fees. Further, the chapter concludes with a section summarising the law on champerty, which was the Insurers' first big challenge to the credit hire industry but which is now only of historical interest.

This chapter does, however, contain some of the most significant updates. Recent litigation has seen increased focus on topics such as non-party costs orders against credit hire companies and issues of illegality. The updates to these sections are found in this chapter.

This chapter is not intended to address all the procedural issues that can arise during credit hire cases, or in civil litigation more generally. It is intended as a helpful guide to issues that the authors have frequently encountered in the courtroom.

B. Procedural Issues

The Pre-Action Protocol

We will not rehearse all the civil procedure rules or pre-action protocols here. Nevertheless, the introduction and expansion of the Pre-action Protocol for Low Value Personal Injury Claims in Road Traffic Accidents has presented a number of additional opportunities and issues.

The first question is whether a credit hire claim should be submitted through the Protocol. The Protocol applies, as its name suggests, to claims which include a claim for personal injury.[427] Where there is no personal injury claim, there is no need to abide by the Protocol. Where there is both a personal injury claim and a credit hire claim, the position is less clear. The Protocol provides that a claim "may include" vehicle related damages (which include credit hire charges) but that "these are excluded for the purposes of valuing the claim".[428] Further, a later paragraph suggests that "Claims for vehicle related damages will ordinarily be dealt with outside the provisions of this Protocol under industry agreements".[429] The result is that the Claimant can choose to include a credit hire claim of any value within a Protocol claim, although the presumption appears to be that they will be left out of the Protocol.

Claimants should be aware that in certain circumstances they may face difficulties if a credit hire claim is not included in a Protocol claim. First, the Protocol provides that where the original claim has not settled and there remain additional vehicle related damages being dealt with by a third party separate from the claim, "the claimant must in relation to the additional damages (1) notify the defendant that this separate claim is being considered [...] (3) make a separate offer".[430] This appears to require a claimant claiming personal injury to ensure that the defendant is notified of the credit hire claim before settling the personal injury claim.

Second, the Claims Notification Form which starts the Protocol process contains questions requiring the Claimant to indicate whether he is in a

[427] Para. 4.1 of the Pre-Action Protocol.

[428] Ibid., para. 4.4.

[429] Ibid., para. 7.23.

[430] Ibid., para. 7.52.

hire vehicle. In *Smikle v Global Logistics*,[431] the Claimant had indicated on the Claims Notification Form that there was no claim for hire charges. His personal injury claim settled. Subsequently, he issued proceedings with a different Solicitor claiming credit hire charges. His claim was struck out as an abuse of process on the basis that the Defendant was entitled to rely on the indication in the CNF that there was no claim for hire charges. Since it is not uncommon for different solicitors to represent the claimant in respect of credit hire charges and personal injuries, there is potential for Defendants to take these points more often.

In this regard, we should also draw attention to the words of Mr Justice Martin Spencer in *Richards and McGrann v Morris*,[432] which highlighted the importance of the CNF in these terms:-

> *"in my view they are important documents; they provide the basis for possible proceedings for contempt of court, as seen, and they provide valuable information at an early stage in the litigation process. Endorsed with a statement of truth, as they are, CNFs should be reliable documents and should be taken seriously".*[433]

In that case, in due course, inconsistencies between the contents of the CNF and other evidence were amongst the reasons for the Court overturning a finding in the Claimants' favour on a causation issue in a personal injury context.

In *Poku v Abedin*, the Court highlighted that these applications will turn on the facts of the case.[434] In *Poku*, it was decisive that although the Claimant had indicated on the CNF (wrongly) that there was no credit

431 Smikle v Global Logistics, Walsall County Court, DJ McQueen, 3 June 2016.

432 Richards and McGrann v Morris, [2018] EWHC 1289

433 Ibid., para. 9

434 Poku v Abedin, 8 October 2020, HHJ Backhouse, County Court at Central London, para. 24.

hire claim, there had been other relevant correspondence which placed the Defendant on notice of the credit hire claim. Accordingly, performing the broad merits-based judgment required on an abuse of process application, the Court overturned the decision to strike out the claim.[435]

We note that *Poku* solely addressed the issue of abuse of process, the distinct arguments which may arise based on compromise because the first instance judgment was founded on abuse of process.[436] If the Court concluded, based on the facts, that a binding compromise was agreed which included the credit hire claim, then the position might be different.[437]

Important consequences also follow from including the credit hire claim within the Protocol. First, the Protocol sets out a rigid procedure moving through fixed stages designed to resolve cases at relatively low cost. Ultimately, at Stage 3 they move to Court through Part 8 proceedings. If a hearing is required, the Court will consider written evidence only. This means that the Court will have to resolve the credit hire claim on limited evidence in limited time. The Court can only re-allocate the Claim to Part 7 if "(1) further evidence must be provided by any party; and (2) the claim is not suitable to continue under the Stage 3 procedure". In *Phillips v Willis*, the Court of Appeal held that these conditions were not satisfied in relation to a credit hire claim in which the sums in dispute were low and the additional evidence which might be required appeared limited.[438] The claim should therefore have been decided under the Stage 3 procedure. The Court added that the case could have transferred if it

---

435 Ibid., paras. 46-50.

436 Ibid., paras. 36-37.

437 See Hillier v Southern Rock Insurance Company Ltd, 16 December 2019, HHJ Murdoch QC, County Court at Northampton.

438 Phillips v Willis, [2016] EWCA Civ 401.

involved "very high hire charges" or "complex issues of law and fact".[439] Since detailed scrutiny of the hire charges and oral evidence may benefit the Defendant, it may assist Claimants to take advantage of the relatively limited scrutiny afforded by the Protocol procedures wherever possible.

There was further appellate consideration of issues arising from the Protocol in *London Borough of Islington v Bourous.*[440] In a key passage explaining the Court of Appeal's approach to the Protocol, the Court stated that:

> *the RTA Protocol is intended to be a quick and cheap procedure to enable the parties to settle at a cost which is proportionate both to the sums at stake, and to the run of the mill legal issues which arise, and in a way which does not place an undue burden on the courts. The RTA Protocol is designed to enable the parties to narrow and limit the issues in dispute, so that if a decision by the court is necessary at Stage 3, that decision will only concern the narrow issue which the parties' exchanges under the RTA Protocol will already have defined for the court. As Jackson LJ observed, the RTA Protocol has 'an inexorable character'. If the parties do not observe its provisions, they bear the consequences: for example, if an issue is not raised, or evidence is not served when it should have been, it can (in general) not be raised later.*[441]

This statement of principle informed the Court's resolution of the issues in the two appeals heard together on that occasion. The Court confirmed that the Defendant cannot object at Stage 3 to a head of damages, except on the grounds which it raised at Stage 2.[442] The burden is thus clearly on the Defendant clearly to define the scope of objections during Stage

---

439 Ibid. para. 35.

440 London Borough of Islington v Bourous, [2022] EWCA Civ 1242.

441 Ibid., para. 143.

442 Ibid., para. 147.

2. Further, the Court confirmed that impecuniosity cannot be investigated in detail during a Stage 3 hearing, with the result that, if the Defendant wishes impecuniosity to be fully investigated, it must apply to transfer to Part 7 at the appropriate time in accordance with the provisions of the Protocol.[443]

Second, where a claim is started under the Protocol but does not continue under the Protocol and Part 7 proceedings are issued, the fixed costs regime set out in CPR 45.29A – L will apply. The costs regime is restrictive; where a claim resolves at trial, profit costs allowed are £2,655 plus 20% of damages. This might encourage Claimants to issue credit hire claims separately. However, one issue that remains open to Defendants to argue is that fixed costs should apply where a personal injury claim is started through the Protocol but the Claimant elects to issue a claim for credit hire charges separately – so potentially obtaining two sets of costs.

Allocation

It is well known that claims worth less than £10,000 are normally allocated to the small claims track and claims worth more than £10,000 but less than £25,000 to the fast track. However, in credit hire claims, an option open to the Defendant is to admit part of the claim for credit hire charges and so bring the amount in dispute within the small claims track. In *Akhtar v Boland*,[444] the Court of Appeal confirmed that where an unqualified admission of part of the hire charges is made, leaving the amount in dispute below £10,000, the claim will ordinarily be allocated to the small claims track. Of course, this is usually beneficial to the Defendant because it limits the amount of costs recoverable.

However, Defendants should be aware of two related problems. The first is that the Claimant is entitled to enter judgment on the admission and

443 Ibid., para. 151.

444 Akhtar v Boland, [2014] EWCA Civ 872.

to continue to claim the remainder of the hire charges. Having made a partial but unqualified admission, the Defendant is likely to find that any allegations inconsistent with that admission will be disregarded. It may follow, as in *Akhtar*, that "the defendant could not, for example, challenge the entitlement of the claimant to damages for loss of use of his vehicle, or the reasonable need of the claimant to hire a replacement vehicle for a reasonable time and at a reasonable hire charge".[445] Thus the price that the Defendant must pay for limiting their exposure to costs, is that their ability to challenge the remaining hire charges will be limited.

Second, pursuant to the CPR PD 46 para. 7.1(3), the Court may award fast track costs up to the date when judgment was entered for the admitted sum. That may mean costs until the date of judgment, not the date that the admission was first made.[446]

We note the recent trend to allocate credit hire claims worth more than £25,000 to the fast track. In our experience, many courts habitually allocate credit hire claims worth up to £100,000 to the fast track on the basis that the legal and factual issues involved in these claims do not become any more complicated as the value increases. That may well be correct in some cases. In others, however, the number of issues which need to be resolved (and which it is proportionate to spend some time addressing in a higher value case) particularly where there may also be a liability dispute mean that the case is ill-suited to being finished in a day and requires more preparation than standard fast track matters. It is suggested that allocation in these cases should be decided on a case-by-case basis, taking care to see whether a particular claim can be fairly decided within the confines of the fast track. The issue may be ameliorated by the advent of the intermediate track, which would allow

---

445 Ibid., para. 21.

446 Cameron v Office Depot (UK) Ltd, Bromley County Court, DJ Brett, 13 July 2016.

more valuable credit hire cases to be addressed outside the fast track but without engaging the multi-track.

C. Costs

It is not intended to provide a comprehensive summary of the law in relation to costs. There are specialist textbooks on this subject alone. The paragraphs which follow are intended to indicate some of the issues which may arise in credit hire cases and to highlight significant credit hire cases in which these issues are discussed.

In a personal injury claim, the claimant is now protected against the defendant's costs by qualified one way costs shifting. These rules do not apply to credit hire claims which do not include a personal injury claim.

Where both personal injuries and credit hire are claimed, we draw attention to CPR 44.16(2) which provides that "Orders for costs made against the claimant may be enforced up to the full extent of such orders with the permission of the court, and to the extent it considers just, where – (a) the proceedings include a claim which is made for the financial benefit of a person other than the claimant […] or (b) a claim is made for the benefit of the claimant other than a claim to which this Section applies."

An issue may arise as to the application of the qualified one way costs shifting regime to mixed cases, with personal injury and non-personal injury elements. The Court of Appeal held in *Brown v Commissioner of Police of the Metropolis* that the protection of qualified one way costs shifting does not apply to the non-personal injury aspect of the claim; therefore the automatic application of qualified one way costs shifting (usually referred to as QOWCS or QOCS) does not apply and the Court has a discretion as to costs.[447] However, the Court continued that the

447 Brown v Commissioner of Police of the Metropolis [2020] EWCA Civ. 1724, paras. 31-33.

qualified one way costs shifting regime remained relevant to the exercise of discretion and that, if proceedings could fairly be described in the round as a personal injury case, then the Court should endeavour to achieve a cost neutral result.[448] In exercising its discretion, the Court may, of course, allow only a percentage of costs.[449]

As to CPR 44.16(2)(a), the Practice Direction to Part 44 adds at paragraph 12.2 that "examples of claims made for the financial benefit of someone other than the claimant [...] are subrogated claims and claims for credit hire".

Further paragraph 12.5 provides that:

> *"In a case to which rule 44.16(2)(a) applies (claims for the benefit of others:-*
>
> > *a) The court will usually order any person other than the claimant for whose benefit such a claim was made to pay all the costs of the proceedings or the costs attributable to the issues to which rule 44.16(2)(a) applies, or may exceptionally make an order permitting the enforcement of such costs against the claimant;*
> >
> > *b) The court may, as it thinks fair and just, determine the costs attributable to claims for the financial benefit of persons other than the claimant"*

Thus, where the claim fails and QOWCS applies, the effect of the Practice Direction appears to be that the Court may award costs against the credit hire company.

The High Court has indicated that CPR 44.16, and the practice direction, did not create a new discretion to award costs against a non-party. Rather they identify a potential example of the Court's general

---

448 Ibid., para. 57.

449 Ibid., para. 70.

discretion to award costs against a non-party as set out in section 51 of the Senior Courts Act 1981.[450]

The leading case on this issue is *Tescher v Direct Accident Management Ltd* [2025] EWCA Civ 733. In that case, the Court of Appeal[451] heard two conjoined appeals which both arose from mixed personal injury / credit hire claims, in circumstances where the Claimant had lost and the Claimant was protected from paying the Defendant's costs by QOWCS. The Court of Appeal concluded that courts dealing with applications for non-party costs should approach their discretion in two stages, determining: (1) whether in the circumstances a non-party costs order of some kind should be made against the hire company; and (2) if so, the amount of those costs.[452]

At the first stage, the clear guidance from the Court of Appeal was that "absent some reason why not, when a claimant has been ordered to pay the costs and QOCS applies, a non-party cost order against the credit hire company is likely".[453] The Court later repeated that an order of non-party costs "will be likely absent special circumstances".[454]

The factors which led the Court of Appeal to conclude that the credit hire companies had sufficient control over the litigation so as to justify a non-party costs order, included that:-

450 Select Car Rentals (North West) Ltd v Esure Services Ltd, [2017] EWHC 1434, paras 28-29.

451 Permission to appeal to the Supreme Court was refused.

452 Tescher v Direct Accident Management Ltd, [2025] EWCA Civ 733, para. 66.

453` Tescher, para. 74.

454 Tescher, para. 81.

- The credit hire cases in question were founded on impecuniosity, so that the credit hire company had no realistic commercial basis to expect to recover its charges from the Claimant;[455]

- The credit hire contracts in question made provision for payment to be deferred until the conclusion of the action for damages (possibly subject to a long-stop provision);[456]

- Since litigation was the only realistic means by which the hire company could be paid, it followed that the hire charges were a cause of the legal costs incurred by the Defendant;[457]

- Sufficient control over the litigation can exist even where the hire company does not appoint the solicitor who acts for the Claimant;[458]

- Similarly, the alleged link between the credit hire company and the solicitors representing the Claimants was not taken into account in assessing whether to make a non-party costs order and "there should be no need for evidence of this kind".[459]

The Court of Appeal's guidance was plainly intended to assist Judges in resolving future applications for non-party costs orders. Defendants may rely on *Tescher* to argue that, absent special circumstances, the general rule in such cases is that the credit hire company should be ordered to bear costs. Claimants may, however, respond that the Court also

455 Tescher, para. 68.

456 Tescher, para. 69.

457 Tescher, para. 70.

458 Tescher, para. 73.

459 Tescher, para. 91.

emphasised that the only immutable principle is to do justice.[460] In individual cases, there remains scope on the facts to show that there are 'special circumstances' justifying a different conclusion.

More specifically, the cases before the Court of Appeal were both cases in which Claimant asserted impecuniosity. This was a relevant factor in the Court of Appeal's determination. It is arguable that different considerations would apply where impecuniosity is not asserted by the Claimant.

At the second stage (determining the amount of costs), the Court of Appeal suggested three possible outcomes: (1) an order for all the costs of the litigation; (2) an apportionment based on the sizes of the credit hire claim and the PI claim; and (3) an award of the extra costs attributable to the credit hire as compared to the litigation without it.

The Court indicated that "[w]hen the credit hire claim is several times larger than the PI claim (as in both DAML and Spectra) an order for all the costs of the litigation would be likely, absent some special feature".[461] Thus, in one of the conjoined appeals, the Court of Appeal ordered the hire company to pay all of the costs, and in the second case, there was no appeal against the first instance apportionment of 65% of the costs against the hire company.[462]

In light of the guidance given in *Tescher*, earlier cases are unlikely to provide much assistance. For completeness, and as an indication of factors that prior Courts deemed relevant in determining non-party costs applications against credit hire companies, in *Select Car Rentals (North West) Ltd*, the High Court summarised the factors relied upon in the decision as follows:-

---

460 Tescher, para. 65.

461 Tescher, para. 77.

462 Tescher, paras. 83, 90.

1. Select [the credit hire company] had actually retained solicitors, Samuels Law, to act on their behalf in the claim. It was no coincidence that these solicitors were also instructed by the claimants. Select's retainer eventually was terminated by letter dated 9 July 2015, nearly two years after the accident;

2. Select was in direct email contact with Esure concerning the progress of the claim saying that Samuels Law was acting on their behalf and expressly inviting Esure to comment to them on the issue of liability;

3. There was a close association between Select and a company by the name of Roy Lloyd Limited. They shared a common director, Mr Justin Lloyd, who was the author of the witness statement relied upon by Select in resisting Esure's claim for costs. In a written agreement between Miss Mee [the claimant] and Roy Lloyd Limited in respect of credit storage, recovery and repair Miss Mee was contractually obliged to cooperate in the appointment of a solicitor nominated by the company in pressing a claim for damages. In the event that Miss were to choose another solicitor her credit would automatically be terminated;

4. Under her rental agreement with Select, Miss Mee gave Select the power to deduct directly from any monies she may recover in respect of her personal injury claim to pay for any shortfall in damages relating to Selects own claims against her;

5. Miss Mee gave an irrevocable authority to her solicitors to provide any engineering report in respect of her vehicle and further updates relating to that vehicle to Select;

6. Miss Mee further granted Select the right to pursue an action in her name; and

7. Select were not merely providing Miss Mee with a hire car on credit, they were operating as de facto claims managers as is

> evidenced by their pro forma letter heading which states: "Revolutionising the way your claims are managed".

The High Court endorsed the decision to award costs against the credit hire company, holding that the Judge had carried out a careful balancing exercise and that he "reached a result which not only fell within the broad bounds of his discretion but one which I would probably have reached myself if, hypothetically, I had found some flaw in his approach which would have required me to exercise it afresh".[463]

Further, in *Kindertons Ltd v Murtagh*, the High Court noted as a procedural matter that the application for non-party costs should have been determined by the trial Judge.[464] The High Court also confirmed that a credit hire company has a "very strong financial stake" in a typical credit hire claim.[465] It continued that "control" of the litigation is a question of degree – and the greater the degree of control, the more likely it is that a non-party costs order will be made.[466] In terms of control, the Court highlighted the importance of contractual terms which tied the claimant to bringing and continuing a claim.[467] The High Court therefore declined to overturn a decision imposing a non-party costs order.

The High Court also found that, prior to making a non-party costs order, it is not necessary for the Court to find 'but for' causation in the sense that costs would not have been incurred 'but for' the non-party.[468]

---

463 Select Car Rentals, para. 43.

464 Kindertons Ltd v Murtagh, [2024] EWHC 471, para. 29.

465 Ibid., para. 43.

466 Ibid., para. 44.

467 Ibid., para. 46.

468 Ibid., para. 57.

In the County Court appeal in *Shahzad v Royal Sun Alliance*, by contrast, the Court held that a non-party costs order should not have been made against the credit hire company.[469] The Court highlighted that these decisions are fact specific and depend on the degree of control exercised by the non-party.[470] Benefitting from the litigation alone is not sufficient, without evidence of control.[471]

On that occasion, the facts were distinguishable from *Select Car Rentals (North West) Ltd*, amongst other things because the credit hire organisation did not retain solicitors for the claimant, the credit hire organisation was not in direct email contact with the insurer, the credit hire organisation was not able to deduct hire charges from any personal injury damages, and the credit hire organisation was not acting as de facto claims manager.[472] It is doubted that this decision would be followed after *Tescher*.

The Court thus has a discretion to order costs against the credit hire company in QOWCS cases. The exercise of that discretion will depend on the nature and degree of the credit hire company's control over the proceedings, though *Tescher* suggests that the general rule is that a costs order is likely to be made absent special circumstances.

It is perhaps worth mentioning that this discussion only applies to cases involving personal injury because QOWCS only applies to cases involving personal injury. In cases where only credit hire or special damages are claimed, costs will normally be ordered against an unsuccessful claimant in the usual way.

---

469 Shahzad v Royal Sun Alliance, 6 April 2023, HHJ Gosnell in the County Court at Leeds.

470 Ibid., para. 54.

471 Ibid., para. 64.

472 Ibid., para. 58.

It would be open to the Defendant in a claim with no personal injury element to seek a non-party costs order against the hire company. *Tescher* would not directly apply to such cases. Instead, the general principles applicable to non-party costs orders would be relevant, including that "the critical factor in each case is the nature and degree of his [the non-party's] connection with the proceedings".[473] Although not directly applicable, Defendants may argue that some of the guidance in *Tescher* about the meaning of control over the litigation remains persuasive.

Finally, we note the procedural rules contained in CPR 46.2, which require that the non-party should be joined into proceedings and given a fair opportunity to make representations before any costs order is made. Practically, before making an application, it is also likely to be beneficial to have put the non-party on notice in correspondence.

D. Fundamental Dishonesty

The concept of fundamental dishonesty may arise in credit hire litigation in different ways. First, where a personal injury claim is dismissed, the Court may disapply qualified one way costs shifting if the claim is found on the balance of probabilities to be fundamental dishonest pursuant to CPR 44.16(1). Second, section 57 of the Criminal Justice and Courts Act 2015 provides that on a personal injury claim where the Court finds that the Claimant is entitled to damages, but is satisfied that the Claimant has been fundamentally dishonest in relation to the primary claim or a related claim, the Court must dismiss the primary claim (unless satisfied that the Claimant would suffer substantial injustice).

The test for 'dishonesty' requires the Court to consider whether, judged by ordinary standards, the Claimant was dishonest. As the Supreme Court put it in *Ivey v Genting Casinos (UK) Ltd*, "When dishonesty is in question the fact-finding tribunal must first ascertain (subjectively) the

473 Deutsche Bank v Sebastian Holdings, [2016] 4 WLR 17.

actual state of the individual's knowledge or belief as to the facts. The reasonableness or otherwise of his belief is a matter of evidence (often in practice determinative) going to whether he held the belief, but it is not an additional requirement that his belief must be reasonable; the question is whether it is genuinely held. When once his actual state of mind as to knowledge or belief as to facts is established, the question whether his conduct was honest or dishonest is to be determined by the fact-finder by applying the (objective) standards of ordinary decent people. There is no requirement that the defendant must appreciate that what he has done is, by those standards, dishonest."[474]

As to whether dishonesty is fundamental, the Courts have held that dishonesty is not fundamental if it is collateral, incidental or related only to a minor self-contained head of damage. Dishonesty is fundamental if it goes to the root of the whole or a substantial part of the claim.[475]

In *Haider v DSM Demolition Ltd*,[476] qualified one way costs shifting was disapplied on the grounds of fundamental dishonesty. In that case, the claim had failed because the Claimant had not established negligence. On appeal, the Court held that the Claimant's failure to disclose two credit cards and one additional bank account in his list of documents and responses to Part 18 Questions was dishonest in the context of a credit hire claim. The Court considered the dishonesty was fundamental given the size of the credit hire claim and the well-known importance of impecuniosity in credit hire litigation.

Other cases have considered fundamental dishonesty in the context of section 57. In *Roberts v Kesson*, the High Court concluded that a claim for the pre-accident value of a vehicle which was in fact repaired was

---

474 Ivey v Genting Casinos (UK) Ltd, [2018] AC 391, para. 74.

475 *Howlett v Davies*, [2018] 1 WLR 948, paras. 16-17.

476 *Haider v DSM Demolitions Ltd*, [2019] EWHC 2712.

fundamentally dishonest and hence dismissed the whole claim.[477] Significant to that finding was that the Claimant had lied in his first witness statement, only made limited corrections in a second witness statement and only accepted that the first statement was untrue in the course of cross-examination.

The opposite result was reached in *Michael v D Hurford Ltd*,[478] where the dishonesty was said to arise in particular from claiming the cost of eight physiotherapy sessions when the Claimant actually only attended one, and failing to disclose credit card statements in relation to impecuniosity. In declining to overturn the factual finding that the Claimant was not dishonest, the appeal Court relied on the Claimant's unfamiliarity with his own statement and that he happily volunteered information detrimental to his own case when questioned about it.

The obvious conclusion from these cases is that the application of these principles will turn on the specific facts of each case. Much depends on the impression made by the Claimant. It was the plainly untrue answer to a straightforward Part 18 Question and the absence of any credible explanation that led the Court to disapply costs shifting in *Haider*. By contrast, the Claimant's willingness to accept errors in his statements in *Michael* appears to have been disarming.

Finally, it is noted that the application of section 57 to credit hire cases remains contentious. If a Claimant is fundamentally dishonest in relation to personal injuries, should an entire credit hire claim (potentially many times more valuable than the injury claim) be dismissed? The language of section 57(1) and (8) refers to personal injury claims in defining both the 'primary claim' and a 'related claim'. Claimants may therefore submit that even fundamental dishonesty in relation to the personal injury aspect of the claim, should not lead to the dismissal of the credit hire claim (because the credit hire claim cannot be the "primary claim" which must

---

477 *Roberts v Kesson*, [2021] EWHC 521.

478 *Michael v D Hurford Ltd*, [2021] EWHC 2318.

be dismissed according to s57(1)). This submission is supported by extracts from parliamentary debates which show that a proposed amendment which would have had the express effect of dismissing linked claims such as credit hire claims in cases of fundamental dishonesty was rejected. These arguments were accepted at first instance in *Senay v Mulsanne Insurance Company Ltd*,[479] with the result that having found fundamental dishonesty, the Court dismissed the personal injury claim but allowed the claims for vehicle damage, recovery and storage and loss of use.

In appropriate cases, there may also be arguments in relation to substantial injustice in section 57(2).

E. Illegality

The Defendant may argue that a claim for damages should fail for public policy reasons where the Claimant's claim is founded on an illegal act.

In a credit hire context, this may arise in various scenarios, for instance:-

- the Claimant did not have a valid driving licence;
- the Claimant did not have insurance on his own vehicle (or sometimes the hire vehicle);
- the Claimant's vehicle was not lawfully on the road, either due to a technical defect or not having a valid MOT; or
- the Claimant may have been using the vehicle to commit a crime.

In Patel v Mirza, the Supreme Court had to address whether a claim in unjust enrichment was prevented where the claimant was seeking to

[479] Senay v Mulsanne Insurance Company Ltd, 24 May 2024, HHJ Charman, Birmingham County Court.

recover money paid pursuant to a contract to carry out an unlawful activity.[480]

The Supreme Court reviewed the disparate authorities on illegality from different areas of the law to identify the core principles. Lord Toulson concluded that:

"*one cannot judge whether allowing a claim which is in some way tainted by illegality would be contrary to the public interest, because it would be harmful to the integrity of the legal system, without (a) considering the underlying purpose of the prohibition which has been transgressed, (b) considering conversely any other relevant public policies which may be rendered ineffective or less effective by denial of the claim, and (c) keeping in mind the possibility of overkill unless the law is applied with a due sense of proportionality. We are, after all, in the area of public policy.*"[481]

The Courts must also keep in mind the distinction in role between the criminal and the civil courts. Punishment for wrongdoing is the responsibility of the criminal courts. Whilst the public interest requires the civil courts not to undermine the criminal courts, the civil courts should also avoid imposing "what would amount in substance to an additional penalty disproportionate to the nature and seriousness of any wrongdoing".[482]

In assessing proportionality, one important consideration is the seriousness of the criminal conduct involved. In *Vellino v Chief Constable of Greater Manchester*, having reviewed the authorities, the Court of Appeal stated "[g]enerally speaking a crime punishable with imprisonment could be expected to qualify. If the offence is criminal, but relatively trivial, it is in any event difficult to see how it could be integral

---

480 Patel v Mirza, [2016] UKSC 42.

481 Patel v Mirza, para. 101.

482 Patel v Mirza, para. 108.

to the claim."[483] Commenting on this passage in the later case of *Joyce v O'Brien*, the Court of Appeal noted that minor traffic offences are unlikely to qualify.[484]

An interesting illustration of the principles arose in *Hewison v Meridien Shipping PTE,*[485] where the Claimant claimed damages for personal injury including a substantial claim for future loss of earnings. He was employed as a crane operator. He was epileptic. He had not disclosed his epilepsy to his employer: such disclosure would have prevented him working in this capacity. He was thereby committing the serious criminal offence of obtaining a pecuniary advantage by deception.

After a detailed review of the authorities, the majority of the Court of Appeal concluded that "where a claimant has to rely upon his or her own unlawful act in order to establish the whole or part of his or her claim the claim will fail either wholly or in part".[486]

However, where the illegality is purely "collateral" or "insignificant"[487] the Claimant can still recover. It is for this reason that Claimants can recover loss of earnings even where they did not pay tax or national insurance on their pre-accident earnings.[488]

On the facts of *Hewison*, the majority went on to hold that in order to prove his claim for future loss of earnings, the Claimant had to assert that he would have continued in his job but for the accident. In order to keep working in that capacity he would have had to continue to deceive his

---

483 Vellino v Chief Constable of Greater Manchester, [2001] EWCA Civ 1249, para. 72.

484 Joyce v O'Brien, [2013] EWCA Civ 546, para. 51.

485 Hewison v Meridien Shipping PTE, [2002] EWCA civ 1821.

486 Ibid., para. 29.

487 Ibid., para. 36, 43.

488 See, Newman v Fowkes, [2002] EWCA Civ 519.

employer. In so doing he would commit the criminal offence of obtaining a pecuniary advantage by deception. Accordingly his claim for loss of earnings was dismissed.[489]

The issue of illegality has now been considered by the Court of Appeal in the context of credit hire in *Ali v HSF Logistics Polska*. The allegation of illegality rested on the finding of fact that the Claimant did not have a valid MOT certificate for his own vehicle, though there was no finding that it was actually unroadworthy.[490] The Court of Appeal rejected the Defendant's causation submission that the accident had not caused a loss; the claim for credit hire charges was a claim for loss of use and the absence of an MOT certificate did not alter the fact that the Claimant had been deprived of the use of his vehicle.[491]

The Court of Appeal went on the address the illegality issue directly, holding, by reference to the relevant statutory framework, that driving without an MOT was "self-evidently" a "relatively minor offence which does not carry very great weight when considering proportionality".[492] The Court plainly considered that both driving without an MOT, and other minor offences such as having defective lights or windscreen wipers, were insufficiently serious to justify the dismissal of the whole or part of the claim.[493]

Further, the Court of Appeal made it clear that it would have been disproportionate to dismiss the claim for credit hire charges on grounds of illegality. The claim was for more than £21,000. The potential fine for driving without an MOT was up to £1,000. Denying recovery of the

---

489 Hewison, para 45. Note that the majority thought the result would have been different had the deception not been deliberate.

490 Ali v HSF Logistics Polska, [2024] EWCA Civ 1479, para. 3.

491 Ali v HSF Logistics Polska, paras. 47-48.

492 Ali v HSF Logistics Polska, para. 49.

493 Ali v HSF Logistics Polska, paras. 49, 54.

credit hire charges would, in those circumstances, amount to the imposition of an additional penalty disproportionate to the wrongdoing.[494]

The criminal conduct in *Ali v HSF Logistics Polska* was clearly relatively minor. The Court of Appeal has not yet pronounced on the, arguably, more serious criminal conduct that would arise from driving without insurance or driving without a licence. In such cases, however, the Courts could be expected to apply similar considerations, including evaluating the seriousness of the criminal conduct and the proportionality of rejecting the claim for hire charges.

In relation to driving without insurance, in the first instance case of *Agheampong v Allied Manufacturing (London) Ltd*,[495] the Court accepted that in order to succeed on the evidence, the Defendant must establish that the Claimant would have continued to drive his own car without insurance throughout the hire period.[496] Whilst the standard of proof remained the balance of probabilities, in light of the allegation of criminality "more cogent evidence" was required to cross that threshold.[497]

On the facts of *Agheampong*, the Defendant was able to discharge that burden of proof. The Court concluded that the Claimant had deliberately misled the Court about his historical insurance position.[498] He had driven without insurance for around 16 months, and given his "general behaviour" and "devious attempt to explain it away" the Court

494 Ali v HSF Logistics Polska, para. 50.

495 Agheampong v Allied Manufacturing (London) Ltd, HHJ Dean QC, unreported, 30 June 2008.

496 Ibid., para. 85.

497 Ibid., para. 86 – 87.

498 Ibid., para. 112.

was satisfied that he would have continued to drive without insurance in the future.[499]

The Court concluded that the Claimant did have to rely on this illegality in order to establish his claim for loss of use. Taking into account the losses caused by uninsured motorists, the length of time without insurance and the fact that the Claimant was also driving without paying road tax, the illegality was not insignificant. The Court concluded that the case therefore "falls squarely within" the principle identified in *Hewison*.[500] The claim for hire charges was dismissed.

In *Ali v HSF Logistics Polska*, the Court of Appeal referred to *Agheampong* as a previous decision on illegality but without obviously endorsing or criticising it.[501] The Court of Appeal did highlight that driving without insurance is a more serious offence than driving without an MOT certificate, since the potential penalties include an unlimited fine, obligatory endorsement of driving licence, discretionary disqualification and the vehicle may be impounded.[502] Defendants may argue that this suggests that driving without insurance should be treated in a different category from driving without an MOT. Claimants may, however, argue that driving without insurance is still not an imprisonable offence, the likely penalty (at least for a first offence) would be a fixed penalty notice involving a fine of £300 and six penalty point, and that it would therefore remain disproportionate to dismiss any substantial claim for credit hire charges.

As *Agheampong* demonstrates, it is also important in such cases to consider the gravity of the Claimant's conduct. Not all cases of driving without insurance are equally serious; there may, for example, be a

499 Ibid., para. 116.

500 Ibid., para. 137.

501 Ali v HSF Logistics Polska, para. 34.

502 Ali v HSF Logistics Polska, para. 32, see also para. 49.

distinction between a Claimant who had no insurance at all and a Claimant who had an insurance policy in place but was using the vehicle outside the terms of the policy (for instance, a Claimant insured for social and domestic purposes only who used the vehicle for business purposes). Further, a Claimant can, of course, obtain insurance at any time.

At the time of writing, there are no reported illegality cases regarding driving without a licence or on a forged licence. Such cases must be determined on their own facts, applying the considerations discussed above, including proportionality and the seriousness of the offence. In practical terms, the additional element of dishonesty which may be present in the use of a forged document, may have a broader impact on the Court's assessment of the Claimant's credibility.

F. Engineering Evidence

The old practice of claiming the fee of the engineer who inspected the Claimant's vehicle as damages has now largely vanished: such engineers' fees are not ordinarily recoverable as damages. Thus, in *Burdis v Livsey* the Court of Appeal held:

> *"He [the Claimant] can recover the cost of the repair unless it be shown that he has not taken reasonable steps to mitigate his loss. Of course a number of quotations or one engineer's report can be good evidence to rebut an allegation of a failure to mitigate and may be useful in settlement negotiations; but the costs are not part of the loss. The fact that insurers use engineers to report on damaged cars and agree the costs of repair is irrelevant to the assessment of the amount of loss. Helphire use an engineer to negotiate the repair charges with the repairer with no doubt the view that the engineer's report will lead to a quick and satisfactory settlement of the claim and protect Helphire. As such they would not be recoverable."*[503]

[503] Burdis v Livsey, para. 156.

In fast and multi-track cases, it remains open to Claimants to attempt to recover the hire charges as part of their costs but not as damages.

Note further that where proceedings are brought simply to recover an engineer's fee, this has been held to be an abuse of the process of the court in issuing solely to recover costs (see *Warriner v Smith).*[504]

Issues remain about the status of inspection reports on the Claimant's vehicle prepared by an engineer. An issue frequently arises as to whether such inspection reports are expert evidence and therefore subject to Part 35 (a submission which is assisted by the format of many inspection reports, which purport to include a Part 35 declaration). Claimants may, however, argue that Part 35 does not apply because the inspection report was not prepared 'for the purpose of proceedings' (CPR 35.2(1)) but in order to assist the Claimant mitigate his loss at any early stage of proceedings.

G. Miscellaneous Expenses

Claims for the inconvenience associated with the accident and for miscellaneous expenses such as postage and telephone costs for pursuing the claim are often tagged on to a credit hire claim.

Defendants may argue that "damages for worry and for the nuisance caused by having to deal with the consequences of an accident are not recoverable."[505] Further that claims for miscellaneous expenses are claims for costs and not damages, though this is a point on which different courts take different views.[506]

504 Warriner v Smith, [1999] 4 CL.

505 per Scott VC in Dimond v Lovell.

506 Taylor v Browne [1995] CLY 1842 suggests that they are not recoverable, but they were recovered in Marley v Novak [1996] CLY 2112.

H. Recovery and Storage Charges

Very often a claim is made for the cost of (1) recovering the Claimant's damaged vehicle and (2) storing it until repairs can start or it can be disposed of. There is nothing wrong with such a claim in principle. However, it can be challenged on the similar grounds to the main claim for credit hire charges e.g. if there has been a deferment of the debt the Defendant may raise consumer credit arguments.

In such cases the first question is likely to be what the Claimant actually agreed to: what he contracted for, when and with whom and whether he is liable for anything on that contract. Unlike credit hire contracts, there is often no written agreement in relation to the storage charges. This means that if there is a deferment of the debt, there may well be enforceability issues.

Furthermore, issues of mitigation may arise. The general principles applicable to mitigation are set out in earlier chapters in relation to hire charges. The Defendant may argue that it was open to the Claimant to store the vehicle at his house for free. The value of the car is also relevant. It may well be argued that it is unreasonable, for example, to incur storage charges which approach or exceed the value of the vehicle.

In some cases, Claimants may be able to argue that the vehicle is being stored pending the Defendant insurer inspecting the vehicle (or confirming that it does not intend to inspect). If this is correct then the responsibility for any delay rests with the Defendant. For instance, in *Zurich Insurance Plc v Umerji*, where the vehicle was stored for over four months, the Court of Appeal did not accept the Defendant's submission that the car should have been disposed of as soon as the Claimant was advised that it was written off.[507] Instead, whilst expressing sympathy for the Defendant's position, the Court of Appeal held that it was not wrong for the trial Judge to hold that the Claimant acted reasonably in storing

---

507 Zurich Insurance Plc v Umerji, para. 44.

the vehicle until the Defendant had either inspected it or made clear that it did not wish to inspect.[508]

In *Motor Insurers' Bureau v Houston*, regarding a claim for storage charges in excess of £5,000, on appeal the High Court declined to interfere with the trial Judge's conclusion that the charges were not unreasonable because the Claimant had nowhere to store the damaged vehicle and stored it until he was paid the scrap value.[509]

I. Delivery and Collection Charges

The issue of delivery and collection charges was dealt with authoritatively in *Burdis v Livsey*. Before the Court of Appeal, all the parties agreed that these charges would sometimes be recoverable. The Court of Appeal concluded that:

> *"If injury causes damage then the injured party can recover the loss caused by the injury. But the need for a replacement car is not self-proving (see Giles v Thompson at 167 D); neither is the need for delivery self-proving. If the injured person lives next door to the car hire company, he can walk round and collect the replacement car and a delivery and collection charge is not part of the loss. However, the cost of obtaining the replacement car can be recovered subject to the duty to take reasonable steps to mitigate the loss. What is reasonable is a question of fact, which can usually be deduced from the surrounding circumstances. If there is suitable public transport, it would be reasonable to expect the car to be collected. If part of the loss is the cost of delivery and collection, that must be proved."*[510]

---

508 Zurich Insurance Plc v Umerji, para. 45, 47.

509 Motor Insurers Bureau v Houston, para. 52.

510 Burdis v Livsey, para. 153.

The result is that it is for the Claimant to prove that he needed the delivery and collection service with reference to his own specific circumstances.

J. Interest

In *Giles v Thompson,*[511] Lord Mustill said of the award of interest, *"The exercise of the right should correspond with reality"*. In that case there was no liability to pay the hire charges until judgment was given and therefore no award of interest was made.

The Court of Appeal returned to the issue in *Pattni v First Leicester Buses Ltd.*[512] In that case the Claimant argued that he was under a contractual obligation to pay interest pursuant to the hire agreement. The Court of Appeal held that contractual interest was not recoverable because it represented a charge for credit, hence an irrecoverable additional benefit.[513] In the same decision the Court of Appeal followed *Giles v Thompson* in refusing to exercise the Court's discretion to award interest.[514]

The same result was reached by HHJ Harris in *Corbett v Gaskin.*[515]

The general position is therefore that interest is not recoverable on credit hire charges. However, if insurers have already re-imbursed the credit hire company, they may be entitled to interest. Thus in *Clark v Ardington Electrical Services and others,*[516] HHJ Harris allowed interest to be

---

511 Giles v Thompson, [1994] AC 142 at page 168.

512 Pattni was heard together with Bent no2: [2011] EWCA civ 1384.

513 Ibid., para. 61 – 62.

514 Ibid., para. 70.

515 Corbett v Gaskin, Unreported, 21 April 2008.

516 Clark v Ardington Electrical Services, HHJ Harris, Oxford County

awarded to a subrogated Claimant from the date of payment. He was upheld on this point in *Burdis v Livsey.*[517] The result is that if there is evidence that the hire charges have been paid (eg by an insurer so that the claim is subrogated) interest is recoverable.

K. Champerty

Champerty consists of wrongfully interfering in the disputes of others. In *Giles v Thompson*, the Defendant insurers argued that the credit hire contracts were champertous because the credit hire companies were instigating the litigation, had a financial interest in the outcome and often were funding them. Therefore, they argued, the agreements were illegal and unenforceable against the Claimant.

In the House of Lords, Lord Mustill asked the single question whether there was:

> *"wanton and officious intermeddling with the disputes of others in where the meddler has no interest whatever, and where the assistance he render to one party or the other is without justification or excuse."*

This is essentially a question of fact. Consideration must be given to all aspects of a transaction, bearing in mind that the public policy behind the law of champerty is to *"protect the purity of justice and the interests of vulnerable litigants"*.

The House of Lords held that the credit hire agreements were not champertous. There was no realistic prospect of the administration of justice suffering. Where the Claimant retained what Steyn LJ in the Court of Appeal had termed a *"residual liability"* to pay for the hire charges, the contract would be enforceable. It was not right to say that

Court, 14 September 2001.

517 Ibid., paras. 157 – 162.

the company was taking a share of the proceeds of litigation, rather the fruits of litigation provided a source from which the motorist could satisfy his liability to the company. This was the case if the Claimant retained a liability to pay for the hire charges whether he won or lost the case against the other side. In *Giles v Thompson* this was held to be so in all of the cases despite the fact that in at least one of them, the publicity material had suggested the cars were free.

Thus provided that the credit hire agreement imposes on the Claimant a residual liability to pay for the hire charges, the Defendant cannot rely on champerty. It is therefore no longer argued in credit hire cases.

The law of champerty has retained importance in two distinct areas of law. First, it remains a rule of professional conduct for a solicitor not to accept payment from a claimant calculated as a proportion of the sum recovered from the Defendant. Second, champerty is relevant to the assignment of bare rights of action. Broadly speaking in these two areas the court will consider whether the transaction bears the hallmarks of champerty. If it does, it is prima facie unlawful unless it can be validated by the third party having a legitimate interest in supporting the action. The law of champerty is still occasionally relied on in other contexts. Thus in *De Crittenden v Bayliss,*[518] the Court of Appeal were asked to determine whether an agreement was champertous. The Claimant and Defendant shared business interests. The Defendant was involved in litigation which, if he lost, would have damaged his financial standing and hence the Claimant's business interests. The Claimant agreed with the Defendant that he would assist him with the litigation in return for 50% of the proceeds. The two later fell out and the Claimant sued on the contract. The Defendant argued that it was champertous and hence unenforceable. Outside these unusual factual scenarios however, the issue of champerty is no longer relevant to credit hire cases. The modern battlegrounds are mitigation and rates issues.

[518] De Crittenden v Bayliss, [2002] EWCA Civ 50.

L. Hire Vehicle Damaged in Subsequent RTA

It is convenient to end by discussing an issue which recently reached the Supreme Court – what damages the Defendant is liable to pay, in circumstances where the Claimant was driving a credit hire vehicle at the time of the accident?

In *Armstead v Royal Sun Alliance*, the Claimant was driving a credit hire vehicle when the Defendant negligently caused an accident damaging the vehicle. By a clause in the credit hire agreement, the Claimant was obliged to pay a defined sum to the credit hire company in compensation of its loss of use whilst the vehicle was repaired. The Claimant sought to recover that contractual sum from the Defendant.

The Supreme Court considered that the Claimant was entitled to recover that sum, subject to well-established principles on remoteness of loss.[519]

As to remoteness, the Supreme Court recalled the basic principles. The test of remoteness is concerned with whether the type of loss is reasonably foreseeable. If the type of loss (in this case loss of use) is reasonably foreseeable, it does not matter whether the precise manner in which the loss occurred is itself reasonably foreseeable.[520] Subject to one point, developed below, the contractual charge for loss of use was therefore recoverable.

The one point of difficulty was that the contractual charge must be a reasonable pre-estimate of the hire company's loss of use. If exceeds a reasonable pre-estimate of the hire company's loss of use, then it is not reasonably foreseeable.[521] Further, if the contractual charge exceeds a reasonable pre-estimate of the hire company's loss of use, then it would

519 Armstead v Royal Sun Alliance, [2024] UKSC 6, para. 22.

520 Ibid., para. 47.

521 Ibid., para. 47(iii).

likely be an unfair contract term as set out in Schedule 2 of the Consumer Rights Act, Part 1 para. 6.[522]

The Supreme Court held that the burden of proof lies on the Defendant to show that the contractual charge is not a reasonable pre-estimate of the hire company's loss of use.

On that issue, however, it had not been pleaded that the contractual charge was not a reasonable pre-estimate. As a result, no evidence had been led on relevant issues including whether the hire company had other vehicles available or whether the contractual charge was an overpayment.[523] As a result, on the facts, the case for a reduction was not made out.

Armstead thus confirms that a claimant who is involved in an accident whilst driving a credit hire vehicle can, in principle, recover damages for the claimant's contractual liability to pay loss of use to the hire company. This is, however, subject to the important restriction that the contractual charge must be a reasonable pre-estimate of the hire company's loss of use. Future litigation on this issue is likely to focus on determining whether the contractual charge is a reasonable pre-estimate, including by investigating the other vehicles potentially available to the credit hire organisation.

522 Ibid., paras. 49-51.

523 Ibid., para. 71.

INDEX

MORE BOOKS BY LAW BRIEF PUBLISHING

A selection of our other titles available now:-

'A Practical Guide to Probation Breaches and Other Applications' by Mark Thomas
'A Practical Guide to Remarriage and Divorce' by Cordelia Williams & Claire Howard
'A Practical Guide to Privacy, Transparency, Reporting Restrictions and Closed Proceedings in the Court of Protection' by Laura Mannering
'Beaumont on Barristers – A Guide to Defending Disciplinary Proceedings (Second Edition)' by Marc Beaumont
'A Practical Guide to Payments for Environmental Services' by Ben Sharples
'A Practical Guide to the Law of Pregnancy and Maternity at Work' by Rebecca Thomas
'A Practical Guide to Redundancy – Second Edition' by Philip Hyland & Collette Moore
'A Practical Guide to International Issues for Scottish Family Lawyers' by Susie Mountain, Donna McKay, Ken MacDonald
'A Practical Guide to the Law on Deprivation of Liberty' by Ben Troke
'A Practical Guide to Rights over Airspace and Subsoil – Second Edition' by Daniel Gatty
'A Practical Guide to the Law in Relation to Inquests' by Ramya Nagesh
'A Practical Guide to the Construction and Rectification of Wills and Trust Instruments (Second Edition)' by Edward Hewitt
'A Practical Guide to Data Protection in Social Housing' by Clare Paterson
'A Practical Guide to Spousal Maintenance – Second Edition' by Liz Cowell
'A Practical Guide to International Parental Child Abduction Law (England and Wales)' by Dr Onyója Momoh
'A Practical Guide to Deprivation of British Citizenship' by Sean Ell
'A Practical Guide to Commercial Property Service Charges' by Rachel Garton
'A Practical Guide to Clinical Negligence – Third Edition' by Geoffrey Simpson-Scott (Geoff)
'A Practical Guide to the Rights of Grandparents in Children Proceedings – Second Edition' by Stuart Barlow

'The Electronic Communications Code: A Practical Guide – Second Edition' by Kerry Bretherton KC, James Castle, Mark Loveday
'A Practical Guide to the Independent School Standards – September 2023 Edition' by Sarah McKimm
'A Practical Guide to Estate Administration and Crypto Assets' by Richard Marshall
'A Practical Guide to Parental Alienation in Private and Public Law Children Cases' by Sam King QC & Frankie Shama
'Contested Heritage – Removing Art from Land and Historic Buildings' by Richard Harwood QC, Catherine Dobson, David Sawtell
'The Limits of Separate Legal Personality: When Those Running a Company Can Be Held Personally Liable for Losses Caused to Third Parties Outside of the Company' by Dr Mike Wilkinson
'A Practical Guide to Transgender Law' by Robin Moira White & Nicola Newbegin
'A Practical Guide to 'Stranded Spouses' in Family Law' by Mani Singh Basi
'A Practical Guide to Residential Freehold Conveyancing' by Lorraine Richardson
'A Practical Guide to Pensions on Divorce for Lawyers' by Bryan Scant
'A Practical Guide to Challenging Sham Marriage Allegations in Immigration Law' by Priya Solanki
'A Practical Guide to Digital Communications Evidence in Criminal Law' by Sam Willis
'A Practical Guide to Legal Rights in Scotland' by Sarah-Jane Macdonald
'A Practical Guide to New Build Conveyancing' by Paul Sams & Rebecca East
'A Practical Guide to Inherited Wealth on Divorce' by Hayley Trim
'A Practical Guide to Practice Direction 12J and Domestic Abuse in Private Law Children Proceedings' by Rebecca Cross & Malvika Jaganmohan
'A Practical Guide to Confiscation and Restraint' by Narita Bahra QC, John Carl Townsend, David Winch
'A Practical Guide to the Law of Forests in Scotland' by Philip Buchan
'A Practical Guide to Health and Medical Cases in Immigration Law' by Rebecca Chapman & Miranda Butler
'A Practical Guide to Bad Character Evidence for Criminal Practitioners by Aparna Rao
'A Practical Guide to Extradition Law post-Brexit' by Myles Grandison et al
'A Practical Guide to Hoarding and Mental Health for Housing Lawyers' by Rachel Coyle

'Stephens on Contractual Indemnities' by Richard Stephens
'A Practical Guide to the EU Succession Regulation' by Richard Frimston
'A Practical Guide to Solicitor and Client Costs – Second Edition' by Robin Dunne
'Constructive Dismissal – Practice Pointers and Principles' by Benjimin Burgher
'A Practical Guide to Religion and Belief Discrimination Claims in the Workplace' by Kashif Ali
'A Practical Guide to the Law of Medical Treatment Decisions' by Ben Troke
'Fundamental Dishonesty and QOCS in Personal Injury Proceedings: Law and Practice' by Jake Rowley
'A Practical Guide to the Law in Relation to School Exclusions' by Charlotte Hadfield & Alice de Coverley
'A Practical Guide to Divorce for the Silver Separators' by Karin Walker
'The Right to be Forgotten – The Law and Practical Issues' by Melissa Stock
'A Practical Guide to Planning Law and Rights of Way in National Parks, the Broads and AONBs' by James Maurici QC, James Neill et al
'A Practical Guide to Election Law' by Tom Tabori
'A Practical Guide to the Law in Relation to Surrogacy' by Andrew Powell
'A Practical Guide to Claims Arising from Fatal Accidents – Second Edition' by James Patience
'A Practical Guide to Asbestos Claims' by Jonathan Owen & Gareth McAloon
'A Practical Guide to Stamp Duty Land Tax in England and Northern Ireland' by Suzanne O'Hara
'A Practical Guide to the Law of Farming Partnerships' by Philip Whitcomb
'A Practical Guide to the Law of Unlawful Eviction and Harassment – Second Edition' by Stephanie Lovegrove
'A Practical Guide to Costs in Personal Injury Claims – Second Edition' by Matthew Hoe
'A Practical Guide to the General Data Protection Regulation (GDPR) – Second Edition' by Keith Markham
'A Practical Guide to Working with Litigants in Person and McKenzie Friends in Family Cases' by Stuart Barlow
'Protecting Unregistered Brands: A Practical Guide to the Law of Passing Off' by Lorna Brazell
'A Practical Guide to Secondary Liability and Joint Enterprise Post-Jogee' by Joanne Cecil & James Mehigan

'A Practical Guide to the Pre-Action RTA Claims Protocol for Personal Injury Lawyers' by Antonia Ford
'A Practical Guide to Neighbour Disputes and the Law' by Alexander Walsh
'A Practical Guide to Coercive Control for Legal Practitioners and Victims' by Rachel Horman
'A Practical Guide to the Law of Driverless Cars – Second Edition'
by Alex Glassbrook, Emma Northey & Scarlett Milligan
'A Practical Guide to TOLATA Claims' by Greg Williams
'A Practical Guide to Elderly Law – Second Edition' by Justin Patten
'A Practical Guide to Responding to Housing Disrepair and Unfitness Claims' by Iain Wightwick
'A Practical Guide to the Law of Bullying and Harassment in the Workplace' by Philip Hyland
'How to Be a Freelance Solicitor: A Practical Guide to the SRA-Regulated Freelance Solicitor Model' by Paul Bennett
'A Practical Guide to Prison Injury Claims' by Malcolm Johnson
'A Practical Guide to Advising Clients at the Police Station' by Colin Stephen McKeown-Beaumont
'A Practical Guide to Antisocial Behaviour Injunctions – Second Edition' by Iain Wightwick
'Practical Mediation: A Guide for Mediators, Advocates, Advisers, Lawyers, and Students in Civil, Commercial, Business, Property, Workplace, and Employment Cases' by Jonathan Dingle with John Sephton
'The Mini-Pupillage Workbook' by David Boyle
'A Practical Guide to Crofting Law' by Brian Inkster
'A Practical Guide to the Law of Domain Names and Cybersquatting' by Andrew Clemson
'A Practical Guide to the Law of Gender Pay Gap Reporting' by Harini Iyengar
'NHS Whistleblowing and the Law' by Joseph England
'Employment Law and the Gig Economy' by Nigel Mackay & Annie Powell
'A Practical Guide to Noise Induced Hearing Loss (NIHL) Claims' by Andrew Mckie, Ian Skeate, Gareth McAloon
'An Introduction to Beauty Negligence Claims – A Practical Guide for the Personal Injury Practitioner' by Greg Almond
'Intercompany Agreements for Transfer Pricing Compliance' by Paul Sutton
'Zen and the Art of Mediation' by Martin Plowman
'A Practical Guide to Adoption for Family Lawyers' by Graham Pegg

- 'A Practical Guide to Industrial Disease Claims' by Andrew Mckie & Ian Skeate
- 'A Practical Guide to Conducting a Sheriff Court Proof' by Andrew Stevenson
- 'A Practical Guide to Vicarious Liability' by Mariel Irvine
- 'A Practical Guide to Applications for Landlord's Consent and Variation of Leases' by Mark Shelton
- 'A Practical Guide to Relief from Sanctions Post-Mitchell and Denton' by Peter Causton
- 'A Practical Guide to Equity Release for Advisors' by Paul Sams
- 'A Practical Guide to Financial Services Claims' by Chris Hegarty
- 'A Practical Guide to Financial Ombudsman Service Claims' by Adam Temple & Robert Scrivenor
- 'A Practical Guide to Running Housing Disrepair and Cavity Wall Claims – Second Edition' by Andrew Mckie & Ian Skeate
- 'A Practical Guide to Holiday Sickness Claims – Second Edition' by Andrew Mckie & Ian Skeate
- 'Arguments and Tactics for Personal Injury and Clinical Negligence Claims' by Dorian Williams
- 'A Practical Guide to Drone Law' by Rufus Ballaster, Andrew Firman, Eleanor Clot
- 'On Experts: CPR35 for Lawyers and Experts' by David Boyle
- 'An Introduction to Personal Injury Law' by David Boyle

These books and more are available to order online direct from the publisher at www.lawbriefpublishing.com, where you can also read free sample chapters. For any queries, call us on 0844 587 2383 or email us at mail@lawbriefpublishing.com.

Our books are all generally in stock at www.amazon.co.uk with free next day delivery for Prime members, and at good legal bookshops such as Wildy & Sons.

We are regularly launching new books in our series of practical day-to-day practitioners' guides. Visit our website and join our free newsletter to be kept informed and to receive special offers, free chapters, etc.

You can also follow us on Twitter at www.twitter.com/lawbriefpub.

www.ingramcontent.com/pod-product-compliance
Lightning Source LLC
LaVergne TN
LVHW052250200926
848481LV00002B/325
* 9 7 8 1 9 1 8 2 4 1 3 8 9 *